STRANGLEHOLD ON AFRICA

STRANGLEHOLD ON AFRICA

René Dumont
and Marie-France Mottin

translated from the French by
Vivienne Menkes

 ANDRE DEUTSCH

First published 1983 by
André Deutsch Limited
105 Great Russell Street London WC1

English translation © 1983 by Vivienne Menkes

Originally published in French under the title
L'Afrique Etranglée © 1980 by Editions du Seuil

Printed in Great Britain by
Ebenezer Baylis and Son Ltd, Worcester

ISBN 233 97471 7

To the forgotten peasant women of tropical Africa carrying their never-ending buckets of water and bundles of wood; to the young people living in the rural areas and shanty towns who are after all the hope of Africa. May they never allow themselves to be strangled.

For centuries they have stifled almost the whole of humanity in the name of a so-called spiritual experience.

In fact, the bourgeois phase in the history of under-developed countries is a completely useless phase. When this caste has vanished, devoured by its own contradictions, it will be seen that nothing new has happened since independence was pro-claimed, and that everything must be started again from scratch.

Fritz Fanon *The Wretched of the Earth*

Contents

Preface by René Dumont

We are to blame

More and more books about Africa are being published. Those written in French speak of the continent being betrayed, disenchanted and bewildered, of hands being laid on Africa, of giving Africa to the Africans, of Africa with its fifty different faces. But in choosing our title we decided to borrow the words of Tanzania's prime minister, Edward Sokoine, when we left him in mid-August 1979: 'They're going to strangle us,' he said. Marie-France Mottin★ and I were on our way back from four months' travel through Tanzania, visiting regions, districts and villages. We had also made a tour of Guinea-Bissau before that. I had studied a large number of West African countries on various occasions, and we were subsequently able to carry out similar work in Zambia, between August 1979 and January 1980, and then in Senegal and the Cape Verde Archipelago in March and April 1980.

I should like to start by expressing our thanks to the various heads of state and ministers who asked us to carry out these studies. Particular thanks go to Mwalimu Julius Nyerere, Edward Sokoine and Jackson Makweta in Tanzania, and to President Kenneth Kaunda of Zambia, for the quite exceptional facilities they were kind enough to offer us in our work. Most of all I should like to express my appreciation of the trust they placed in us, for in spite of growing difficulties we were able to hold far-ranging discussions on technical, economic, social and ultimately political topics with no limitations placed on us whatsoever. We were able to speak to people both at the highest level – in government circles, in the Party and in the civil service – and to regional or provincial authorities, to those at district level and even to people living in the villages. We were touched by our encounters with

---

★ Marie-France Mottin and I are now working as a team. She has given me a much greater understanding of the human problems involved.

African peasants, both men and women, the true modern proletariat who scarcely ever get a mention unless they are dying of hunger. Few foreigners are able to make such first-hand contact with the villages.

As a result we were able to prepare a very detailed critique of the agricultural, rural and general policies adopted by these countries. We were not afraid to criticize – though we tried to make our criticisms constructive – for we had been specifically asked to express our views freely, and to cover the whole field, even though our hosts knew that many in their own circles would not be happy with the situation. And so indeed it turned out: in Zambia virtually everyone was dissatisfied; in Tanzania many of the top Party officials, including the central committee, were busy defending their entrenched privileges; and in all the countries we visited the heads of parastatals disapproved of our work.

In October 1914 I was ten and living in Arras on the front line. Throughout the war I used to listen to the complaints of the men on leave, while those removed from the scene of operations were having a whale of a time, showing no concern for the unspeakable sufferings and loss of life among those on active service, brought about by the stupidity of the military authorities and the dereliction of duty by the rulers of Europe, which lost its world supremacy in the process – and good riddance. In 1982 we are in the middle of another world war, a very different one, but certainly no less terrible. This time the front is made up of the peasant populations in tropical countries and the shanty towns of Tehran, Calcutta, Bangkok or Hong Kong, where a growing number of people from rural areas are seeking 'refuge' from a life of poverty, oppression and exploitation. Millions of children die in such places every year, thanks to our economic system, which has killed more people than Hitler, Stalin, the Shah of Iran and Pinochet put together. Others live in abject poverty, or indeed in Hell. I have seen the seventh circle of Hell on the pavements of Calcutta.

We are the prime cause of this appalling poverty. By 'we' I mean the industrialized countries, those who again are removed from the fighting and show no concern for the sufferings of those at the front. We are living in unbelievable luxury, beyond our means, beyond the limited wealth of our small planet. We are using up its non-renewable energy and ore resources far too quickly; we are destroying the world's forests to plant crops that sap the soil's fertility, or to make paper which we promptly proceed to waste. We are like the sorcerer's apprentice, increasing the carbon dioxide content of the atmosphere even though we cannot assess the impact on the world's climates. When we do manage to do so, it may well be too late.

The industrial revolution triggered off what is now known as 'development', followed by the mass consumer society, which is like one vast jumble sale selling off non-renewable resources dirt-cheap. Since 1946 the pace has hotted up because of our policy of frenetic urbanization and a lifestyle based on the private car, and on the assumption that oil would be more and more plentiful and cost less and less. This has led us to a totally deviant form of pseudo-civilization, and has destroyed truly convivial societies. In those days W. W. Rostow and Herman Kahn were promising that this 'standard of living' could be enjoyed by everyone the world over, if only those 'backward' Third World nations could manage to wait patiently and obediently.

This is either criminal ignorance or a criminal lie. It is *development* that has brought about the worst destruction in the history of the world, on an even more lunatic scale than during the two world wars. The arms industry, which is worth 500,000 million dollars per annum (1980 figures), is wasting the world's finest brains, its richest ores and the dwindling supply of energy. World hunger is an unforgivable crime, since we could put a stop to it within a few years if the world's resources were more evenly distributed and our economic system were rethought to ensure giving everyone enough work to meet the essential needs of the population of the whole globe. Instead, the chief hallmark of our civilization is growing inequality. Our planet could not possibly support on a worldwide scale the squandering of resources practised by the so-called 'developed' nations. This habit of squandering therefore depends on the frequently worsening poverty of a growing percentage of mankind. We refer to ourselves proudly as 'the free world', and claim that we live in a 'democracy'. This is debatable enough within our own countries; in relation to the rest of the world it is sheer hypocrisy. We are first and foremost exploiters of the poor, because of an economic system based on dominance that has been cunningly devised by and for the rich nations.

Many people in France do not think of '*Cartiérisme*' as being dead, for they still hold to the theory of the journalist Raymond Cartier, who claimed that the abject poverty of the Third World nations is due entirely to their own leaders. We shall admittedly be criticizing these privileged leaders in our turn, but we urge our readers to remember that we, the developed nations, form the bulk of the privileged beings busily exploiting our planet. The prime responsibility for world famine therefore rests with us. We are the real hypocrites.

I should like to acknowledge the very valuable help I've been given by Jacques Bugnicourt.

René Dumont

Preface by Marie-France Mottin

When I was a little girl they used to teach us that Africa was a huge continent covered with forests and full of savages whom we had to evangelize. The forests have virtually disappeared now and the 'savages' are independent, even though some of them do still go to Mass.

What exactly is Africa? Those who are fond of the quick and cosy generalization, in spite of living in the twentieth century, still think of it as one single unvarying and uniform 'land'. Those who look at the maps see it as a huge indeterminate thing, a solid mass plonked down below Europe, a bottomless well of ores, peanuts, bananas and other so-called 'exotic' crops, but also as the place where our 'civilizing' mission came unstuck.

Somewhere or other there are all those populations we do our best to forget, because they aren't 'civilized'. So we toss them back into the abstract void known as the Third World, and they won't start leading a proper existence in our eyes until they begin to mimic us. Our Eurocentrist outlook is merely a form of racism, and although nowadays we daren't be more than paternalistic, we still think in racist terms.

There's the Africa of the intellectuals who never leave Europe – a vast territory they like to think of as virgin, on to which they can freely project their dreams of revolution (which can never come true in their own countries) and of new societies – and they've certainly made the most of the opportunity. All they know about this Africa of theirs are their own counterparts, the men and women with 'black skins and white masks', because they all speak the same hollow language. They theorize, talk in Marxist terms and would dearly love to hold forth about relations and modes of production to all those 'ignorant', illiterate peasants slaving away with their hoes. When the various countries became independent they entertained great hopes, and some of them still do. When it comes down to it the responsibility lies as much with the theorizing Left as the pragmatic Right in that although they don't know much about Africa they unquestioningly justify any self-styled 'socialist' policy and are only too ready to excuse departures from the straight and narrow, to atone for imperialism. Theirs is a romantic, simplistic view; it does no good to anyone.

Then there is the Africa of the press agency dispatch which tells us, via the anonymous certitude of the telex, about politics and international relations. That particular Africa is a mere chapter of accidents – the Biafran War, the attacks on Shaba, diamond scandals, children massacred. Every now and then the telexes refer laconically to a coup or famine. When a dictator is toppled we hypocritically remember the scandals he was connected with, and it never occurs to us that it was our silence or complaisance that kept him in power for so long. To be honest, we're a bit disappointed to see these larger-than-life characters vanish from our sensation-loving media. Their macabre clowning had reinforced our racism ('We told you so!'). But at bottom Africa interests us only when our own interests are involved. We talk of 'a French presence' or 'unwarrantable interference by Cuba'. 'We [i.e. France or the United States] have to stay on there, otherwise the Russians will . . . etc., etc.' It's true that there are those barbarians in Pretoria, the ones we sold our arms to, and who invade their neighbours at regular intervals, but that all seems a long time ago.

There's also the more peaceful Africa known to large numbers of ethnologists, those observers (and preservers) of traditional primitive societies, contemplators of the status quo, encouraging our taste for folklore. And there's the Africa of the polluting tourists who adore sunbathing in underdeveloped lands and pop out of their Hiltons and other executive clubs to see 'how the other half dies'. More often than not they're so busy stuffing themselves and luxuriating in exoticism that they don't see anything much, apart from their swimming pools and the servile domestic staff who keep alive the nostalgic memory of some grinning creature dreamed up by the ad men. Alongside this variant we can set the Africa of the centurions, and of the merchants and predators, but then that's an old tradition on a continent that seems destined to suffer looting and pillage.

Then there's one last Africa, a more modern and gloomier continent this time – the Africa of the experts, of the United Nations and other international organizations who submerge reality and deny life in a coded language, a computer language that does equally well for Latin America or southern Asia. This new version of Esperanto will come in very handy in the not so distant future when we shall all be talking like machines; it makes everybody toe the international technocratic line and be thoroughly well behaved. For instance those barefoot women with their dirty loincloths and babies slung behind, who come to Lusaka's avenues to chop wood for their shanty dwellings, are transformed into an asepticized and universalized category known as 'the informal sector which increases energy output to serve the needs of the peri-urban zones'.

And so they draw up a detailed balance sheet of extreme poverty which leaves out nothing except the true face of the destitute. If these do get a look in they are reduced to a mere 'human factor', as though all they are entitled to be is a subsidiary and often disruptive element in a reality that no longer affects them. This is no way to shake up the so-called 'developed' nations, to create the necessary motivation for change and lay the foundations of a dialogue. For the problem is after all a problem of dialogue, at a time when a plethora of communications seems to have made things more incommunicable.

In the end, these caricatures of Africa and the constant harping on 'development' have made us forget the crucial point – that Africa is made up of Africans. Even if they are a bit of an embarrassment. 'Zaïre would be fine,' Mobutu used to say, 'if it weren't for all those Zaïrians.' He was speaking with greater honesty than many other people who daren't say this.

For Africa – that huge cake sliced up by greedy foreign powers – is also people. Populations split by arbitrary boundaries mapped out to suit the marching pace of the marines, or drawn by the pencils of distinguished negotiators; whole civilizations repudiated and societies demolished by enforced development that is out of the question today. The people of Africa are not only the pastoral peoples who reject 'our' development; the mighty warriors doomed to live as farmers; the obstinate and 'backward' peasants whose children die off at the drop of a hat; the millions who live rock-bottom existences in the rural areas and whose one and only concern is to stay alive – to find water and wood for cooking. They also include the young men and women who've been uprooted and befuddled by a Western-style education, and find it very hard to come down to earth and live the humdrum daily life of Africans; and, lastly, they include the much criticized élites who've been disoriented by Western dreams and are desperately trying to take the place of the former colonial authorities, so that they can forget the centuries of humiliation and recover their identity, but often find themselves struggling with government jobs for which they are quite unprepared. From capitals set up away from their country's centre to suit the purposes of colonial trade and the slave economy, they struggle to run countries that are ungovernable.

When you really think about it, could Africa have got off to anything but a false start? How could we ever have thought it would be easy, with such handicaps?

When we were received by President Léopold Senghor on 2 April 1980 he said to René Dumont: 'I must confess I was very critical of you at first. But now I have to admit that I was wrong – and you were right.' To which René Dumont replied: 'I only wish I'd been wrong.'

Marie-France Mottin

Editor's Note: in April 1982 Editions du Seuil published a pocket-book edition of *L'Afrique étranglée* revised to include the authors' study of rural development in Senegal carried out during a four-month visit to that country, at the invitation of President Abdou Diouf, the previous year (1981). The present translation is of the du Seuil edition of 1980 but incorporates significant changes and in particular up-dated statistics, that appear in the later edition.

1 A downtrodden, plundered and polluted continent

1 *False start for Africa*

We must never forget the genocide perpetrated against the people of Africa, millions of whom were transported as slaves to the plantations of North America; or the wars of conquest that disseminated the slave economy and the system of trading valuable raw materials in exchange for the rejects of our own industrial production; or the colonial economies which were run solely in the interests of the parent state, with no industry allowed. This period was followed by the granting of independence. Some of us had fought hard for this and had the highest hopes of it. Between 1958 and 1961 the French government asked me to draw up a series of outline schemes for agricultural development in the colonies that were to be granted independence, though de Gaulle had wanted to keep them inside the framework of a community dominated by France. I therefore went off to Madagascar, the Ivory Coast, Chad, the Congo, Dahomey, Senegal and the Cameroons. During the summer of 1959 I went with Charles Bettelheim and Jacques Charrière to study the potential of Guinea, from which all the French officials had been recalled by de Gaulle the previous October, in a bad-tempered gesture that did him little credit. Then in 1961 the socialist government of Mali asked me to prepare the same type of study, working with Samir Amin.

I wrote lengthy reports for each country,[1] but I soon felt that the politicians, particularly in the Congo under Fulbert Youlou, were quite incapable of promoting any real agricultural 'take-off', the basic prerequisite for overall progress in these so-called 'underdeveloped' economies. An increase in agricultural output keeping largely in step with population growth could have strengthened the fragile political systems in the early days of independence. But I soon realized that this increase could not be achieved in the circumstances then prevailing. The French government, backed up by Jacques Foccart's secret police, was busy promising the moon and stars to anyone prepared to follow them in their allegedly 'generous' policy of aid and cooperation. I felt that if I let it be thought that I approved of this policy, in that I had been involved in it, I would be betraying my friends in Africa and jeopardizing, if only by omission, the future of the whole continent.

I therefore decided to bring these problems of development in general and rural development in particular to the attention of the public at large – and so to politicians – by writing, rather too fast I must admit, a kind of pamphlet called *L'Afrique noire est mal partie*, which was published in 1962 (and subsequently appeared in English as *False Start in Africa*). It rapidly became my best-selling title, but many of those who read it used it to further political aims that were different from my own. Those who deplored the loss of our colonies and the short-sighted and self-centred advocates of *Cartiérisme*★ had a field day with the defects I pointed out, although many of these were virtually inevitable in the circumstances, and anyway were largely our fault, a fact which I should have stressed more forcefully. Rereading the book in 1980 I realized that the historical and, more important, the *sociological* data on which it was based were inadequate. It gives off a strong whiff of Eurocentrism in its approach to the realities of life in Africa. This applies particularly to the advice I gave on modernizing agriculture (most of which I deleted for the pocket edition, published in 1966). In those days little was known about the very wide range of peasant communities in Africa, ranging from the Fulani nomads on the edge of the Sahara to the cereal growers on the savannahs or the itinerant farmers in the evergreen forests, plus many others.

I had admittedly (not that anyone took any notice) advised against a large number of instances of modernization carried to excessive lengths, such as the overmechanized peanut farming in the Casamance region of Senegal, which was copied from the 'peanut scheme' in Tanganyika. But I hadn't made enough allowances for the gaps in my knowledge of Africa during the precolonial and colonial periods, and of the very wide range of traditions, economic systems and sociological factors within those peasant communities. The Betsileo rice growers on the upland plateaux of Madagascar have nothing in common with the women growing cassava in the forests in the northern Congo basin, near Ouesso.

Yet the book did still have the effect of an electric shock on the

---

★ See p. xii (translator's note).

students and the authorities in French-speaking Africa, and even now I am barely tolerated there: in 1978 the Club du Sahel had intended to commission me to draw up a report, but the African authorities would not agree to this. The book was banned and I was declared to be *persona non grata*, as though I had committed an act of *lèse-majesté*. Before writing it I had resigned from the steering committee of the Aid and Cooperation Fund (Fonds d'aide et de coopération or FAC) set up in France by the infant Fifth Republic, whose policies I criticized in the strongest terms.

The impact of the English-language edition in English-speaking Africa was very different. In Tanzania, Julius Nyerere made it compulsory reading for his ministers, and a school textbook. It was eventually translated into Swahili, the language spoken in Tanzania.[2] *'Mwalimu'* (a term of affection meaning 'schoolmaster', used for President Nyerere) then asked me to come to Tanzania to 'criticize' his agricultural policy – he at least does not believe himself to be infallible. Kenneth Kaunda invited me to Zambia for the same purpose, but whereas the Tanzanian report was published and distributed in Tanzania, and criticized incidentally, the Zambian one was never made public. In 1979 it was the other way round.

Twelve years later a second invitation from the same two heads of state, who were still in power despite growing difficulties both at home and abroad, gave us an opportunity, after a large amount of travelling in the 'socialist' countries and the Third World, to confirm our belief that the situation in tropical Africa, far from improving, is deteriorating and indeed becoming positively dramatic. This situation affects each and every one of us. No one who is concerned about the future of our small planet, and about his or her descendants – to whom we are answerable – can continue to ignore it.

2 *France's share of the blame*

I feel that it is only right for me to refer to France first, although the same applies to many other countries too. The funds provided by the FAC chiefly covered expenditure and steered the 'development' of our former colonies in directions that suited our interests, within a neocolonial framework. As early as 1959 France took up arms in defence of allegedly friendly governments such as Ahidjo's in the

French Cameroons against the popular revolt led by the Union of the People of the Cameroons, whose leaders were murdered by France's secret service.

The French army also intervened to defend the neocolonialist government in Gabon. They did the same in the Republic of Chad, where they merely succeeded in fomenting an appalling civil war and the Libyan invasion. In Mauritania the government that ruled with our support did eventually have to surrender its territory to the Polisario. Miners have lost their jobs in Lorraine, which still has huge reserves of iron ore, on the pretext that Mauritanian ore is cheaper, as indeed it is – but this only goes to show that we are paying too little for it. Naturally we take up arms in its defence.

Zaïre was falling apart, under leaders universally acknowledged to be totally corrupt. But this did not stop the French army intervening in May 1977 and again in May 1978 in Shaba to prop up Mobutu. The point is that if a group with stronger 'African nationalist' leanings were to take power, they would give effective support to the 'Front Line' states which, ranging from Angola to Botswana and Zambia, from Tanzania to Mozambique, are backing the freedom movements (which have now achieved victory in Zimbabwe) in Namibia and Azania (South Africa).

Finally, a more recent intervention saw the French army, which had so belatedly backed the vile Bokassa (even as recently as 1979 to describe him in this way would have led to a charge of insulting a head of state) and his ludicrous coronation (which incidentally was partly paid for by South Africa), replacing him by another of our protégés, his cousin David Dacko, who had handed over power to him without a fight on 31 December 1965. An even more serious example is the fact that for many years France has been providing equipment for the South African army, and has even helped them to build up a nuclear industry that may already have assisted the manufacture of atomic weapons – an appalling threat to black Africa.

On the economic front, the FAC is still funding the infrastructures and export crops that supply us with cheap groundnuts and cotton from the savannah, and palm oil, coffee and cocoa, rubber, bananas, pineapples, tropical timber and so on from the forest belts. After them came uranium and various ores, which are more crucial to our economy nowadays. (The only exception here was the short-lived price rises for coffee, which aroused vociferous protests from the wealthiest consumers in the United States, who refused to admit that they were exploiting the Africans; when prices dropped back to their previous depressed level, they referred to them as 'normal prices'.) I therefore resigned from the steering committee of FAC, since it generally refused to finance food crops and the industries upstream and downstream from agriculture such as fertilizers and tools, and factories giving added value to the raw products straight out of the plantations and fields.★ I was told that these industries must be set up by the private sector. After all, we weren't living under a socialist system!

At that point a friend handed me a confidential document from the Banque de l'Indochine advising those of its customers who were prepared to invest in West Africa to go for breweries and other aerated drinks firms, because they were the only industries liable to turn in big profits. Why should a private investor put the national interest first? Even de Gaulle stood up for his policy of cooperation by showing that it in fact gave France more in real terms than it cost her. Gunder Frank has shown us that the flow of capital between the United States and Latin America was very much in favour of the States, even though the country prides itself on its aid record. The same applies to trading between Africa and Europe, which invariably favours Europe.

3 Looting the Third World

The 'old international economic order' (though 'disorder' would be a better word) is taking a long time a-dying, in spite of countless declarations in favour of a 'new order' that would bring about a fairer distribution of the world's wealth. In fact the looting of the Third World has never stopped since the period of slavery and colonization. It is continuing in our own day in the form of an unfair system of trading in which raw materials – initially agricultural and subse-

---

★ Another reason was that on 15 September 1961 I made some harsh criticisms in an Antananarive (known as Tananarive in those days) of France's neo-colonial policies, whereupon the then prime minister, Michel Debré, asked 'my' agriculture minister, Edgard Pisani (who failed to comply), to 'mete out to Professor Dumont a form of punishment that is more than merely symbolic'. Another of Debré's actions was to sponsor mercenaries in the Comoro Islands.

quently mineral – are bought far below their value, while manufactured products and hard goods produced by factories in the developed countries are sold at too high a rate. With freightage, brokerage, insurance, banking, factorage, patents and transfers of technology and other 'invisibles', this type of exploitation is continually being added to.

Our so-called 'developed' world is admittedly collapsing beneath us, with unemployment and inflation completely uncontrolled. But it manages to cover up its bankrupt state by using various banking devices, such as the devaluation of the dollar; and it invents new methods of looting the Third World. France imports African labour when it's needed, then tosses it out like a squeezed orange.

We export our inflation and pollution and take advantage of cheap Asian labour. Countries ranging from South Korea to Singapore (and even Hanoi) supply us with labour at moderate cost because wages are kept low by means of strict policing. The multinationals transfer to the poor countries technologies that have already been written off in the rich countries, without bothering to find out whether they are suitable. These suggestible new nations are pushed into buying sophisticated plant and equipment that mean they have to import white (or yellow) technicians who are allegedly qualified. These technologies ruin the local craftsmen and at the same time fail to provide new jobs for them. As a result unemployment is becoming *the* major problem in the Third World. This army of young jobless could easily produce all the essential commodities that are now available, but only within a sensible economic framework. We plug 'our' model of development in an economic and social setting to which it is totally unsuited, and soon we'll start seeing the extent of the damage. Well played, gentlemen!

4 The 'generous' Common Market – the First and Second Lomé Conventions

The EEC is a club whose members are the rich countries, their purpose in getting together being to get even richer. France, Belgium, Holland, the United Kingdom and even Germany down to 1918 were all colonial powers. On another front this Europe that has had such difficulty in seeing the light of day stands up for its own interests in the face of North American imperialism and that of the so-called 'socialist' camp. Because the European countries have largely exhausted their own sources of raw materials, they feel the need to appropriate new sources, by force of arms if need be, though preferably by recourse to the standard economic ploys. And they also have to find new markets for their over-equipped industries. Yet the European countries would like to present a picture of themselves as generous, and sympathetic to the interests of the nations they have exploited for so long and on such a large scale, and whom they are now starving. They hope in this way to wipe out the very memory of the original sins of capitalism and the Industrial Revolution, of slavery and colonization, but in fact they are merely repeating them.

The European Development Fund (EDF) gives priority to expenditure on infrastructures, prestige projects for hospitals and stadia, and most of all for export crops. For instance it provided ample funding for oil palm plantations in countries ranging from the Ivory Coast to Dahomey. Admittedly this did help to step up output of fats, but it also helped to lower world prices on the world markets, which meant that the Common Market got back a lot more than it put in – another example of generosity paying off. In Togo in 1974 the Fund was financing only coffee and cocoa, so as to ensure that there was something approaching a glut that would favour the buyer rather than the seller. It provided no funds at all for food crops, which are still in very short supply there. And in 1970–1, when the peasants in Senegal turned their backs on groundnuts, the EDF stepped in to help the groundnut crop, which, as we shall see, helped to ruin the soil in Senegal through erosion (wind erosion in the north, water erosion elsewhere).

Once Britain had at long last joined the Common Market, the number of African, Caribbean and Pacific countries (ACP) 'supported' by the Common Market rose to forty-six, and an agreement known as the First Lomé Convention was signed in the Togolese capital in February 1975. This agreement provided for development aid for these countries totalling 3,500 million European units of account (or approximately 4,300 million dollars at the end of 1979). This aid was to be granted solely for projects approved by the bureaucrats in Brussels, whose speed of action is far from being 'developed'. At the end of 1979, shortly before the First Lomé Convention expired (in March 1980), only a little over 25 per cent of this aid had actually been paid out, according to the December 1979 issue of the journal *Africa*.

Stabex* wanted to stabilize the income derived from agricultural exports from the ACP, so they decided to pay compensation if the income from one of a list of thirty-four agricultural products fell more than 7·5 per cent in a year. For instance, Tanzania was paid a small amount to offset the drop in sisal prices and so was Senegal for the drop in groundnut prices. But there is no provision for adjustments to take account of rising inflation, and this lessens the effectiveness of the system. Also, since 1981 Stabex's funds have not been enough to pay for the planned compensation. The discussions leading to the Second Lomé Convention were very protracted and on several occasions the negotiations very nearly broke down altogether. By this time there were sixty ACP countries and they were to receive 5,200 million units of account spread over five years. They asked for twice this figure, producing watertight arguments to back up their claim. It would have been easy to agree – it only meant lowering the very high level of protection afforded to surplus production in Western Europe. 'Protection' for Europe's milk lake alone costs 4,000 million dollars per annum – a figure far in excess of the aid given to the ACP – and we mix powdered milk in with animal feedstuffs. This is a good example of the wasteful economic system we put forward for these countries to copy, and we shall soon see the extent of the muddle that taking such a model can lead to.

The European leaders must utterly despise Africans to be able to go on cracking up such a model to them. The ACP countries would have liked to see the aid allotted quite simply shared out between them, but Brussels will only ever grant aid on the basis of a single scheme at a time, and this inevitably means the money arrives too late. A degree of control is probably needed, though. Ten new agricultural and fisheries products are covered, but very little cash is earmarked for ores. Also, products manufactured in the ACP can be imported into the Common Market without payment of customs duty only if everything that has gone into their manufacture comes from the country of origin, which is often no easy matter.

---

* Fund for the stabilization of exports, created by the EEC.

5 *The United Nations and 'development'*

In early 1960 John F. Kennedy launched in the United Nations the first 'development decade', which promised all sorts of miracles: its first aim would be to satisfy the basic needs of the world's population by taking full advantage of local resources and ensuring that all young people had jobs. A fine-sounding programme, but . . .

Kennedy, who was under threat from the Cuban revolution, promised Latin America, by means of an Alliance for Progress scheme, 20,000 million dollars' worth of aid, though by no means the whole of this sum was eventually paid out. Reforms in agriculture and the tax system were necessary preconditions, but these were never implemented, except in Chile, and we all know how the United States reacted.

In 1969 the World Bank commissioned Lester Pearson, the former prime minister of Canada, to head a large-scale study designed to see 'how development was getting along'. The Pearson Report pointed firmly to a large number of shortcomings, but recognized only part of the overall failure of the system; it didn't put forward any far-reaching proposals for change. It laid constant stress on the increasing integration of these poor countries into the world market through developing their exports. Now exports represent the main means of exploiting the Third World countries. They would be better advised to satisfy first the basic needs of their own people by using to the full all locally available resources and putting all their young people to work.

The second development decade was planned on the same lines, but when it came to an end in 1980 at least there was a greater appreciation of the shortcomings. And this time there was no sounding of trumpets, particularly in view of the fact that the third decade started with the all-out failure of the UN Industrial Development Organization (UNIDO) conference held in New Delhi in January and February 1980. In its *World Development Report* dated August 1979 the World Bank calculated that, taken together, the developing countries' overall GNP had gone up by 6·2 per cent per annum between 1965 and 1974, and by 5 per cent between 1974 and 1978. These figures are slightly higher than those for the developed countries. But an advance of 5 per cent on an annual per capita output ranging from 80 to 300 dollars (in the case of thirty-seven countries officially classified as 'very poor') – and it must be stressed that this figure is relative and open to question –

9

represents *nothing* in comparison with the 3·4 per cent growth in the developed countries, which relates to per capita GNP ranging from 3,000 to 10,000 dollars. Let me make this quite clear: the gross product per head of the population is increasing much less fast in most of the poor countries, where the population is going up by 2–3 per cent per annum, or even more, whereas population figures are increasing only very slowly in the developed countries, and indeed are already beginning to level off, or even to fall.

Africa south of the Sahara comes right at the bottom of the league table, with a figure of 1·6 per cent per annum for GNP growth over the period 1974–7. This means that the availability of resources per head of the population decreased and that a situation of absolute poverty ensued. We can illustrate this more clearly by looking at the case of Zambia.

In 1964 the first United Nations Conference on Trade and Development (UNCTAD) met in Geneva. Conferences have subsequently been held in New Delhi (in 1968), Santiago (1972), Nairobi (1976) and Manila (1979). Although the poor countries had deepseated political differences, they did their best to present a rather more united front against the rich countries. They therefore set up the Group of 77. The name came from its seventy-seven founder members and has been retained, even though it now has 122 members. The Group's main demands were the setting up of a joint fund to protect their export prices, easier access to the developed countries' markets, a stepping up of 'aid' and a decrease in their indebtedness. But none of these has ever really come to anything. They ran into the selfishness of the capitalist nations (the North-South 'dialogue' provided a clear illustration of this down to Cancun in October 1981) led by North American imperialism, which has both rivals and considerable backers in Japan and West Germany.

During the first decade the stated goal for public development aid was a minimum of 0·7 per cent of the GNP of the developed countries. But since then the percentage has steadily decreased for the richest nations. In 1977 the overall figure was 0·31 per cent, but for the United States it was a mere 0·22 per cent, with 0·27 per cent for West Germany and 0·21 per cent for Japan. And let us not forget the generosity of the Swiss, who gave 0·19 per cent, whereas their banking system and multinational companies largely owe their survival to the exploitation of the Third World (cf. Ziegler, *Main basse sur l'Afrique*, Le Seuil, 1978, who tells us that the total figure for Swiss bank accounts opened by the privileged minorities who are in power in the Third World is very nearly equal to the total figure the Third World countries receive in aid).

Only a few countries are exceptions to this rule, and may therefore be said to be slightly more favourable to the Third World. A few of the oil-exporting Arab nations, the Scandinavian countries and Holland have reached or are about to reach a figure of 1 per cent of GNP, i.e. above the target figure. Australia, Belgium and Canada come somewhere between the two groups. So does France, which claims to give 0·5 per cent but omits to point out that the lion's share of this figure goes to her overseas *départements* and territories, whose populations are given 'aid' to encourage them to remain under the French flag. After all the various islands govern a huge stretch of ocean that may turn out to contain the greatest wealth of tomorrow's world.

6 *The new international economic order*

Now that the underdeveloped nations are in the majority in the United Nations (North America and Europe originally predominated), they naturally try to lessen the extent to which they're exploited. In 1973 the Algerian president Houari Boumedienne put forward the idea of a new order to the non-aligned countries and subsequently to the United Nations, who agreed to it on 9 May 1974. It ran as follows:

> We, the members of the United Nations . . . *solemnly proclaim* our united determination to work urgently for the ESTABLISHMENT OF A NEW INTERNATIONAL ECONOMIC ORDER based on equity, sovereign equality, interdependence, common interest and cooperation among all states, irrespective of their economic and social systems, which shall correct inequalities and redress existing injustices, make it possible to eliminate the widening gap between the developed and the developing countries and ensure steadily accelerating economic and social development and peace and justice for present and future generations.

Fine words – but they are still merely words. The 'old order' is still in force and the World Bank (yet again!) assures us that absolute poverty will not have been wiped out by the end of the century. With the growth rate allowed for in the Bank's basic scenario, it is predicted that there will still be at least 600 million 'absolutely poor' people in the developing countries at the end of this century. Dom Helder Camara★ refers to 'subhuman' living conditions and there is no need to go as far as the border of Cambodia/Kampuchea to see them at first hand. We are living in a truly horrific world, though many of the privileged few claim to be Christians, humanists and even socialists.

Yet, again according to the World Bank, these extrapolations presuppose that 75 per cent of the anticipated growth in incomes will go to the 40 per cent of wealthy people. If very firm wealth-redistribution policies were adopted 60 per cent might benefit from this income growth. But even if the most optimistic scenario, suggesting a very rapid increase in production, is taken, there would still be 300–350 million 'absolute poor' by the end of this century.

This is a crucially important statement. The institution that most accurately reflects the mood of central capitalism, i.e. the capitalism of the wealthiest or 'developed' countries, has admitted that it is utterly incapable of overcoming abject poverty by the end of the century. So what do they think they are capable of doing over the next twenty years? All the necessary resources are there, quite enough to fulfil everyone's needs. Yet most of these resources – manpower, land, minerals, water, energy and know-how – are squandered, first and foremost on arms (which also leave the most appalling threat hanging over us), and then on the incredible abuses perpetrated by our appalling consumer society, which culminate each year in Christmas gluttony.

We shall therefore have to look for other solutions and recognize here and now that it won't be easy, in view of the large number of failures chalked up by various 'socialist' systems. But I must make it clear that we are posing a question mark over industrial society in general, not just the central capitalism of the West. Once the 'socialists' had come into power in Ethiopia they organized a tank parade in Addis Ababa to glorify modern industrial methods. And the Eritrean war justifies our use of inverted commas round the word 'socialist'.

★ The progressive Roman Catholic archbishop of Recife in Brazil.

7 *The oil crisis tightens the noose*

Development progressed at unprecedented speed between 1948 and 1973 at the heart of the capitalist world, relying first and foremost on the existence of ever more plentiful oil supplies at continually falling prices. Indeed, the Iranians claim that in 1970 they had to sell three barrels of oil to obtain the same quantity of durables as cost them one barrel in 1950. When the Organization of Petroleum Exporting Countries (OPEC), which was set up in 1960 on the initiative of Venezuela and Saudi Arabia, is accused of continually putting up the price of oil, its accusers forget to mention that for many years the 'Seven Sisters' (the big oil companies) managed to extort black gold out of them at very low prices. In the early days in Saudi Arabia they just gave a few handouts to the local kings. From 1970 onwards OPEC did allow a few minor price adjustments in favour of the producing nations, and then in 1973, when the second Arab-Israeli War took place, they threatened an embargo, terrifying the world's most powerful nations, and eventually managed to increase oil prices drastically.

Although the price rise sounds impressive – from $2 per barrel in 1972 to $36 in 1981 – it isn't quite so impressive in real terms: if you take inflation into account you arrive at a rise from $2 to, say, $12 (World Bank figures). But this does still mean that it rose by a factor of 6 in real terms. The oil-consuming nations laid in stocks regardless of the cost and the rise became even steeper: the price per barrel went above $40 on some occasions on the Rotterdam spot market. The profits made by the major companies reached unprecedented heights. Yet we persist in accusing no one but the Arabs.

On a world scale a price rise of this magnitude, which I hoped and prayed for before it happened (see my book *Utopia or else . . .*), is admittedly beneficial: for a start it forced us to stop increasing the amount of this precious and non-renewable resource we wasted – a first step towards really cutting down on the wastage. But the dominating economic position of the rich countries allows them to keep the lion's share for themselves. Carter never managed to force his fellow-Americans into seriously cutting down on their senseless level of oil consumption. The Americans claim to be democratic, yet with less than 6 per cent of the world's population what possible moral right have they got – they who talk so readily in moral terms – for continuing to waste about a third of the planet's main scarce resources? In December 1979 the Kuwaiti oil minister said on a French television programme: 'The real culprits are the industrialized countries, since they stepped up their consumption very considerably in the sixties and didn't do enough prospecting.'

He was quite right. We've built up a completely unnatural civilization based on waste, relying on the theory – now recognized as absurd, but the recognition came too late – that we had unlimited supplies of energy and that the price we paid for it would go steadily down. This dramatic situation became totally unacceptable once we started projecting the selfsame development model, mistermed 'civilization', on to the countries over which we held sway – our colonies and later our independent ex-colonies. This so-called 'civilization' is in the process of strangling them, and only too often we look on unmoved. The rise in oil prices mopped up their last foreign currency reserves and tragically increased their indebtedness. It's true that between 1974 and 1977 the oil-producing nations paid 2 to 2·7 per cent of their GNP to the OPEC Special Fund for Third World aid, which is much more than the previously rich countries have ever given. But in 1978 the figure fell to 1·1 per cent. And this goes nowhere near compensating for the increase in oil prices. Is it possible to change your economic model to prevent yourself being strangled? It certainly isn't easy.

8 *We call them 'underdeveloped', but we're the ones who are ruining the planet!*

The European nations set off like conquering heroes to 'colonize' the world because they had highly efficient ships and arms. During the same period they were making improvements to their agriculture in Lombardy and Flanders – that was as early as the sixteenth century. Improvements spread in Britain in the eighteenth century, with the 'clover and turnip' revolution, when fodder planting superseded the system of letting the land lie fallow one year in three, enabling farmers to keep more livestock (both cows and horses) and thus increase the amount of energy and animal manure at their disposal. But this 'revolution' also ruined the small-scale peasant farmers. With productivity rising by 40 per cent over a fifty-year period, capital and labour were now available for the Industrial Revolution – which was largely financed by plundering the colonies, particularly India, and which reached its peak during the later eighteenth century.

The Industrial Revolution (and the closely related development of capitalism) changed the face of the world, but not always for the better. The world's natural wealth was wasted and destroyed faster than before, and inequalities increased. Paul Bairoch tells us that in 1700 the differential between average incomes in the various major nations was no more than 1·8 to 1, whereas nowadays, he claims, it is 40 to 1. The World Bank refers to a differential of 120 to 1, but Bairoch rightly thinks this figure is too high.

This new capitalist system ruined craftsmen and small tradesmen, in Europe first and later in the Third World. When the capitalist countries had to give up the idea of trying to dominate the colonies on the political front, their economic system was so firmly rooted there that it was never really questioned at that stage. It was christened 'development' and it was suggested that the Third World should 'catch up', or in other words 'develop' by following our model down to the last detail. One or two did dig their heels in, but the majority avoided asking three crucial questions. Firstly, is the consumer society a desirable goal? Secondly, can it be set up anywhere? Thirdly, is it suitable for Africa?

No society has ever developed activities that have as little justification as our own. Labour that is immediately productive is constantly decreasing and Herman Kahn tells us that by the end of the century farmers in the United States will account for a mere 1 per cent of the population, and that agriculture will produce only 0·5 per cent of their gross national product. So man is increasingly being cut off from the land that feeds him. Many children brought up in towns think that food is produced in supermarkets and they've even put a cow in the New York zoo for the children of the city's poor families.

Our society thus employs most of its members in useless activities, some of which (like the arms industry) are positively harmful. It no longer produces purely to satisfy basic needs; instead, advertising builds up a market for anything that's produced, because it brings in profits. Such a society throws out all those who are of no use to it – young people, the unemployed, those who don't 'fit in'. But most important of all, it is increasingly allowing the Third World to starve.

In the end it is leading the whole world down the road to ruin (including the rich, who would be well advised to give more thought to this). Such is the warning sounded by the Club of Rome and the ecologists and environmentalists, and they are having to shout louder and louder (since we are growing increasingly deaf). After gradually exhausting the non-renewable resources of the rich countries we're now getting our hands on the Third World's reserves. Once pollution had reached unbearable levels in Japan and on the east coast of the United States, capitalist society started setting up pollutant factories in the underdeveloped countries (cf. the plan for an oil refinery in Senegal described in chapter 6). We feel that this society – *our* society – has now become thoroughly undesirable.

Can this type of society be set up anywhere? In about 1965 Jean-Jacques Servan-Schreiber urged us to take up 'the American challenge',[3] claiming that the United States was becoming the Mecca for European productivity. I was sent to the United States in 1946 in connection with the Monnet Plan. The country boasts of having achieved the world's highest levels of agricultural productivity, but this is true only in terms of the amount of labour involved. Land in the United States yields much less per hectare than in Japan, Korea, Taiwan, mainland China – or indeed Western Europe. The Americans can afford to waste and under-use most of their land because the country as a whole (and this applies to Australia too) is underpopulated. But by what right do they have such vast tracts of land at their disposal, considering that they have massacred and wiped out the indigenous populations?

Their energy yield is deplorable – no doubt an even more serious matter. They often need to consume more than 10 calories of oil (in fuel, fertilizers, pesticides and equipment) to produce just one calorie of food, and then they waste most of it. In a Californian feedlot 100,000 head of horned cattle put out to pasture consume 850,000 kilograms of maize. This would feed 1,700,000 East Africans, i.e. very nearly a third of the population of Zambia. Some level-headed Americans have calculated (see in particular the journal *Science*) that their system of producing and consuming food is much too costly to be adopted throughout the world. If we include processing (and adulterating too, often enough) agricultural produce, packing and distributing the food, airconditioning in the supermarket and transporting food by private car to a home in the suburbs, the energy consumption involved is so high that if the same system were followed all over the world, food and agriculture alone would swallow up more energy than is now consumed worldwide.

Any attempt to spread this sytem is therefore an appalling piece of trickery. And yet we've done just that. We've persuaded virtually all the African leaders that our model of progress is the only desirable model for them, and the only valid model for Africa. But we've never asked the most important of the interested parties, the peasants, what they think, and we've never bothered to study the economic, historical, sociological, political and pyschological context into which we were introducing it. This 'rape' wasn't carried out by force of arms alone, or even merely by the much-vaunted interplay of market forces. Another more suitable weapon was also used, and one that's been underestimated far too long – the weapon of cultural dominance.

9 *The West's cultural dominance of Africa*

The British didn't wipe out India's civilization, and certainly not its religion, even though they did destroy many of the continent's craftsmen and small tradesmen. Islam, ranging from the Sahel in Africa right across to Indonesia and the Philippines, successfully resisted all attempts to Christianize it, and to a large extent to Westernize it too. China was never completely conquered, in spite of its lack of military superiority. The point is that a more highly developed society was already in existence in Asia; it had been using writing and coinage for centuries and had consisted of large-scale centralized states. At the beginning of the eighteenth century India and China had reached a level of technology that was roughly comparable to Europe's. And our slave traders bought Indian fabrics as trade goods for Africa.

Admittedly a large number of imperialists spoke far too disparagingly of pre-colonial Africa, but that doesn't mean we should overestimate and idealize it. Although the Koran was written in Arabic in the Sahel, and medieval Timbuktu had a university superior to those in the parts of Europe that were still in the Dark Ages, in most of intertropical Africa the art of writing, that tool for transmitting and spreading knowledge, was unknown. So too was the systematic use of coinage, though iron bars, cowrie shells or lengths of cloth were used instead. A few empires did grow up, but only in one part of western

Africa. This was where most of the continent's weaving was done. Metalworking was another trade practised, involving the use of copper and iron. Wooden tools were superseded by iron hoes, and plants that originated in North America spread quickly. Yet the wheel, and the horse- or ox-drawn plough or cart, the basic tools required for embarking on the first stage of agricultural development, were still unknown – and in far too many cases they still are today.

With such a fragile economic and intellectual base, the arrival of the white man (the first to come were caravaneers, traders and explorers, but they were followed by missionaries and soldiers) brought about the collapse of the African values, traditions and religions that provided man with a link to the land he respected, to his ancestors, his extended family and his tribe. Zimbabwe, Malawi and Zambia are much more Christian than Europe nowadays! The white man taught Africans to read and write, and he set up an urban society, which was a rarity in Africa at that time. He oppressed and exploited the black man. Yet everything he introduced was automatically accepted as 'superior', because he was the master – nothing was ever questioned. The Africans learnt European languages, tried to reason like Descartes or Bacon, and used European consumer goods. They were soon open-mouthed with unreasoning admiration when faced with anything from Britain or France or Belgium, depending on whether they came from English-speaking or French-speaking Africa, or from Zaïre.

The glitter of North American civilization exerted an even greater fascination. As we shall see, the Zambians tried to live out the American dream, yet were incapable of noticing the highly questionable aspects of that dream. European attitudes to 'underdevelopment' are coloured by a degree of paternalism and a degree of contempt for the Africans; and yet the Africans have adopted these same attitudes. They were too easily persuaded by us that they were incapable of working out their own development model suited to their particular environment, their economic situation, their traditions and values. Instead, they went roaring round the world in our planes, sometimes in a bid to forget their anxieties, and careering about in our cars, which gave them the illusion of having virtually unlimited powers. And so they were committed to 'our' type of development without having really thought it through. This attitude constitutes what might be called a second original sin, one which is liable to lead this strangled continent to gradual ruin.

10 *Foreign 'aid' and non-productive capitals*

The European countries started by developing their agriculture and subsequently developed their industry, but they manufactured all the equipment they needed on the spot, whereas we introduced to Africa an urban civilization based on motorcars and airconditioned skyscrapers and all the trappings of the consumer society, without first making the necessary improvements to agriculture, developing technological knowhow or amassing the capital needed for the plant and equipment required. The European countries managed to step up their own development by exploiting their colonies, and later by plundering the Third World. And the African countries are adopting a form of development that actually depends on their being exploited themselves, in that they are paid too little for their agricultural produce, their ores and even their oil.

With agriculture stagnant and industrialization based on plant and equipment, semi-finished products and even raw materials that were mainly imported, not enough wealth was created. Yet the model of consumption, itself imported, turned out to be too expensive to spread to the whole of the population. As a result the Westernized 'élites' holding the reins of power felt themselves entitled to consume as much as us, or even more. They chose to adopt 'our' development model, in that it enabled them to satisfy their longing for a Western lifestyle, and didn't bother about the rest of the population.

Sumptuous capitals sprang up, representing a vast amount of non-productive investment – and the subsequent cost of upkeep of the prestige buildings was underestimated too. The former colonial powers professed to be friends of the élites holding the reins of power, since they were the guarantee that they would continue to enjoy priority in their economic – and political – links with the country in question. During the period 1958–62 France needed African votes at the United Nations to enable her to prolong the deadly mistake of the Algerian War. So, wittingly or unwittingly, we foisted on them a development model that compelled them to go on buying manufactured goods, plant and equipment from their former colonizers for as long as possible. And we were never chary of egging them on to pay for prestige ventures. For instance, as I showed in my book *Paysans écrasés, terres massacrées*,[4] Upper Volta has been given foreign aid over the last few years totalling more than the whole of its internal budget. What real margin of independence does that leave them with? Those who agree to wear the golden chains of aid are soon locked into a vicious circle of increasing dependence.

11 *Increasing inequality; a demolished environment*

So here we have the so-called élites increasingly quenching their thirst for luxury goods by buying Mercedes and other prestige cars. In the precolonial period, or indeed in the colonial period, the gulf between the old chief in his mud hut, surrounded by a perimeter fence and millet stalks, and his subjects was much less blatant than it is today. Inequalities are constantly on the increase inside these nations too.

The only way all this luxury could be made even more sumptuous was to exploit the peasants still further, since aid alone wouldn't cover it. Initially the peasants were encouraged to increase their acreage of export crops: groundnuts, cotton and tobacco, mainly on the savannah; and coffee, cocoa, tea, bananas, pineapples, rubber and palm oil in areas where there was more rainfall, often in forest clearings. All these crops bear very heavy export duties, often over 50 per cent of their prices on the world market. The duty is paid into the various countries' treasuries, i.e. into the pockets of the élites who run the distribution system to their private advantage. And these world market prices are often held down to favour consumers in the developed countries, who thus become exploiters themselves, even if they refuse to admit this.

The environment suffers too as a result of this system, and the deserts keep encroaching all the time. This applies particularly to the Sahara, both to the north and to the south. In 1977 the United Nations Environment Programme held an international conference in Nairobi on desertification. But the cry of alarm it sounded had little impact, and the wealthy countries refused to make any substantial contribution to the expenditure designed to slow down the encroachment of the world's deserts. Every year 8 million hectares of tropical rain forest vanish (i.e. 1 per cent of the total), and we cannot calculate the full extent of the impact of destruction on this scale on the overall world climate. But we do know that crops and plantations on dense forest land produce much higher yields than with a series of annual crops, which soon 'savannah-ize' this type of environment. I pointed this out earlier in the case of Thailand, which will have scarcely any forest land left by the end of the century; the Ivory Coast boasts of having scored a similar success with its agriculture, but if it keeps up the same pace its forests will vanish even sooner. Already the winds blowing in from the ocean are not collecting as much moisture on the coastal strip of Africa as before, because of increasing deforestation, and this is liable to intensify the drought in the Sahel.

12 *With the falling off in food crops, malnutrition and imports are increasing*

Cash crops are constantly being expanded, because they bring in the foreign currency needed for satisfying the demand for luxury goods and prestige of those in power. Because there isn't enough plant and equipment, the increase in cash crops is achieved at the expense of food crops. Funds are more likely to be agreed – or simply skimmed off – for crops that bring in foreign currency. Where technical advice, fertilizers or insecticides are needed, priority is always given to cash crops, ranging from groundnuts in Senegal to cotton in Chad and Tanzania or tobacco in Zambia.

Much less advice and far fewer funds are forthcoming for cereals or other food crops, and the marketing system isn't as well organized. For instance in Senegal growers who aren't close to the road network have had to leave their surplus sorghum to rot, and maize is left to rot in Tanzania because of a lorry shortage. Prices are kept fairly low, because the authorities are more afraid of urban consumers than of the peasants, who are scattered and usually unorganized.

The result is increased malnutrition. The rural districts are affected first, even though it is hard for us in Europe to envisage country dwellers suffering from shortages and even famine. We aren't referring here to large-scale famines such as in the Sahel in 1972 or Ethiopia in 1973, which are the only ones the press and the other media deem worthy of mention. The vast majority of the peasants in tropical Africa, Egypt and North Africa suffer from famine, lasting for varying lengths of time, at the time of year when they need something to tide them over before the next harvest. And peasants ranging from Senegal to Upper Volta told us that the period of shortages is getting longer, sometimes leading to full-scale local famines. A large part of East Africa is hit by drought every five years on average, and those who suffer most are the peasants. Precolonial Africa was better at planning ahead and putting stores aside, stores that amounted in some cases to the equivalent of several years' supplies. The novelties we're so busy spreading around encourage the peasants to sell more than they should, not even keeping back enough to hold out until the next harvest. And the money they spend on such knick-knacks doesn't stay inside the country, as it once did, when local craftsmen could cover all needs. Bata's plastic shoes kill all prospects of expansion for local shoemakers, together with the jobs that could entail.

As a result tropical Africa is importing increasing quantities of cereals: 2 million tonnes in 1960, 6 million in 1970, 10 million in 1976, 12 million in 1978, and so on. The continent's indebtedness is increasing all the time, and indeed this applies to the whole of the Third World. As Africans aren't able to pay for their increasing purchases of cereals, they're forced into even greater dependence and reduced to begging. The megalomania of their élites is a contributing factor here, but so too, indeed even more so, is our development model.

The United States, with its virtual monopoly of the world cereals market, has a 'food weapon' that is highly likely to become increasingly deadly. This explains, incidentally, why we protested about its use against the Soviet Union in January 1980, even though we utterly condemn the Soviet army's occupation of Afghanistan. Basic self-sufficiency – let's not call it autarky – has therefore become the essential ingredient of independence in the case of young nations. It's a surer guarantee than a ruinous arms build-up that's bound to look pathetic compared to the stocks of arms held by the big powers.

13 *Sprawling towns, hotbeds of unemployment and crime*

In a study carried out for the International Labour Office (ILO) Paul Bairoch offers evidence to show that the exodus from rural to urban areas was more the result of people wanting to leave the rural areas than of their being attracted towards the towns. But both these factors play a part in this shift, and the population of African towns is increasing much faster than the amount of housing and the number of jobs available. Shanty towns are mushrooming,[5] and the situation is deteriorating all the time.

The World Bank's vision of the future is distinctly unappealing, since it claims that by the year 2000 the developing countries might well have 1,200 million urban dwellers, half of them without reasonable access to the basic minimum provision of food, clean water, basic education and housing. This headlong urbanization copied from the West's economic model leads to a rise in unemployment and, in the long term, in crime. Half the population of Kinshasa live off prostitution and other forms of corruption.

14 The threat of South Africa

The independent Republic of South Africa has set up a system of apartheid that is universally condemned yet shows little sign of dying out. Asians, Coloureds and Africans are allowed no political rights whatsoever. The Africans suffer most, since they are permitted very little education – just enough to make them good producers. The blacks represent 80 per cent of the population, but only 13 per cent of the land is allocated to them – the very poorest, with no mining or industry. As the women in poor families cannot even scratch a living from soil that has been exhausted and will soon be completely eroded, the men are forced to move to the so-called 'white' areas to work in the mines or factories or on the farms, or do other kinds of manual labour. They're treated as migrant labour, separated from their families, housed in dormitories and compelled to travel back every evening to places on the outskirts, such as Soweto, to which I was driven, illegally, one evening in 1973.

Apartheid could not survive without continual backing from Western investors, mainly in Britain and the United States, but also in West Germany, Switzerland, France and elsewhere. The West is afraid of losing the fabulous mining wealth in a country whose uranium will soon be as valuable as gold and diamonds are today. For many years South Africa felt secure with a buffer zone of friendly states along her northern borders, where Rhodesia and the Portuguese colonies held sway. And even now that these powerful neighbours have become independent, South Africa still isn't out on a limb. Malawi is still a loyal ally (and so was Rhodesia down to March 1980). Making much play of its anti-communist stance, South Africa sought contacts with the allegedly moderate black African states, its most assiduous allies being the Ivory Coast and the Central African Republic under Bokassa. It also struck up friendships with Madagascar during the pre-Ratsiraka era, James Mancham's Seychelles (before he was overthrown by Albert René) and the Comoro Islands, which were 'recaptured' by 'our' mercenaries. And it established contact with Gabon, Senegal, Liberia (before the coup d'état) and even Zambia.[6]

Apart from these peaceful approaches, its army invaded Angola in July 1975 and couldn't be shifted until the Cubans intervened. South Africa is still helping the opponents of the governments in Angola and Mozambique and staging destructive raids on these countries at regular intervals. More recently, with the increase in guerrilla warfare in Rhodesia during the talks leading to the autumn 1979 armistice, it stepped up its raids into Mozambique and Zambia, with increasing instances of sabotage and blowing up of bridges, and thus looked like jeopardizing the development of both countries for many years to come. As a result their governments had to push the Rhodesian guerillas into agreeing, at the end of 1979, to the armistice conditions laid down in London.

15 *Apartheid demeans the Africans*

So the present system in South Africa could not survive if it weren't for the complicity of the major Western powers. The rise in the price of gold (from 35 dollars per ounce in 1971 to over 800 dollars in early 1980, with no way of telling whether, when and at what level it will start to slow down) strengthens its economic position. And it exerts an inhibiting influence, not only from the military point of view but also economically and culturally, over the whole of black Africa, particularly over the southern half, in the Front Line states.

South Africa is a developed country and produces much more on her farms than she needs for home consumption. The Zambians are still obtaining supplies there when they run out of maize, as they did in 1979–80. The South Africans have a very vigorous economy, which they like to attribute to the superiority of the white man. By comparing the economic successes – in spite of sanctions – of what was formerly Rhodesia, they can insinuate that Zambia's problems show how incompetent the Africans are – yet another 'justification' for apartheid! The white colonists in Zambia never miss the opportunity of propagating this theory, in private conversations. The idea is to persuade the Africans that they're inferior, inefficient and ultimately incapable of running their economy properly without white 'assistance'. This aspect shouldn't be forgotten when we come to our chapter on Zambia.

Within the system of imperialist dominance by the West, headed by the United States, the Shah's Iran found easy access to the supplies of arms it needed to maintain its role as watchdog of the Middle East, protecting the world's largest oil reserves. But this plan collapsed beneath the unexpected attacks of Islamic fundamentalism. The emperor of Ethiopia vanished, having attempted to conceal appalling famines from the eyes of the world. There is now a Cuban presence in Ethiopia, aided by the Soviet Union, and the same applies to Angola, Mozambique, the Congo, South Yemen and so on. (Incidentally, France is in no position to criticize the Cuban presence, since it still has troops in Africa, ranging from Dakar to Djibouti and even Réunion.) But the famine that has been raging in Ethiopia since 1977–8 became appalling when the dictatorship withdrew the rights that had been granted to the peasants. Libya's intentions in Chad are beginning to look clearer. Gaddafi certainly hasn't improved his image by offering protection to Amin.

All this strengthens the United States' feeling that they must maintain the status quo in South Africa because if the black majority were in power they might be more willing to look for support to the socialist camp. They are therefore urging Botha to make minor concessions on so-called 'petty apartheid', such as allowing Africans to move about more freely in places that have been restricted to whites up to now, to take jobs now held only by whites and also to set up their own trade unions. Since South Africa is now at a stage in its development where it needs a higher proportion of skilled labour, educational opportunities for the blacks are improving.

Yet the substantial profits from investments in South Africa depend first and foremost on the low salaries paid to Africans, and this is bound to mean that the process of granting them full emancipation will be slowed down. The standard of living enjoyed by the

English-speaking middle classes, who are always speaking out against apartheid, is much higher than their counterparts enjoy in the United States, because of the availability of domestic help and the many other services provided so cheaply by the black population. Apartheid has been taken to such extremes that it seems to us that it will be difficult to put matters right by slow stages, as so many capitalists and 'friendly' governments recommend. Few whites in South Africa, and this applies particularly to the Afrikaners, have a true homeland in which they can seek refuge if a black government comes to power, unlike the *pieds-noirs* in Algeria, Morocco and Tunisia, who poured into France. So they're fighting with their backs to the wall, and a full-scale flare-up with the Front Line states, who aren't so well armed, is not beyond the realms of possibility. But the Soviet Union clearly would not remain on the sidelines if that happened.

16 *Dialogue, triologue and the Brandt Commission*

People with wealth and power in the developed world are at last beginning to worry about the world's future. In 1972 the Club of Rome warned that the world was bound for disaster if the present pace of demographic and industrial expansion was maintained, through exhaustion of scarce resources and pollution of the environment. As this threat mainly concerned the twenty-first century our leaders soon rallied – after all they won't be in power by then.

They are much more worried about soaring oil prices and the even more frenetic rise in the price of gold, and about growing unemployment and inflation. But the brightest of them rightly see the growing poverty of the Third World as presenting an even more fearsome threat. For instance Valéry Giscard d'Estaing tried to set up a North-South dialogue between the developed and poor countries, but this soon collapsed because the deep-seated selfishness of the 'haves' would not allow them to agree to any major concessions. The gap between rich and poor is widening all the time, though the rich see nothing scandalous in this. Subsequently Giscard put forward the idea of a 'triologue', thinking that if Africa's raw materials, the petro-dollar and European technology could all be brought into play simultaneously, this would enable the process of development to spread further and faster. By 1981 it was obvious that this theory was doomed to failure. The idea of North-South dialogue was taken up again at Cancun in October 1981, with François Mitterrand standing up for the South against President Reagan.

The World Bank refused to give up. Just as it had commissioned the Pearson Report at the end of the first development decade, so in 1977 it entrusted Willy Brandt and a team of politicians with the task of preparing a report that was presented to the United Nations in February 1980. This time the Bank had picked on a European social democrat to head the study, and the report, which is called *North-South: A Programme for Survival*, gives a solemn warning (the very same warning that I have been giving over and over again, with little result, for a good twenty years) that the eighties and nineties may be fatal for mankind. But the report's contents are too moderate for us; it is essentially a reformist document. The measures it sets out come nowhere near solving the problem, though they do represent a slight improvement on the present situation.

So what are these measures? It's true that a more substantial *net* transfer of funds to the less developed nations (50,000–60,000 million dollars in 1985) and an increase in loans from the IMF and the World Bank are clearly essential, but if waste continues on the present scale, or becomes even worse, these measures won't do the trick. We believe that the international energy strategy which the Brandt Report puts forward is nowhere near bold enough. The rich countries ought to slash their consumption (or rather their squandering) of oil, scarce ores, water and so on. And the world food programme it sets out is reminiscent of the one the FAO has been unsuccessfully putting forward for very nearly twenty years now (it was reiterated by the international conference held in Rome in 1974).

17 Questioning our own 'Civilization'

It's salutary to remember that all nations have many interests in common. The first of these is to cut back drastically on their suicidal arms spending. It would have been better to make a formal recommendation to transfer an increasing share of arms spending to the world's most underprivileged peoples, and to initiate effective measures to ensure that inequalities, both between nations and within nations, are rapidly reduced. The Brandt Report doesn't clearly bring

out either of these points, which seem to me to be crucial prere-
quisites, since it fails to mention the plundering of the Third World.

We're told that if the needs of the poor countries could be
transformed into effective demand, this would give work to the
under-used factories in the 'rich' countries. But this would only step
up the industrial explosion which presents such a serious threat to the
environment. So at the same time the waste practised by the rich
societies would have to be reduced so as to cut down on pollution and
the squandering of scarce resources, since otherwise the rampant
destruction of the environment would increase to dangerous levels.
We'll therefore have to take a long, hard look at out whole lifestyle.

It's true that all the various monetary, financial and trade measures
could offer some temporary relief, and the same applies to the Second
Lomé Convention if it were implemented worldwide. The idea of an
international tax to finance a World Development Fund could help to
keep the capitalist system alive. But, as I pointed out in my book
Utopia or Else . . . , as long as our economy is based on the search for
profit, and on that alone, we are heading down the road to
destruction.

Before we start advising the poor countries to put their economies
in order we should look more closely at where we want to go
ourselves. We'll be coming back to this in our conclusion, but
meanwhile we should like to point out that our aim is to devise an
economic system based on the husbanding of the earth's scarce
resources, the protection of the natural environment, and fewer
inequalities.The Brandt Report is right to ask the communist
countries to play a greater part in solving the problem, but it could
have shown more concern for ecological questions, and put forward
more dynamic measures, to be implemented immediately, in favour
not only of the poor nations, but of the poorest people within these
poor nations. But, once again, we must admit it won't be easy.

18 *Increasing poverty in Africa and the Third World*

Diplomats in the rich countries, plus all sorts of technocrats, experts,
Peace Corps or vso members and their various international equiva-
lents, and representatives of the United Nations and its various
specialist bodies, are always going on about the increasing poverty

experienced by the Third World. They are (too) well paid for saying so.

They speak out against underdevelopment, yet when all is said and done they live very well off it. More and more people and organizations are handing out aid and advice, and funds are forthcoming, in considerable quantities. As a result the various capital cities are getting bigger and more splendid all the time, and more and more meetings are being held all over the world, convoking not the peasants and the working classes, but the privileged minority in positions of power. It is they who benefit most from aid, because funds are creamed off and embezzled at every level.

But Africa's poor, both in the rural areas and in the shanty towns, have been suffering from increased malnutrition and the increasing scourge of unemployment over the last twenty years of independence. ('Independence is for townspeople,' a Congolese peasant told me in 1961.) It's true that there are far more schools and dispensaries now, but the education system is still totally unsuited to these countries' real needs, at this stage in their development. Preventive and traditional medicine for the poverty-stricken rural masses is still being neglected, in favour of sophisticated forms of treatment that are virtually restricted to town-dwellers and in particular to the well-off, i.e. those who can afford it.

Road maintenance is increasingly being neglected and in Zaïre the roads are actually disappearing. In most factories production has been slowed down and a large number of them are simply closing down owing to a lack of maintenance or a few spare parts, both of which could easily be remedied. A growing percentage of vehicles are breaking down. The rural areas are increasingly being abandoned, with fewer buses running, and fewer lorries to transport crops and essential goods – not to mention the sick. There are shortages of salt and soap, and in many cases malnutrition is worse than it was before the colonial era. All this isn't true just of Bengal or the Nordeste region of Brazil.

More and more people in Africa's poverty-stricken rural areas are going hungry, and this is endangering African independence and enhancing its dependence. In the chapters that follow we shall be stressing the responsibility for this deplorable situation by examining the role of the power 'élites'. But by far the greatest culprit is the developed capitalist world, 'central capitalism', as Samir Amin calls it.

Development in Africa, as we shall try to show in our concluding chapter, must be completely rethought. And it must be rethought by the Africans themselves, relying first and foremost on their own strengths. Meanwhile we shall try to show what is happening in the villages and on the outskirts of some of the big towns.

2 Zambia – the copper curse

1 *A disjointed country*

A quick glance at the map shows that Zambia was an artificial creation of those appointed by the great powers to mark out boundaries that were plonked down in the midst of tribes to whom boundaries mean very little (smuggling is merely trading between members of the same family). Although the boundary commissions were fond of straight lines, they showed greater subtlety when it came to Katanga's copper, which explains why the famous 'Katanga pedicle' jutting into Zaïre came about: everything vanishes into it, Zambians in a hurry to reach the north of the country, sacks of maize, and products made in the state-run factories that are unobtainable inside the country.

Zambia is a huge and underpopulated country, cut in half by the railway line linking the mines to Zimbabwe, with the population concentrated on either side of it. It is a landlocked country, far away from the sea and ports and hemmed in between its neighbours, all of them undergoing varying degrees of upheaval. Zaïre is in a state of collapse and apparently 'sending in bandits'. In Angola and Mozambique, where there was war for so many years, guerrilla warfare is still raging, with South Africa stoking the flames. Then there is Zimbabwe, the source of all the trouble, whose fate has at last been decided. Malawi was the Cinderella of southern Africa but is now doing remarkably well, albeit within a questionable sociopolitical framework; by late 1979 it was even able to give 15,000 tonnes of maize to help Zambia through a difficult period. Zambia's last neighbour, Tanzania, is a 'friend', though the Zambians like criticizing it; the Tan-Zam, the Chinese railway, passes through Tanzania on its way to Dar es Salaam, which has just put up its port duties, to the fury of the Zambians.

Lusaka, the capital, lies in the centre of the country and is a caricature of our Western civilization in the middle of the savannah. The Lusakans decided that they were living in North America, whereas their cousins in their village huts had barely emerged from the Stone Age. The dream continues in the Copperbelt, the local Hollywood, where copper has brought swimming pools and British-style golf courses. Lusaka forms an enclave of development inside an undeveloped country, full of Mercedes and concrete tower blocks. In the luxury Pamodzi Hotel, decorated in a style that makes you think of nowhere at all (though it was in fact flown in from Spain), the élite jostle one another to drink their Coca-Cola or whisky, looking gloomy and trying to forget Africa. They feel perfectly comfortable in their three-piece suits and dignified ties because the hotel is aircon-ditioned – over-airconditioned in fact, since the temperate climate doesn't justify it. Nor does it justify the shorts worn by those who like harking back to the colonial days, who can still be seen there. Many of them have never managed to shake off their arrogantly paternalistic attitude. The white farmers in their luxury ghettoes keep themselves to themselves, importing whatever they need for their parties by plane from Britain or South Africa and keeping up their nostalgic illusions. But then would it really be true to say that the colonial era is over?

In the streets, crowds of ordinary people – women in dirty chitenges (soap is in short supply) and carrying small children on their backs, men in torn shirts (but they'd look even poorer if their shirts were patched) – huddle together, resignedly queuing for a sack of maize flour that may never materialize. Most of the population in Zambia is undernourished to a greater or lesser extent, and the children are dying of malnutrition. Agricultural output is falling and increasing quanti-ties of cereals and other food products are being imported.

Yet the country's agricultural potential is enormous, with its highland plateau (at an altitude ranging between 1,060 and 1,370 metres, except for two low-lying valleys and some mountainous regions), pleasant climate with temperatures never going to extremes, and fairly well watered soil (there is a bit too much rainfall in the north, with its leached soil, while the south, with less, sometimes suffers from drought). Even though only part of the country's 750,000 square kilometres, say 12 per cent, is really fertile, this ought to be plenty to feed the population of 6 million (1981 figures), with a large surplus for export. But this is certainly not the case.

2 *A classless and self-sufficient society in the precolonial era*

Before colonization the people of Zambia were grouped into districts or 'chieftainries', varying in size from a large village to a small kingdom, which ensured that local customs were respected and levied a tribute in the form of labour, game, grains or craftwork. The chief kept stores for use in times of famine and offered presents in return for people's tribute. This meant that salt, iron tools and imported foreign textiles circulated. But the justice he meted out was harsh.

Before long Zambians came into contact with foreign traders travelling in search of African ivory, which was suppler and more highly prized in India than the Asian variety, and in greater demand in Europe once the Industrial Revolution had produced wealth there. But the developed world at that time was particularly eager to acquire products resulting from slave labour, such as cotton, sugar, coffee and cocoa. Livingstone reported: 'We are guilty of keeping up slavery by giving increasing prices for slave-grown cotton and sugar. We are the great supporters of slavery.'[1] Even France under the Third Republic, 'the Home of Revolution and Freedom', was still prepared as late as 1880 to accept Réunion's recruiting 'committed workers' – who were in fact slaves under another name. Appearances had to be kept up! And even in the 1980s the world still has plenty of slaves.

In that precolonial society copper and iron were mined and worked, spears, axes and hoes, pottery, nets, mats and baskets made, timber and bamboo were worked and tree-grown cotton spun and woven. The population was almost entirely self-sufficient, and adaptable to growing all sorts of new crops. To the local millet and sorghum they added maize, cassava, groundnuts, sweet potatoes, tomatoes and so on, imported from America, plus sugar cane from India. In a normal year, with game and fish plus what they could pick in the fields or forests, they often ate really well.

But the country was being laid waste by civil war. At the end of the nineteenth century the population was dying from smallpox, crops were destroyed by grasshoppers and livestock were decimated by rinderpest. Famine wasn't unknown either. The explorers and caravaneers were followed by a new breed of white man – missionaries come to convert the people to Christianity. This was a first form of Westernization, of de-Africanization. Once the Africans had accepted that the white man's religion was superior, they were soon eager to adopt his lifestyle, his form of dress, his whole civilization and customs. This was not necessarily an improvement, but they appreciated the fact that he could teach them to read and write and act as a bridge between them and the world outside, of which they knew so little; they also liked the fact that 'he wasn't a slave or elephant hunter'.

3 *The colonial regime's need for labour leads to rural underdevelopment*

The British South Africa Company, a British chartered company on the same lines as the East India Company, was founded by Cecil Rhodes as a first step towards his scheme of flying the British flag 'from the Cape to Cairo' (which explains why Lusaka's main street, which leads north, is still called Cairo Road). The company acquired mining rights from the Lozi tribe (Upper Zambesi) and signed treaties with various chieftains. This enabled it to occupy, somewhat high-handedly, what was soon to be known as Northern Rhodesia. The region had very little in the way of ores, but it did have people, that crucial means of production needed by South Africa for its farms and gold mines and by Katanga for its copper. A tax of three shillings per hut was therefore imposed on all able-bodied adult males. The tax had to be paid in cash (whereas up to then barter had been the sole method of trading) and the only way to get hold of the necessary cash was to find employment with the white man, either with the government, in which case a month's work paid for the tax, or, as happened in the majority of cases, in the mines or on the farms of Southern Rhodesia or South Africa. In fact it was merely another form of slavery.

By this method the colonial powers soon weakened the power of the chiefs – already stripped of their religious privileges by the missions – and destroyed the social structure, the whole fabric of village society. The women and children left behind in the villages were not as strong as their menfolk when it came to cutting branches for burning in the *chitemene* system of fertilizing millet (Eleusine or yard-grass), the finest cereal of all. They increasingly had to fall back on cassava, which contains virtually no protein, just a small amount in the leaves. With colonization, malnutrition soon worsened and affected more people, and the rural areas became underdeveloped in the true sense of the term, whereas the so-called 'primitives' had never known malnutrition, or rural underdevelopment. The independent state of Zambia hasn't so far managed to get rid of this twin scourge within a socioeconomic framework that is still typically neocolonialist.

4 *The white man takes the best land*

Before long some colonists, many of whom had lived poor and overcrowded lives in South Africa, had settled on the Tonga plateau in the south, beside the railway line that had been built between 1906 and 1910 to transport food supplies from Southern Rhodesia to the Katanga mines. The settlers went for fertile land that wasn't infested by the tsetse fly, which caused sleeping sickness in both men and animals. The places where they settled, mainly beside the railway line and later to the east near Malawi and to the north near Lake Tanganyika, still tally on the map with most of the best land in Zambia. On it they produced maize, for the Africans, and beef, chiefly for the Europeans and primarily for Katanga, plus Virginia tobacco for export. Although they only took about 3 per cent of the land, compared to 50 per cent in Rhodesia, it was the best land.

In many cases the land was already being cultivated by Africans, but this was no problem for the colonial authorities, who evicted them into reserves that were not only poorer but farther from the railway and the roads, as is still happening in the Bantustans in South Africa. Although the country as a whole is very sparsely populated, the reserves were soon overcrowded. The system of leaving land to lie fallow at intervals had to be abandoned and soon permanent cultivation was damaging the soil. The hillsides had to be planted too, because suitable land was in short supply, and erosion naturally resulted.

The colonial authorities woke up rather late in the day to the fact that the reserves were overcrowded, and so they made them bigger, but in some cases they expanded on to land infested by the tsetse fly. The Africans were soon aware of this, but the white powers failed to notice it. On the other hand some Tonga tribesmen who were more advanced did rear oxen and buy iron ploughs of the type they'd seen the settlers using. A tiny handful of agricultural advisers taught them the use of a leguminous green manure (*Crotalaria juncea*). Anyone who wanted to sell maize or groundnuts to the cooperatives was forced to combat erosion, chiefly with strips of grass, which took up space and were quite useless, as well as being unpopular. The mission schools, which were very few and far between, and anyway only offered primary education, also taught their pupils to bake bricks, to do stonework and work with wood and iron. They even built their own schools, and the elderly peasants who were once pupils there feel that present-day schools ought to be still teaching their sons to use their hands. These concrete, though limited, lessons were soon forgotten. Sad to say, most of what our friends in Zambia have learned from our examples is liable to jeopardize their potential for development, since the examples we set them were quite unsuited to their situation at the outset, which was very different from Europe's. In Britain the Industrial Revolution and the period of large-scale urbanization were preceded by an agricultural revolution, whereas in Zambia the colonists cultivated only 1 per cent of the country intensively, if that.

5 Copper and towns – a class-ridden, poorly Westernized society

Eventually, in 1930, the discovery of methods for processing deep-lying copper ores set off a 'copper rush' in Zambia. Mines, accommodation for immigrant labour and apartheid towns mushroomed in the Copperbelt, and Lusaka, in the centre of the country, which became the official capital in 1935, grew up in an equally haphazard way. Villas surrounded by huge lawns fringed by ornamental shrubs and trees were built beside avenues planted with jacarandas, coral trees and frangipani, covered at the end of the dry season with blue, blood-red and cream-coloured flowers. These were the prosperous districts, made up of what was referred to as 'low-density housing', i.e. houses for the white colonists, a class whose privileges were based on the colour of their skin, the power they wielded, their knowhow, the jobs they held and their incomes.

Further away, set well apart from these districts, are the round huts of the 'developed' Africans, placed close together ('high-density housing'). Writing of Lusaka in the 1950s, John Gunther says:

Africans were not allowed in most European shops, but had to make their purchases through hatchways. They stood in line outside each shop, in a dark, uncovered passageway sometimes in the rain, and when they reached the peep-hole into the wall they called out their wants. Merchandise was pushed through to them from inside. They were not allowed to touch or handle anything, try things on, or look at several items in order to make a choice.[2]

So 'two-tier' towns grew up, with blacks practically always accepted only as seasonal migrant labour, as is still the case today with Johannesburg and Soweto. They came in from their villages for a few months at a time, or perhaps a year at the most, leaving their women and children behind. In theory the women and children were supposed to feed themselves by growing crops, so the wages paid by the mines were only enough to keep the workforce fit. There was no provision, as in Europe, for ensuring that the workforce was perpetuated – the villages were supposed to see to that, but often failed to do so properly. As a result a very poorly paid sub-proletariat was created and big profits could be made, and then exported. The expatriates (i.e. the 'colonials') – engineers, technicians and even white skilled labour – were paid high salaries and wouldn't allow blacks to enter any of their trades.

This is a classic form of apartheid, and one that is still in force in South Africa. The poor blacks never questioned the superiority of the whites, who had a monopoly of authority and knowledge. To them, civilization could only mean British civilization, and they believed in the Western model of development because it was the only one they knew. The 'colonials' lived in large houses with large numbers of servants and never did any manual work themselves. The Africans dreamed of leading the same life as them, seeing it as the acme of civilization. Years of humiliation and arrogant treatment had thoroughly convinced them of their own inferiority, and in order to be accepted they tried desperately to copy the white man, starting with his way of dressing. Frantz Fanon[3] has shown how as soon as they moved a few rungs up the social ladder they tried to anglicize their whole lifestyle. Even now, the trappings of this 'Englishness' – the wigs worn by magistrates, judges and the Speaker, mayoral chains of office, teachers' gowns, army and police uniforms with their lavish use of gold braid, even school uniforms – represent a heightened form of de-Africanization, a repudiation of many traditional African values.

What a pity this is.

Some mission-educated Zambians put up a skilful fight for independence, in order to recover their dignity and eventually find themselves on an equal footing with the whites. Britain granted them independence – somewhat late in the day, in 1964 – without bloodshed. As a result, once they acquired power the Africans did not reject the civilization of their masters but instead adopted it, propagated it, and sometimes even exaggerated it. It is an essentially urban civilization, its symbol the private motorcar for which its oversized towns were built. In fact their civilization itself, sad to say, is suffering from elephantiasis.

6 Independence leads to greater Westernization and non-productive towns

Kenneth Kaunda came to power in 1964. The British and other white men turned out in force to watch the new flag being run up the flagpole and listen to the national anthem. There were large numbers of whites in the mines, the civil service, factories, construction companies and some businesses, and they still enjoyed considerable influence. Copper was selling well in those days ('We were born with a copper spoon in our mouths,' Kenneth Kaunda remarked to us), the state's coffers were filling up nicely, and Zambia tried – quite rightly – to step up its share of the income from this semi-precious metal. But the country wasn't as rich as the Zambians thought, and they were wrong to think that this 'wealth' would go on for ever. The expatriates encouraged spending and the World Bank appeared on the scene, along with various United Nations bodies, offers of bilateral assistance, technical advisers, volunteers (who did rather less harm) – in other words all the various 'aid-donors'. Their funds swelled the country's resources, precious little cautionary advice was given – and what little there was was rarely listened to. I wrote a warning report in 1967 but it wasn't printed, because it 'caused displeasure'.

The 'colonial' towns now started growing bigger and more splendid. There were 21,300 houses in Lusaka in 1964, 2,215 of them in the 'desirable residence' and 'very desirable residence' categories. By 1973 the figure had risen to 73,200, with 23,000 'desirable' and 'very desirable', i.e. ten times more. The dwellings of the poor, in the shanty towns or 'squatter areas', housed 14 per cent of the population in 1964 and 42 per cent in 1973. By 1979 the figure had no doubt gone up to 50 per cent of the city's 600,000 inhabitants. Incidentally Zambia had the greatest urban density in the whole of tropical Africa in 1979, with 40 per cent of the population living in towns or cities. It had reached the same degree of urbanization as southern Europe, but not the same level of production. In recent years the most expensive houses cost an average of 70,000 kwachas (in 1980 1 kwacha was worth $1.28 at the official exchange rate and a third of that on the black market).

The leafy districts lived in by the wealthy have long, attractive avenues. The houses with their large gardens are well spaced out, so the provision of water, electricity, sewage and telephones is a very expensive business. But the community is happy to provide these services – nothing is too good for the Zambian state. The new parliament building, the Mulungushi Hall conference centre, the international airport, the university hospital and most of all the twenty-two-storey tower blocks in Cairo Road – money has been spent hand over fist, and all on totally unproductive investments. The money from the country's copper, the only developed sector, has been used to build an urban civilization that's turning out to be ruinously expensive in terms of upkeep. Yet the basis of this civilization is agricultural, and still very largely African and traditional, with very few industries. So the towns have feet of clay. The Zambians confused buildings with development, and foreigners have egged them on.

In 1977 Zambia had 107,000 private cars, virtually all of them in the towns, but only 1,373 buses or coaches, 16,000 lorries, 32,000 light vans, 6,500 motorbikes and very few bicycles, far fewer than in 1964, even though cycle tracks have been built. Rural districts had far too few vehicles, and anyway hardly any of them were in running order because vehicle maintenance and repairs were so badly organized. With the whole economic structure starting to break down, the only form of urban transport that continued to run smoothly were the private and company cars of the ruling class in power.

7 *A poor imitation of the Western development model*

Even before independence the Constitution of the party that subsequently gained it stressed the political aspects of the new country. Its economic proposals were too vague, speaking merely of achieving an African democratic socialism, raising living standards and distributing wealth more fairly.

After independence the new Constitution referred to wage-earners and to the health and education of working people, but didn't mention the peasants. It immediately opened the door to the development of what was then only an embryonic state bourgeoisie, since it expressed a desire to 'protect and promote trade, industry and agriculture in the interests of the people by legislation and to protect the interests of commercial traders and help them in their progressive businesses and schemes'. In the first part of his *Humanism in Zambia*, written in 1967, Kaunda adds: 'We are vigorous on this programme, because it gives economic opportunities.'[4] This gives us a slightly clearer idea of what he means by socialism.

The economic model Zambia inherited from the colonial era was never really questioned, any more than the idea that the white man was superior. The idea was to 'Zambianize' the colony, which meant taking over a system that could work efficiently only if the expatriates stayed behind, thus perpetuating the danger of exploitation, cultural dominance and, most of all, dependence. The élites who were in power weren't fully aware of this, not in the first place anyway, but it wasn't long before some of them discovered that it was in their interest. The ruling class and the country's president were soon building up, under cover of vague philosophical rhetoric – but then humanism isn't an economic theory – a form of neocolonialism that could never lead to true economic and political independence. But had they really set their hearts on independence, or were they merely eager to increase their privileges and prosperity?

Anyway, can we really blame the underdeveloped nations for being dazzled by our model of development? A tiny handful of them are just beginning to realize that our economic system is breaking down completely, with unemployment and inflation out of control, in spite of all the 'economic summits' our leaders attend. If we don't always notice exactly how ludicrous their constantly broken promises are, we've only got to look at the staggering rise in the price of gold. The only way this 'model' can survive is by exporting its inflation and pollution, and by plundering the Third World even more – as, for instance, with the low prices paid for Zambian copper. There isn't a Fourth World for the Zambians to plunder, so in adopting the Western economic model they have to restrict it to the wealthy urban dwellers; it's too expensive to be available for the whole population, as in Europe or North America. The division of society into separate social classes – and we must remember that this started under the colonial system – was soon becoming more marked.

8 *The widening gulf between urban and rural areas*

As early as 1969 the Turner Report stressed that wages had gone up steeply in the towns, but that productivity had dropped by 25 per cent since 1964, if allowance was made for the large-scale investments that had been made. The report points out that the work discipline of the colonial era had disappeared and never been replaced. In fact many of the workforce knew that with friends and relatives in high places, and with the Party to back them, they were protected against dismissal or could be taken on again. So they took unfair advantage of this situation: nepotism and tribalism are still rife in many African countries.

Five years after independence the urban population's consumption had shot up by 20 per cent, leading to a higher level of imports. The income of the rural population, who at that time made up over 70 per cent of the total population, had moved from 112 million kwachas in 1964 to 116 million in 1968; but allowing for inflation, the figure had gone down considerably in real terms. Over the same period the income of the 330,000 wage earners had gone up by 32 per cent and, according to President Kaunda, now totalled 780 million, i.e. seven times the income of the rural population, for an urban population less than half that of the rural areas. This meant an income differential of 15:1, which was soon seen as unacceptable.

So as early as December 1969 the Party conference in Kitwe officially agreed that the rural areas had been neglected and that the situation there was deteriorating, to such an extent that a 'very radical change' in their favour would have to be made.

9 Villages in distress

'Our peasants are lazy, conservative and backward; they don't want to work,' was the explanation given to us by the middle classes in Lusaka, parroting the language used in the colonial era. But why should they want to work? For the pleasure of feeding the people of Lusaka, who give nothing in return but hot air? For years now the country's leaders have harangued the working millions day in and day out with a string of hollow phrases.

Our travels in the rural areas soon grew monotonous, with the same complaints voiced everywhere and the same sights to greet us. All the villages were so poor, with their mud huts built round poles, each as wretched and tiny as the last, often housing large families packed in like sardines. Ragged children covered with scabies would be playing in the dust, or in the mud if it was raining. The women would be furiously scrubbing away at old, faded clothing, with no soap to help them. New clothes are exorbitantly expensive and hard to come by, with fewer shops than in the colonial era. The state-run factory at Kafue produces poor-quality fabrics with less attractive patterns than in neighbouring countries. Anyway, most of the fabrics are sold on the black market. They aren't obtainable via the official channels.

Sometimes the women would start shouting angrily: 'There've been shortages of everything for years and years – salt, oil, cloth. And it's so long since we saw any soap we can't even remember what it costs!' The official price, that is, for every now and then we'd come across a boy proudly displaying cakes of soap that he was selling for five times the official price. 'I'm a black marketeer,' he'd tell us. There's no other way he could earn a living. Shopkeepers, too, take advantage of the shortages. Anyone who has some soap can swap it for beans, and thus get them five or six times cheaper than the normal price. 'What d'you expect us to do?' say the peasants resignedly. If one of them does manage to get hold of a 25-kilo sack of salt he can get one of his neighbours to do a day's work for him in exchange for a kilo of salt. Now the minimum day wage for an agricultural labourer is equal to 5 or 6 kilos of salt. The peasants invariably do badly out of this type of barter: they usually sell their own produce – this is certainly true of maize – at the official rate, yet everything they buy has to be at black market rates.

We reminded one old lady that you can cook with crushed

groundnuts, but her only answer was: 'Yes, I have tried that. But they've got us used to cooking with oil.' And 'they', i.e. the so-called modern economic system, can no longer supply the oil. That's the tragedy of Zambia's villages. In the heady days when copper was fetching high prices the villagers were encouraged to acquire such habits, with offers of imported wealth and promises of future modernization which was feasible in the early days, but is impossible now that the economy has collapsed. Hence the very characteristic atmosphere of stagnation and apathy verging on despair. They were promised all sorts of wonderful things after independence, but none of these marvels has materialized. 'Civilization' raised their hopes and expectations, but all it has managed to do is to upset the traditional life of the people without offering any concrete advantages or improvements. 'Nothing's changed for us since independence,' claimed one disillusioned peasant woman. 'Except that they do buy our maize now,' chipped in her ragged neighbour. But payment is often very slow – some peasants have time to starve to death before the money turns up.

There are hardly any tractors left for them to hire, and they've forgotten about hoes. The fertilizers they've been brainwashed into using never reach them in time nowadays, and anyway they've got too expensive. 'It's you whites who've spoilt us with your modern agriculture,' one elderly chief accused. 'In the old days we used to have our maize as we'd always had, and at least we'd got enough to eat. You made us think that chemical fertilizers would solve all our problems. And now we're even poorer than before.' By the end we felt ashamed at asking questions, and so did the civil servants travelling with us. They were shattered: 'You must go and tell them in Lusaka what's happening here.' We did, but they just called us 'sham progressives', accusing us of wanting to introduce alternative technologies so as to keep the peasants at the stage where they were mere hewers of wood and carriers of water, but clean forgetting that that's exactly the stage they stand at now, because modernization is too expensive to reach the villages. The cost of a tractor and a truck for the few has been such that most of the population has never even had a bicycle or a cart. Peasant women still carry things on their heads, wasting time on unproductive and exhausting labour – and are promptly branded as lazy!

So there the peasants are – forgotten by the towns and authorities who refuse to look reality in the face (how could they possibly

43

envisage the peasant's lot, living as they do their American-style lives?), helpless, bewildered, drowning their distress in *chibuku*, the local beer brewed with maize and sorghum, during the slack season. What else can they do in villages where there's no hope left? We'd speak to the large number of gatherings we attended about the government's two main slogans: 'Back to the land!' and 'Grow more food!' They were greeted by shouts of laughter. 'All right, let's talk about them. They make us laugh, those big shots in their Mercedes. That fellow from the Party's central committee who told us to stay here in the village made sure he took his family off to Lusaka first – he came from here, you see.' 'Those blokes from the Party came to see us and told us to "vote the right way". They made us all sorts of promises, but they haven't been back once since the elections.' Yet thousands of bicycles had been handed out to Party workers so that they could spread the two slogans we mentioned round all the villages. They kept them for their own private use instead. It would have been much better to give them to the farm labourers who are so badly paid and so poorly housed. The villagers pay virtually no attention to the Party, though they do still listen to the chiefs.

During our travels through the rural areas we paid courtesy visits to a large number of tribal chiefs, ranging from the paramount chief to senior and ordinary chiefs. In one village in the north we saw a fat chief of the Bemba tribe leaning on his Mercedes and listening condescendingly to kneeling women pouring out their grievances and telling him that all their poultry had died because they couldn't get enough grain. Most of the chiefs don't flaunt their wealth in this way, and ride round on bicycles, but all of them are still surrounded by a sort of aura and they are all treated with respect by the authorities. Chief Empezeni, a descendant of the fierce Ngoni warriors who crossed the Zambezi to escape from the Zulus, has recently and reluctantly – and more prosaically – had to buckle to and till his own fields. He sent us a message to the effect that he would receive us at a specified time in his 'presidential palace', which turned out to be a fairly modest place, but officials invariably addressed him timidly and in the third person via an intermediary, bowing and scraping as they did so. The Lozi chief's palace is grander (many people still refer to the king and royal family of Barotseland), but we weren't allowed in because the chief wasn't back from his summer residence. It's interesting to note that before the great plain of the Zambezi is flooded, the 'king' sails back up to his winter residence along the canals with his subjects lining the banks. The 'modern' chiefs living in Lusaka, and other élite groups, come from the capital specially to take part in this traditional ceremony.

In Kaoma his cousin – he too is a grandson of the famous paramount chief Lewanika – received us with great pomp, the men going in by the main door while the women slipped in by a little hidden door, and everyone was on bended knee (especially the officials). America certainly seemed a long way off! Even the servant who brought the tea would drop to his knees every time he touched anything. (The receptions given by the president are much less formal and he likes to pour the coffee himself.)

The chiefs are represented in Lusaka by the House of Chiefs, but the government now has a right of inspection over all appointments (and is sometimes allowed to go further). When Queen Elizabeth II visited Zambia the chiefs were extremely disappointed not to be sent for. 'After all,' they said, 'she's a chief too.' Apparently the British paid more attention to this type of thing.

But the chiefs have in fact lost some of their traditional powers, though this may not always be apparent. Their religious authority waned with the coming of the missions and their political authority with first the colonial administration and then the Party. The peasants are aware of this. Lusaka and the single political party now have the monopoly of power, so they invariably turn to them, realizing that they owe everything to Lusaka.

The villages that have adopted religions opposed to the authorities, such as the Jehovah's Witnesses or the Lumpa Church (which was forcibly disbanded at the time of independence), stand on their own feet and do their own organizing, knowing that no one will ever help them. They build attractive villages with flowers everywhere and run their farms better than their neighbours who are affiliated to the Party and sit back expecting to be given government aid for everything. Such expectations are never fulfilled. The top government men are more colonialist than the colonials and never do more than roar through the villages in a cloud of dust. Visits from agricultural or veterinary advisers are few and far between. Just as well sometimes – in one village they were carving up the carcase of a cow killed by the vet's attentions.

10 *How can agriculture be 'modernized'?*

There is general agreement that 'something must be done' to step up agricultural output. Kenneth Kaunda sent us a telegram saying that the problems connected with the country's agriculture had got out of control and he was delighted we were coming. He expected us to criticize the policies that had been followed up to then. After the failure in the late 1960s of an ambitious cooperative farming scheme, the Agriculture Minister set out to create a class of 'kulaks' or 'emergent farmers'. They were given grants to help them expand and were able to hire official tractors for half the cost price. This policy has slowed down the spread of ox-drawn transport, the only kind that 'relies on the country's own resources'. At this time there was war on Zambia's borders, and by the end of 1979 it had encroached on Zambian territory. Fertilizers were very heavily subsidized, which discouraged farmers from using various forms of organic manure and gave them no incentive to use rotation with grassland based on legumes, or with beans, groundnuts and soya beans, all of which can fix nitrogen from the air. Instead preference was given to imported nitrates, which are petroleum by-products and are getting more and more expensive, especially when they're manufactured on the spot.

Groundnuts are declining and sunflowers merely marking time, and oil and oilseeds have to be imported. Yet oil and soap are in short supply everywhere, especially in the villages. There's nowhere near enough cotton to meet the country's needs, so fabrics and synthetic fibres have to be imported. Yet much of the country is highly suitable for growing all these crops. The problem is that the sprawling towns act as magnets, so the peasants have no incentive to work hard on the farms.

Extension staff concentrate all their efforts on hybrid maize requiring large quantities of chemical fertilizers – a Zambian variant of the 'green revolution'. A big effort has also been made to have irrigated wheat grown all over the country, since bread consumption is on the increase, whereas maize and other local cereals are less popular. In 1978 144,000 tonnes of wheat were imported and 8,000 tonnes produced; in 1979 home production fell to only 5,000 tonnes. Even locally produced wheat is expensive in terms of foreign currency, because the hoses and sprinklers needed for watering it are very expensive and liable to break down, and there's the cost of fertilizers and insecticides too. Worse still, major emphasis is being put on potatoes, which are even more expensive and difficult to grow, and were selling in autumn 1979 for more than 1 kwacha per kilo – a luxury product! But wheat and potatoes are prestige crops because those big strong white men eat them! Yet it would be easy to grow an improved variety of sweet potatoes, an easy crop with which the peasants are familiar. The varieties with coloured flesh provide carotene or provitamin A, which could markedly reduce the country's blind population – Luapula has a very large number of blind people.

Strawberries, peaches, apples, grapes, all of them prestige fruits, are grown, whereas it would be much simpler to encourage the whole peasant population to grow papaws, guavas (which are half-wild anyway), mangoes, and even citrus fruits, pineapples and many other tropical fruits. In Tanzania the markets are overflowing with fruit, yet apart from Lusaka Zambia has hardly any. Some places, such as Ndola, the country's second largest town, have literally no fruit at all, as we saw in September 1979, and the same applies to the villages, except for the odd mango tree. Everything is geared to the minority which is in power, to provide luxuries for the rich – most of whom are black rather than white nowadays. And these luxuries take precedence over the basic needs of the poor.

Maize is now the top priority throughout the country. But although it can be grown successfully on fertile soil such as that owned by the white settlers, and on much of the land in the southern half of the country, virtually the whole of the northern half is unsuitable for maize growing because the soil is too acid and too heavily leached. The crops traditionally grown there are millet, cassava, sorghum, sweet potatoes and beans, but nothing has been done to improve these 'poor peasant' crops. Yet even with priority going to maize, the acreage allocated to it continued to drop, and this was the case until 1979. Drought made things worse, with production dropping even further. This was when Zambia pleaded for help, since it was unable to put its agriculture back on its feet.

When we held meetings outside the capital the officials didn't try to hide their grievances: 'We have to refer everything to Lusaka, but they've got no idea what's going on in the rural areas. . . . Lots of projects never get beyond the planning stage, they're never carried out at all. We haven't been able to pinpoint the real problems.' The extension service comes in for some strong criticism: 'Why help just the large-scale farmers and neglect the peasants who can't read or write. . .? We've been spoilt by Western technology.'

The only competent agronomists are to be found at regional level. The district agronomists are only partly trained or not trained at all, while the agricultural assistants in the wards haven't had any practical training whatsoever, and we came across some who were totally ignorant. As inspectors have stopped coming to check up on them, they take things easy. The only people to be given grants are the planters beside the railway line; nothing ever gets through to the remoter districts, or at any rate not enough to meet the basic needs. Although research into agronomics is a crucial factor in the development of the country's agriculture, the funds available for it total only 1½ million kwachas per annum, a pathetic sum. But in 1979 the Agriculture Minister was still handing out, even after a large number of cutbacks, subsidies worth 30 million kwachas for foodstuffs for the urban areas. Namboard, the national marketing board, doesn't buy any of the traditional peasant crops (millet, sorghum, etc.) and the level of nutrition in the villages is dropping all the time; they really have been disinherited and abandoned by the urban authorities.

11 *Pigs and chickens 'American-style'*

Rich Africans copy the Europeans in liking a large amount of meat with their *nshima* or maize porridge, and they're the only people with genuine purchasing power. So a super-modern breeding industry has been set up solely for them, with two large factories turning out fodder for the pig and chicken breeding units, which are fairly modern in themselves. Namboard transports maize grown in the area round Petauke, in Eastern Province, to the provincial capital of Chipata, 180 kilometres away (the man in charge likes to collect all his maize round him). He then sends it on another 600 kilometres to Lusaka (via Petauke, which means 360 wasted kilometres!). As some of the maize is used as an ingredient in the cattle fodder, it then travels back to Chipata (via Petauke) and eventually back to square one in Petauke, where it is supplied to local pig- and chicken-breeding units!

There was a maize shortage in autumn 1979 and the whole elaborate structure collapsed, since there wasn't enough food to keep it upright. The starving chickens started eating one another and pigs were slaughtered before they were fully grown – total chaos in fact. It would have been perfectly possible to set up breeding units depending chiefly, like those in Europe down to about 1950, on local-grown resources, just as the basic foodstuff for pigs in China is sweet potatoes. The essential prerequisite for such costly 'modern' methods was to sell pigs and chickens at high prices. Later on the state decided to pay the same price for maize throughout the country, and agreed to cover all transport costs, which explains the subsidies of 12 million kwachas to Namboard (though they claim this is nowhere near high enough), plus 74 million in the form of cancelled debt repayments. In so doing the state denied the most elementary principles of economics and encouraged people to squander transport resources, since it was in no one's interest to keep costs down, and some people found it more lucrative to move fertilizer shipments about needlessly.

12 *Everything is always late and the machine is breaking down*

So here we have a form of agricultural modernization which presupposes regular and substantial inputs imported from far away at vast expense. All sorts of transport difficulties have to be overcome, and these were considerably heightened by attacks from outside, with bridges blown up and so on. This should have encouraged the Zambians to cut back on these inputs. The white minority took over power in Rhodesia in 1965. Now most of Zambia's goods traffic had to cross Rhodesia to reach the port of Beira in Mozambique. The Chinese funded and supervised the building of the Tan-Zam railway running between Dar es Salaam and the Copperbelt, which was completed in 1975. It was expected to transport an annual total of 2 million tonnes of freight in either direction, but by 1978 the figure was still less than 600,000 tonnes, and half the locomotives were out of order, while the others were running a third below capacity. Strikes and general disorganization were common. Then in October 1979 a bridge over the river Chambeshi was destroyed by the Rhodesians. And so it went on.

These factors should have encouraged the Zambians to rely much more on local resources in the way of earth, labour and manure – as indeed the Chinese recommended – but they were set on American-style 'total modernization'. Yet if they were going to achieve this they had to be able to organize themselves properly. This form of modern agriculture is dependent on loans, and a large number of colonists turned up with virtually nothing in the way of capital except their briefcases. The loans made to the cooperatives have never been repaid. Another bank was set up, but the rate of repayments was so poor that it soon went bankrupt.

A new start was made with the Agricultural Finance Company (AFC), which provided government loans. Between 1969 and 1974 as much as 91 per cent of agricultural loans were repaid, but the wealthier farmers, many of whom had previously been high-ranking civil servants or leading figures in the Party, or even ministers – which had made it easier for them to amass the necessary starting capital – had such influential contacts in the world of politics that they started repaying less and less. Their less well-off colleagues followed their bad example, and between 1975 and 1978 the repayment figure dropped to 71 per cent. As a result the AFC was short of capital and had to turn down applications from potential customers. It did continue to lend money to its old customers, but it often arrived too late: in tropical climates with only one rainy season the only way to get a good yield – and therefore to be in a position to pay back loans – is to sow early.

Namboard is often very late in collecting grains, particularly maize, and at least 15 per cent of the sacks stacked up in the open air in their rural depots are spoiled. Fertilizers are often stored in places with little shelter too, and here the losses can be as high as 30 per cent. Payment for crops comes weeks or even months late. In September 1979 the rice growers in the Chambeshi Valley couldn't start on their new campaign in time because they still hadn't been paid for the previous crop, several months after delivering it. As a result they hadn't got any money to pay for fertilizers, labour and so on. Agricultural output has been falling since 1976.

13 *The IMF and the finance minister deliver the coup de grâce*

Although allegedly a 'rich' country, Zambia is getting more and more heavily into debt. In 1979 she owed 1,500,000,000 dollars, an amazing figure when you bear in mind that Britain's debt of 3,000,000,000 was deemed excessive by the IMF a few years ago. Imports of luxury goods have been scaled down a bit, but they haven't been stopped altogether.

For instance a hundred new cars were delivered for the Common-wealth Conference in August 1979. The Fiat assembly plant at Livingstone was equipped with machinery that was already obsolete in Italy by then; it produces a mere handful of mediocre vehicles, with very little value added. A bicycle factory is at last being set up, ten years on!

But the West wants to go on selling, and in spite of its claim to donate 'aid' the IMF invariably puts the interests of the capitalist world first. It therefore made Zambia a standby loan in 1978 of 356 million kwachas in foreign currency, to enable the country to continue importing goods. But at first it laid down harsh conditions, insisting on cutbacks in credit, budget expenditure and so on. Kenneth Kaunda did manage to obtain slightly less harsh conditions by stressing the constraints imposed on him from outside, i.e. the costs resulting from his country's position in the front line against the Rhodesian guerrillas.

The Zambian government therefore received a rather politer request to cut its spending, squeeze credit, and raise its farm prices, so the finance minister slashed all the various budgets, by roughly the same amount in each case. But he knew nothing whatsoever about the problems facing the rural areas and disregarded the peasants. He concentrated solely on the figures in his budget, ignoring the economic consequences of his decisions. He had no concept of the need for proper economic planning and control. Far too much money had been going to the towns, so they still had enough, and the frenetic merry-go-round of cars continued, more often than not on journeys that weren't really necessary. On Sundays forty-five cars could be seen parked around the cathedral, but only one bike (or sometimes none at all). Meanwhile in the rural districts everything ground to a halt because the previous level of funding was already quite inade-quate. Even the World Bank stressed that over the last few years Zambia had been spending a mere 10 dollars per head of the population per annum in the rural districts. This figure covered spending on all sectors (the civil service, the police, education, health, agriculture, local roads and so on). Yet subsidies to lower the cost of basic foods sold in the towns (for rich and poor alike) amounted to as much as 30 dollars per head in 1978 – three times higher than the rural expenditure figure.

After the budget cutbacks in 1979 the agricultural training centres, which used to seek out 'emergent farmers' in their own areas and provide them with board and lodging throughout their training courses, could no longer operate. The staff were kept on, but they didn't do anything; they didn't even try to offer advice to the neighbouring villages. Few of the ward agricultural assistants now had bikes, and those who did had no tyres or inner tubes, so they couldn't ride round their large districts, which have many remote hamlets. Most of the district agronomists' Land-Rovers had broken down, or else there weren't any funds available for the petrol which was still being wasted in Lusaka. As a result the rural administrative machine, which has been virtually starved of the funds needed to keep it going, is more or less totally unproductive. Yet it goes on costing money in the form of salaries, building maintenance and so on. That's what the IMF likes to refer to as its contribution to development – but it isn't the only culprit!

14 *The failure of agriculture run on military lines*

Once the villages had been officially declared to be on the bread line, everyone tried to lend a helping hand. In 1975 funds were provided to enable the army to help the rural areas to develop. They were to set up five Rural Reconstruction Centres (RRCs) in each of the country's fifty-three districts. Three hundred young people of both sexes were to attend the centres for three years, practising farming and learning various rural trades and crafts. In the first year one centre was set up in each district, but then the scheme ground to a halt, as all sorts of difficulties arose.

The initial funds earmarked for the scheme totalled 17·5 million kwachas. In an attempt to be 'different', the organizers started out by spending 5 million on hundreds of thousands of saplings of exotic fruit trees from South Africa. They bought peach, plum and apricot trees, vines and even apple trees, without knowing whether they were suitable for the soil where they were to be planted. They did add local citrus fruits and papaws, but they didn't listen to advice from the extension service on how to maintain their orchards. They rarely weeded them, so when the weeds had grown to over two metres high, in the dry season, it was quicker to burn them – and the trees went up in flames too! Some of them even planted their trees on marshy ground so they wouldn't need watering.

The land handed over to the centres varied considerably in quality; some of them had to be moved three times. With sound equipment they should have made a go of it and turned in a profit – if the young people had been prepared to work, that is. But for the last five years they've been getting 2 kwachas per day for their food – twice the average wages for a farm worker – and they are single, with no families to support. With no real leaders and no incentive to put in some proper work, many of them haven't even grasped what they are doing there – they simply let themselves be fed and housed.

As soon as they have learnt a trade they go off to practise it elsewhere, where they are better paid. The girls soon leave and the young men follow them. When we visited the centres there were only forty to seventy young people there, or very occasionally a hundred. The local peasants, who get no aid and no equipment, were annoyed at the sight of so many tractors lying idle. They referred to the centres as 'schools of laziness'.

In the previous season, in the Kaoma district RRC on the Lukulu road, the seventy-two young people, with plenty of equipment, including a tractor, grew a mere 15 hectares of maize and 2·5 hectares of cotton, even though they had excellent land, 90 per cent of it already cleared. But they see little point in their work, since they have everything they need. We visited the centre on 3 November 1979. It had rained during the night – a good start to the rainy season – and in the nearby villages all the women were busy sowing their first maize. But the young people at the centre were playing volleyball, even though the neighbouring field was all ready for sowing. 'But it's Saturday,' was their reply. Civil servants in Zambia take two days off per week (the Chinese get two days a month) and, like all good civil servants, are fed in return for doing nothing at all.

Yet the Third National Development Plan (TNDP), indulging, as ever, in wishful thinking, says that they must be given more money, because 'there are only two trucks per centre and these are hardly adequate for their needs'. They've got all the equipment and land they need, but they must still be fed like soldiers. The Zambian army is good at spending ever-increasing sums of money, but doesn't know how to produce on an economic basis. But then what army does, apart from the Chinese army?

15 *Deforestation and erosion – an environment under threat*

Trees in Zambia are public property and Zambians squander them as
the fancy takes them, making no attempt to husband them – after all,
they're free. It is forbidden to cut down trees on hillsides because of the
danger of erosion, but when you live near a town like Chipata in the
east, the need for timber becomes more urgent and the ban is hardly
ever respected. Every day a few more trees are cut down on the
hillsides overlooking Chipata, and this gradual deforestation is
already leading to soil erosion, with the bare rock starting to show
through. Anyone using a bulldozer to clear land for planting will
simply remove *all* the trees, since this makes easier going for the
tractors. With ox-drawn ploughs there's no need whatsoever for this.
Wherever the land slopes slightly it would be better to leave strips of
forest – even on flat ground, they act as a windbreak – and to leave the
young trees that could produce high-quality timber, and provide
much-needed shade, in ten or twenty years' time.

Trees are squandered on buildings or cattle shelters – because
they're worthless. Every year Zambia is reckoned to lose forest to the
tune of 100,000 hectares to obtain timber and charcoal, which are also
in demand in the towns. Even more land than this is cleared for crop
growing, though a lot of the cleared land is never in fact cultivated, or
not properly cultivated, and once the land has been laid bare it
deteriorates. Felled trees are burned on the spot, so they don't even
provide heat; and there is no attempt to use them for building timber
or joinery or anything other than firewood. The country doesn't have
enough sawmills to cut them into planks, and anyway it imports a
large amount of timber. Rural craftsmen are a dying breed throughout
the country, and their children are unemployed. All this ill-considered
deforestation is offset by very little reafforestation, which is restricted
to the Copperbelt, where timber is needed for the mines, and for a
paper-pulping plant which is taking far too long to materialize, with
the trees already mature. A total of 14,000 hectares were planted with
eucalyptus and pines during the six years of the Second National
Development Plan. Acacias with their tannin and forage trees (*lucaena
glauca*) with their leaves that can be used as fodder improve the soil and
should be used. Apart from those 14,000 hectares there's nothing but
the odd plantation in the provinces. Nothing has been done in the
villages at all, though the foresters have made a few half-hearted

attempts to reafforest. Now most of the energy consumed in tropical Africa comes from wood or charcoal, and they are often squandered. Wood stoves could lead to large savings, if it were made worth people's while. If the country had true village communities their members would be able to grasp how advantageous it would be for them to protect their forests and expand their plantations. Tanzania does have village communities of this kind, and reafforestation in the villages is making headway there, albeit on far too small a scale.

The dangers of erosion were pointed out as early as 1930, and the Africans were supposed to combat it by contour ploughing and maintaining strips of permanent fallow grass. The traditional authorities were in charge of this, but all their rules and regulations were abolished and this has discredited all these soil-protection measures, since the people fighting for independence proclaimed them to be 'colonialist'. The new rural district committees don't enjoy any real authority in this field and the chiefs – the only people who are listened to – are no longer responsible; they are too dependent on the government to act on their own initiative.

Soil conservation is nominally the responsibility of the extension services, but they have neither the equipment nor the necessary training. They're geared solely to short-term output.

Meanwhile thoughtless deforestation and various forms of erosion, ranging from what is known as sheet erosion, where the surface layers of humus-rich topsoil are swept away, to deep gullies, are degrading most of Zambia's cultivated land and thus present an ominous threat for the future. Flooding is getting worse and will soon jeopardize the rice fields in the valleys. If the environment is to be properly protected a wide-ranging information campaign must be organized, as with sanitation and malnutrition. But it can't be run with the necessary dynamism unless the country's political leaders are genuinely concerned about the country's future, and not merely with their own short-term interests as a privileged class.

Ill-considered use of tractors, which are powerful enough to cause great damage, adds rapidly to the erosion as soon as the land slopes even very slightly (even with a 1 per cent gradient) if the conventional method of soil preparation – i.e. ploughing and disc harrowing – is used. In many cases, especially if the soil is sandy, the minimum amount of work will do, affecting only drills where the seed will be sown, or even what is known as 'zero tillage', in which a combined drill covers the ground only once, broadcasting both seeds and fertilizer, plus the use of weedkillers. But then weedkillers may turn out to be dangerous in the long term.

Another problem that is frequently discussed is bush fires. As early as 1944 the alarm was sounded by J.-P. Harroy.[5] If fire didn't sweep through the thinly planted forests every year a mass of humus would build up and then when the land was cleared for cultivation the soil would be much more fertile. If the grass was cut at the end of the rainy season to make hay or silage the oxen would have more energy for drawing the plough at the end of the dry season. The tall grasses used for roofing could also be used for paper making, and so on. But then all that would mean a great deal more work.

But these tall grasses (*Hyparrhenia*) are the haunt of snakes, tsetse flies and mosquitoes. No wonder the peasants don't care for them. When the fires are over the cattle like eating the fresh growth of young grass. Early and carefully controlled fires fulfil these various functions and do a great deal less damage, but when we were in Zambia in September 1979 we saw a lot of late fires, which do much more harm. Some of them had been lit to drive out a handful of rats or mice, which birds of prey caught before the hunters – what a sorry sight!

16 *The widening gulf between urban and rural areas*

A survey carried out by Alan Marter[6] shows that 40 per cent of rural households are short of labour (through emigration, families being separated or illness) and so can't get enough food and income from their fields. They are in a much worse position if they live outside the rich areas, in the north or west of the country, where cattle rearing is impossible because of the tsetse fly and they therefore can't use animal traction or make dairy products. These poor families living in areas with poor land have no oxen, ploughs or carts – and no money to hire them with either. Even in the fertile areas only the rich, i.e. 10–20 per cent of farming households, own cattle.

So there is a fairly wide discrepancy within farming households, since the wealthiest also have a larger acreage of more fertile land (even if the land can't be sold). Even though each family can usually be allocated enough land to ensure their livelihood, they are very often short of genuinely rich land, which is owned by the upper-class families, influential people, those who have contacts with the powers-that-be, district chiefs, top officials, or even by Party leaders. Even in the three wealthy provinces (Central, Southern and Eastern) 58 per cent of rural households were below the poverty line of 120 kwachas per household per year in 1974, and the figure for the rest of the country was 92 per cent. Since then the situation has only got worse.

Even the better-off rural families, with an annual income of 900 kwachas, had less than the average earnings paid to a miner (1,700 kwachas), or even to those working in other industries (1,100 kwachas). The average rural income was only 123 kwachas, or a mere third of the lowest official salary paid to an urban worker, which was 360 kwachas at that time. Given this state of affairs, Marter concludes that the opportunity of achieving a far higher income by moving to a town was such that it was worth running the risk of being unemployed. The informal sector does provide some jobs, so even if it is merely a dream, there will always be some way of getting by, and the fear of being out of work is lessened if you know you've got some relative in a good job. So people flock from the rural areas to the towns. The thought of the shanty towns never enters their heads – all they see is the luxury mansions. The rural population is dwindling (in Northern and Luapula provinces, for instance), or is growing by a mere 1 or 2 per cent per annum. The urban growth rate is 6 per cent. In Lusaka the figure is 9 per cent; its population shot up from 260,000 in 1969 to 600,000 in 1980.

Between 1964 and 1976 average urban incomes rose by 50 per cent, and the figure was even higher in the case of the wealthiest town-dwellers. But average peasant incomes went down during the same period. In 1964 the price of a 90-kilo sack of maize could buy you *three* shirts; in 1979 you could sell it for 9 kwachas, but the cheapest shirts cost 15 kwachas *each*. In the four years from 1976 the country's overall output (not merely agricultural output) fell by 2 per cent, which means a per capita income drop of 15 per cent, with an annual population growth of 3·2 per cent. Urban incomes, too, are falling now. But the gulf between urban and rural lifestyles must be calculated much more in terms of services – water, health care, education, electricity – than of earnings. Electricity, after all, makes a huge difference to people's lives – just think of the bright lights!

17 *Prevention is better than cure*

The first complaint voiced in many villages is about the dispensary:
'We have to walk for ages to get there, and when we do, there aren't
any medicines.' It wouldn't be fair to say that Zambia has done
nothing to improve public health in rural areas. The Health Minister
prides himself on the number of centres that have been set up – 565 in
1979, with another 77 due over the following five years. But here
again there is a confusion between the number of buildings and their
effectiveness, and this salves many people's conscience: 'Look what
we've done for the masses,' say the well-groomed upper crust of
Lusaka patronizingly.

We saw a large number of these centres, all of them built to the
expensive specifications laid down by the minister. They are always
crowded and the poor staff do their best. But however dedicated they
are, they simply can't cope. More often than not they don't have the
medicines they need. The assistant in charge of preventive medicine
hasn't got a bicycle for his rounds. Some health centres haven't even
got any qualified staff. We saw district hospitals without a single
doctor, because no one wants to work in these 'underprivileged' parts
of the country. Then there are the nurses whose main aim in life is
acquiring social status and a rich husband from Lusaka, and who don't
give a damn for these makeshift buildings. The country is riddled with
malaria and special anti-malaria squads have been set up, but there
isn't any foreign currency available for buying chloroquine, in a
country so set on squandering that it manages to find a million dollars
every year for importing cosmetics which – or so the Party newspaper
claims – 'the women of Zambia simply can't do without'. It refers of
course to women in the towns – their sisters in the villages seem to
have more pressing needs. Luckily, these neglected sectors of the
population can still consult medicine men, who are as popular as ever.
But one elderly chief complained that witchdoctors aren't what they
were: 'Nowadays they've been affected by the greed they see all round
them and they've gone very commercial.'

A Western-style approach to health problems, based on curing
rather than preventing, is still the order of the day. The results are only
too obvious: infant mortality at the rate of 127 per 1,000 infants during
the first year of life, and between 30 and 40 per cent up to the age of
five. Life expectancy is 47 years. Zambian children, even those

who've been vaccinated, still die of smallpox. (The problem is that the vaccines are highly unstable and it's difficult to preserve them in a tropical climate. Expensive though they are, in fact they're often unusable by the time they leave the airport.) The children die of other preventable diseases too, but the real cause of death is malnutrition. Malnutrition is the major health problem in Zambia, with a third of all children seriously undernourished and weighing 70 per cent less than the normal figure. What sort of future can children expect if they haven't had the necessary amount of protein in their first three years of life? And malnutrition is an ongoing process, affecting pregnant women, whose health is impaired by anaemia. 'Sometimes you can't even find their veins,' one nurse in a poor district told us. These makeshift hospitals are the mirror image of a society of outcasts.

But, one society lady assured us, 'malnutrition is essentially the result of ignorance'. This is sometimes true, with taboos often preventing pregnant women and nursing mothers from eating rich foods such as eggs, meat or fish (and on top of that it's customary for men to serve themselves first from a dish, so that what the women and children eat depends on the father's appetite). But taboos can't explain the whole picture. For instance women who are left alone with their children have difficulty in feeding them. When their husbands abandon them – temporarily or permanently – to go off and work in the mines, they have to cultivate several acres of land single-handed. They hire themselves out to more prosperous neighbours for a mouthful of maize, or eat cassava so as to be able to sell their cereals or legumes, which have a higher food value but are more profitable. They are so weakened as a result of malnutrition and all the various illnesses caused by it that their output falls and a vicious circle of poverty sets in. And we call them lazy!

18 *Schools of alienation*

In one rural school a teacher greeted us by saying: 'We haven't got any books, or exercise books or pencils. So how do you expect us to teach the children to read and write?' Yet one official had noted in the visitors' book (a British colonial tradition): 'Surroundings very well kept. Pity there aren't any panes of glass left to replace the broken ones. Something must be done about it. It looks bad.' A typical reaction from the authorities, who aren't much bothered how the structures work. It's the building itself that counts.

In village schools of this type the metal-framed doors and windows, and the furniture, come readymade from abroad, often from South Africa, or from factories in the towns, whereas carpenters could easily make them with local timber, as they do in Tanzania, and the same applies to the desks and the various building units. The remoter villages build their schools with what little they have available, but before they can be 'recognized' and provided with teaching staff they have to buy corrugated iron roofing, although they could perfectly well thatch the roofs, as they thatch their houses, using productive labour and saving on foreign currency. All this means that the villagers have no hope of practising productive crafts. Now no village can really get by on nothing but farming. With only one crop per year they spend months out of work. All this equipment is expensive and eats into the education budget. There's nothing left to pay for the books and pencils that the school is supposed to provide. And the modest sums contributed by the parents are supposed to go on football! The pupils are expected to grow maize in their 'production units', but they are frequently badly organized, and if they are successful, the money left over once costs have been paid for has to go into a bank account. Meanwhile the pupils have none of the things they need for better learning.

In remote rural areas many children can't go to school at all, as it may be 16 kilometres away. Often it only goes up to grade 4 (the lower primary section), and a third of the pupils won't get a place in the upper primary section. So the process of elimination starts at that early stage. Primary-level inspectors rarely turn up in the villages nowadays – the pretext is lack of transport. Using a bike, we were told, would mean a total loss of face. The teachers take advantage of this situation, some of them spending their time drinking with the local chief, while others go off to Lusaka and only come back on pay day. Young primary teachers who start out full of enthusiasm are soon given the cold shoulder if they don't toe the line. The best of them dream of jobs in the capital, where they're bound to get promotion. After all why should they choose to slave away in forgotten villages that have nothing to offer them?

'At least in the old days, with colonization, you used to learn something at school,' is a common refrain on the lips of parents from peasant families. The mission schools for African children used to teach them various types of crafts and trades. Kenneth Kaunda told us that he had built a house for his mother with his own hands, and the prime minister, Daniel Lisulo, claimed to be able to do any type of repair. But when the country became independent everyone had to go to 'the white man's school', which prepared pupils for secondary education – and for Oxbridge. To hell with manual skills: they smacked of the old days – education was going to be purely academic. So the technical schools to which pupils used to go straight out of primary school were closed down, and new ones opened for children who'd been through the first stage of secondary education. But here they are taught to use equipment that is far too sophisticated.

In the eyes of an ex-colonial subject, education means learning English, and later on picking up a cushy job as a civil servant. Or even, better still, a scholarship to travel abroad. So right from the first year, and in spite of Unesco's recommendations, children in rural areas who've never heard a word of anything but the local dialect are given all their education in English, the language of the towns, and are thus cut off from their home environment and steered in a very definite direction. The syllabus reinforces this 'programming' of their education, since it's based on preparing them for secondary education, and has been taken up enthusiastically by the teachers, who are themselves fascinated by the bright lights. As a result young people are still further alienated from their villages, whereas in fact most of them would be better advised to stay there, since the secondary education they've been promised will reject four-fifths of them. Every year a hundred thousand bewildered children 'fail' the competitive exams and are contemptuously labelled 'drop-outs', a highly pejorative term for youngsters who've been given no preparation whatever for ordinary working life.

To begin with they'll hang around their villages for a while, full of frustration, to the despair of their parents, who have to feed them but daren't say too much because they're intimidated by their own lack of education. Before long most of them try to get to the nearest town to stay with some distant relative. But jobs are few and far between in a society that's more concerned with acquiring machines than labour, and only about a third ever find paid employment. The rest of them start off by selling cigarettes to scrape a living. They are known as 'mishangas boys' and the pavements of Zambian towns are crawling

61

with them. When they've had enough of kicking their heels in the shanty towns and catching glimpses, through garden gates, of the privileges enjoyed by others and the signs of growing inequality, they begin stealing, gradually growing bolder until eventually they're committing armed hold-ups – a form of redistribution of wealth in an unbalanced society that offers its youngsters neither work nor hope.

19 *Privileges start at secondary level and become more marked at university*

The only hope lies in secondary education. If you get there you've crossed the threshold and are at last on the other side of the fence, where privileges are rife. In 1960 a representative from the World Bank speaking in Chile pointed out that primary schooling merely created a generation of frustrated revolutionaries if they didn't continue their education, whereas secondary education turned out 'good citizens', pillars of society. The ideal solution would therefore be a mixture of submissive illiterates and 'good citizens'. In Zambia, too, the World Bank provides more funds for secondary schools, which are given preferential treatment by the Zambian authorities, as the peasants themselves complain – 'They neglect our primary schools and do everything for the secondary schools.' Northern Province puts three times as much money into its fourteen secondary schools as into its five hundred primary schools. Secondary school pupils are all boarders, but they don't pay any fees, even if they come from wealthy families, as they often do – yet another instance of preferential treatment meted out to the 'haves' in the name of equality. One church secondary school near Ndola with five hundred pupils has a row of handsome buildings that would cost over 10 million kwachas today, which means an investment of 25,000 kwachas per pupil. It also has a huge private stadium.

Even in difficult periods funds are always available for building swimming pools for secondary schools, but there's never enough for pencils for the primary schools. Pupils in secondary schools have grown used to eating large amounts of meat. When their ration had to be cut back and dried beans and fresh vegetables were served instead, some of them promptly went off and killed a pig in the school pigsty. The alleged ringleaders were expelled, but it was hardly their fault.

The blame rests with the environment that has brought them up so badly. The government ought to have made sure that with the equipment they've already received – or should be given – for their production unit, the schools are capable of being largely self-sufficient, as Kenneth Kaunda insisted shortly after independence. But they are nowhere near self-sufficient. Once children have managed to get into a secondary school they think of themselves as members of an élite, entitled to whatever they want. Even those who criticize capitalism and imperialism never question the privileges enjoyed by the pupils. They're never willing to give up any of the advantages they enjoy under the 'system', even when they've been busy criticizing certain aspects of it.

This preferential treatment is even more marked at the next stage up the ladder. For instance the pupils in one school went on strike to back up their demand for more beef and less chicken at mealtimes. In November 1979 university students demonstrated their support for the president, and when he declared a state of emergency they demanded that British firms should be nationalized. Yet they've never protested about their own privileges, which they are incapable of seeing as such. They take it for granted that they shouldn't do any form of manual work in the way of cleaning and maintaining their bedrooms or refectories, lecture rooms and lawns, and a large staff is employed to do this work. Some of them are surprised they aren't still served eggs and bacon for breakfast, as they used to be when the university first opened. Even those from the wealthiest families (and the proportion is still rising) think it perfectly normal that they should pay nothing at all, and be given free books, travel grants for the vacations and so on.

They've left their villages well behind them and in their dreams most of them are already living in Britain or the United States, like the young man who told us that one multinational company would buy tobacco cheap from the peasants in eastern Zambia and sell the cigarettes to the students with unnecessarily deluxe packaging, at high prices. Meanwhile the peasants roll their own cigarettes, using strips of newspaper, and we suggested he might do the same. He bridled: 'If I go to Britain some day I could never do that.' He didn't realize of course that plenty of university teachers in Britain roll their own cigarettes!

Cultural dominance is as strong as ever. Students complain that the number of expatriates at the university is still high, and demand that the top jobs should be rapidly 'Zambianized'. Too many of the teaching staff come from the United States, and many of the Zambians who were also trained there come back in a mood to out-Herod Herod. The teaching is inevitably Western-style, and certainly ill-suited to the country's needs, with some of those who talk about development quite incapable of escaping from the 'classic' economic model, i.e. capitalism. In October 1979 the university awarded 120 degrees in art subjects, 120 in the social sciences and 46 in law, but only 21 in science, 13 in engineering (including one chemical engineer) and 12 in agronomics. Yet Professor Ben Turok, who helped us a great deal, did eventually publish, in 1979, after fifteen years of pseudo-independence (in the economic and cultural sphere genuine independence is a long time coming), a study called *Development in Zambia.*[7] In it he has tried to find concrete solutions and does so, at long last, in the light of the whole country's interests, rather than in those of the privileged few in high-ranking positions. Who wants to go back to the land in this sick society, or at any rate to stay there?

20 *Non-productive activity in Lusaka*

'I've never seen anyone come back,' claims one disillusioned elderly chief. 'Except the ones who come back to steal from the old people who won't hand over their money.' Most of the young 'drop-outs' land up, with no training whatsoever, in the shanty towns. When the Third National Development Plan was drawn up (it started in 1980) it was decided, somewhat late in the day, that something had to be done to counter this growing problem. Provision was made for just 5,000 'drop-outs', 1,000 a year for five years, to be given a form of apprenticeship, with the possibility of being set up in business. The cost was expected to be 3·5 million kwachas, or 700 kwachas per apprentice. But this figure is too low, and it seems likely that the figure of 5,000 apprentices will never be reached.

In the townships in Old Kanyama, west of Lusaka, only a third of the young people have a steady job. The others do various odds and ends and get by somehow. One shamefaced seventeen-year-old who'd failed to get into secondary school told us that he made 3 or 4 kwachas per day selling cigarettes. Shoeshine boys can earn up to 7 kwachas per day. Meanwhile even the highest-earning agricultural day labourers only get 1 kwacha 70 ngwee, and the hardest-working canecutter – it's a very tough job – manages to make 3 kwachas. In Kanyama the average wage in 1973 was 55 kwachas a month, but in 1978 the figure was down to 43 kwachas in real terms (nominally it was 92 kwachas, but the cost of living had increased by over 100 per cent). Living in the shanty towns is expensive, as everything is bought in small quantities: a small saucer of beans costs 20 ngwee, and 2 centilitres of oil (which is unobtainable except on the black market) costs 10 ngwee. The women who sell these items have no other means of livelihood, and even then they are only just scraping a living – the poor exploiting the even poorer.

Shanty town children therefore suffer from malnutrition and fill the children's hospital to bursting. Seventy per cent of those admitted are undernourished, and the situation is getting worse. In fact it's so bad that the doctors told us: 'Socioeconomic deprivation has been a key factor over the last few years, preventing children getting the proteins they need if they're to develop normally.' Whereas in the old days treatment was mainly for *kwashiorkor* (protein deficiency), this has been superseded today by marasmus (100 per cent calorie deficiency). To put it bluntly, the children simply aren't being fed any more. Mortality has gone up and the doctors conclude: 'The cause is malnutrition, and the answer to this appalling waste of human lives is better social conditions, not first aid.'

At any rate there are hardly any hospitals in the shanty towns, because some people in authority are convinced that the one and only problem is clean water. The shanty towns are growing faster than the services provided for them, and the lack of sewerage and earth closets can spread epidemics. Attempts are therefore being made to equip them properly, since the privileged few are afraid of having cholera on their doorstep. They're also afraid of too much discontent, so they're 'improving' the shanty towns and have called on the World Bank for help, as it is favourably disposed towards this type of peace-keeping operation – service roads, water and electricity supplies, the odd palatial-looking school. Plots of building land are let for 3 kwachas per month and those who rent them can buy 100 to 500 kwachas' worth of building materials on easy terms. But wealthy people living in the smart districts are given loans worth tens of thousands of kwachas (in times of inflation these are more gifts than loans). The peasants complain that in some cases 1,000 to 2,000 kwachas are handed out for improving hovels lived in by people who produce nothing. 'All it'll do is attract more people to the towns,' they say. 'With the same amount of money you could equip a poor family in a rural district with an ox-drawn cart or plough.'

The shanty towns aren't properly drained and are often built on marshy ground. In 1972 Kanyama was very badly affected by flooding and a large number of houses were demolished. A public appeal was launched (some funds came from outside Zambia too – a poor country like Tanzania contributed), but a lot of the money was embezzled. Even poor families living just outside the towns are forgotten, and so are their children; only a third of them can get a primary school place, and in the poorest shanty town the figure is only 18 per cent, whereas in the well-to-do parts of town children from wealthy families who don't get into secondary school can still go to the highly profitable private schools.

These huge populations scraping a living on the outskirts of Zambia's towns produce virtually nothing (a few civil servants do live there, because they can't find anywhere else at a moderate rent). But then most of the town-dwellers are unproductive. Armies of men, some of them public employees, others in private employment, can be seen scything the lawns running alongside the avenues or round the luxury mansions with their machetes. And there's a growing number of household servants, gardeners and official chauffeurs, all of them in non-productive jobs. At about 6 pm, swarms of helmeted night watchmen hurry off to work – a new job created by 'well-planned development'. With crime on the increase the walls round the mansions are getting taller and taller and are topped by bits of broken glass. But guard dogs won't do the trick now, so the privileged few are guarded by their night watchmen, who will occasionally let in some accomplice. ('You simply don't know who to trust these days . . .')

Zero productivity is rife at the official level too. On every floor of Mulungushi House, where a large number of ministers can be found, a dozen 'messengers' are busy chatting, dozing, playing draughts or drinking tea. And we mustn't forget the hidden cases of zero productivity in offices, where civil servants may sometimes seem busy, though never excessively so – they knock off at lunchtime on

Friday, which is increasingly tending to be the day when the funerals of distant relatives take place.

Lusaka never stops mushrooming, yet its productivity doesn't keep step. The World Bank predicts that by 1990, 60 per cent of Zambians will be urban dwellers. But what will they eat, when the only people left in the villages are women, children and old people? It's quite out of the question to plant maize on the city's lawns – too humble for a city that prides itself on being one vast garden. (Maize planting was actually forbidden for many years, on the trumped-up excuse that it was a health risk – in fact the malaria-bearing mosquitoes don't breed there, and the real reason was aesthetic.)

We mustn't forget, faced with this swelling unproductive sector, that Zambia wanted to develop and control an extensive industrial sector. We shall now examine the circumstances and results of this project.

21 *Capital-intensive rather than labour-intensive factories*

After Zambia had made massive investments in non-productive towns and buildings, the whole of her economic policy was geared to encouraging capital-intensive factories by means of low import duties for plant and machinery, investment loans and substantial tax write-offs for depreciation. As a result multinational companies were able to sell Zambia sophisticated equipment that requires foreign managers and allows technological supervision from abroad. Another sugar refinery similar to the one at Nakambula is already at the planning stage. At 1980 prices, it could well cost 200 million dollars, to produce 100,000 tonnes of white sugar per annum. That means a cost of 2,000 dollars per tonne of sugar, a high proportion in the form of foreign currency, plus the need for a large number of white technicians and a lot less unskilled labour. Incidentally the 9,000 hectares of canes at Nakambula are burned before the harvest to make it easier work.* But this results in loss of humus (from the dried leaves) and loss of fodder from the leaves at the top of the stem. If we add to this the molasses spread on the roads to lay dust, all this waste

---

* i.e. the dry leaves are burnt off the plants to make the stalks more accessible.

represents foodstuffs for 80,000 head of improved cattle for five or six months during the dry season. No one worries about the future of the soil – so why bother to nationalize?

Indian peasants produce the cane and use the leaves at the top of the stems for fodder – we've already pointed out that they are excellent for this purpose. They transport the cane to the factory in ox-drawn carts. Alternatively they sometimes press it in the village between two or three steel cylinders worked by a pair of yoked oxen walking in circles, and concentrate the juice by burning the dried stems. The only capital required is a few dollars for every tonne of crude sugar (*gur*) produced. Now this *gur* tastes infinitely better, and is infinitely better for the health, than white sugar, and the Indians living in Lusaka import it from their own country at great expense.

The TNDP states clearly that small-scale industries must be encouraged, and a mission from the World Bank came to investigate the problem. After paying grudging lip-service to labour-intensive industries, but making no specific proposals, the Plan calls for three large maize-milling factories, each with a 60,000-tonne capacity. Yet Zambians have maize mills operated by hand, by animals, or by small diesel engines, and all of them would provide work and added value for the villages, save on transport costs, and reduce the cost of investment and foreign currency.

22 *Parastatals have nothing to do with socialism*

In the early days after independence the Zambians were concerned about the preponderant role played by the private sector. As early as 1969 they embarked on partial nationalization, by slow stages, of the copper mines, which were 'dominating' their economy. Then they expanded their industry, which was mainly beer and cigarettes at the time of independence. Wages rose too fast, leading to an increase in demand that was met initially by imports, and later by expanding industry at home. But this process of 'import substitution', which forged ahead between 1964 and 1972, stepped up the need for plant and machinery and imported raw materials so substantially that the local 'value added' soon fell from a half to a third of the GNP. It was aimed chiefly at the better-off and neglected many of the basic needs of the poor majority.

The Zambians had adopted a viewpoint that was in theory socialist (a stage on the road to humanism), and they built up a state-owned industrial sector, within the framework of a mixed economy, to 'expand and control the commanding heights of the economy', in accordance with the well-known Marxist formula. But after reaching a peak in 1972, output levelled off and even fell at certain times during the period 1976–81. Blame for all this was laid at the door of the Rhodesian war, transport difficulties and a lack of foreign currency.

But Ben Turok stresses that these 'parastatals', as they are called, are a form of state capitalism, and that a clear political will is missing. Zambia's so-called socialism has in fact given birth to a state bourgeoisie that is given even more preferential treatment than other types of bureaucracy (in the way of earnings, houses, servants, cars and foreign travel). The managers in their privileged position certainly don't share the socialist tendencies flaunted by Kenneth Kaunda. They keep up links with the private sector and the multinationals, which supply plant and machinery that is too sophisticated and expensive. Hence 'the persistence of Zambia's dependence on foreign capital, expertise, technology, supplies and markets'.[8]

Corruption is on the increase among these top executives, who are changed frequently for tribal reasons. Soap is unobtainable except on the black market, which is supplied with new crates straight out of the factory. The day we went there the head of the soap works had been suspended from duty and one of his employees jailed (note the difference in treatment, depending on your place in the hierarchy). Another example: one top official, a Greek, is said to have made his fortune buying shares in some companies for next to nothing because he spread a rumour that they were about to be nationalized, with no or virtually no compensation. The price subsequently rose, either because the company wasn't nationalized at all, or because large amounts of compensation were paid. But it's hard to prevent this type of practice in the context of a mixed economy. Then there is the fertilizer factory in Kafue: for three years it has been almost complete, but for 8 per cent of its plant and machinery and some tubing. So this highly expensive equipment is totally unproductive, and depreciating fast in the humid tropical climate.

We could quote dozens of examples of this type of waste. But a large number of influential people are jostling for advantage. The most serious aspect of corruption is that those in charge suggest more expensive solutions if they think there'll be more in it for themselves. To satisfy their demand for privileges the 'parastatals' are grouped together in holding companies, in time-honoured capitalist fashion. Except that true capitalists go in for all sorts of speculation on freightage, exchange rates and raw materials, whereas in Zambia it amounts to nothing more than a straightforward concentration at management level to ensure that the firms in question aren't subject to ministerial checks, since it's the holding company that inspects its subsidiaries. Perched on top of what is already too complex a system stands an even more parasitic structure of holdings controlling other holdings, with a twenty-two-storey block called Findeco House (the holding company has in fact been closed down now, but this hasn't had the slightest effect on production, which has actually gone up!), airconditioned buildings, deep-pile carpets, huge offices – and very poor management. These holding companies are quite pointless and totally unproductive, but they do make it easier to cover up losses and irregularities by juggling the accounts – swollen overheads, expensive but pointless business trips, expense accounts, lavish meals in smart hotels, and so on.

We wouldn't want to find ourselves praising the multinationals, but it's true that Lonrho, which has recently been nationalized in Tanzania, still plays a big part in Zambia's economy. Although its top management is much smaller, it seems much more efficient than in the parastatals. They insist that each of their subsidiaries should produce a detailed report covering its economic and financial situation every Friday. If the report isn't in on time, someone is sent along on the Saturday morning to investigate. The incompetent (not to mention the dishonest) do not last long.

Why can't the parastatals be equally well run, yet be geared to the interests of the nation and her large poor population, rather than of foreign capitalists, or the state bourgeoisie who have grabbed the levers of power and kept all the privileges for themselves? Seventy-five per cent of the parastatals investigated by parliamentary commissions are losing money. This isn't necessarily their fault – in some cases their selling prices are fixed too low – but it often is. The whole structure will have to be rethought, though privatization of these firms, which would lead to monopoly situations, still appears undesirable. To let a privileged minority run the country solely in the interests of the various power groups is to set it on the road to ruin.

23 *Zambia's blind alley*

'Over the last fifteen years we've never really enjoyed our independence,' say Zambia's leading figures apologetically, and they put all the blame on the Rhodesians. We mustn't underestimate the external difficulties: the high cost of sanctions and attacks by the Rhodesians affected landlocked Zambia very badly, leading to higher transport costs for both imports and exports (copper). But the trouble is that given her geographical situation, and with a permanent state of war on her boundaries, Zambia relied too heavily on imports, without feeling the need to be self-sufficient, particularly in food, in spite of the slogans that are supposed to mobilize the people and which have been bandied about since 1969. The effect of these slogans is derisory: 'We've been hearing it for so long we don't pay any attention. . . .'

The Zambians put the blame on the colonial administration, international capitalism or various forms of imperialism, yet those very same people who vituperate against 'foreigners' are the first to expect them to fork out aid. They seem to think the world owes Zambia a living. During the food crisis in 1979 they pinned all their hopes on one event – the end of the Lancaster House conference, which was expected to open up the road to the south once again. They didn't even try to find domestic solutions to the crisis. When, in early 1980, the road southwards was at last reopened, maize from South Africa (which the press insisted on referring to as 'Zambian maize', because the Zambians had bought it) made good the shortages. But the whole economic apparatus had ground to a halt, and the next maize campaign got off to a bad start. And this time there was no one to put the blame on.

In the rural areas vehicles lie idle because there is no fuel or spare parts. Most of the biggest factories are working below capacity because they can't get enough raw materials or spare parts, and so can no longer provide the basic necessities, which are in short supply all over the country. In other words the whole machine is out of order, and the development Zambia dreamed of has failed miserably. Although the Western development model worked reasonably well when Zambia was a rich country, she no longer has the means to keep it running. Some people have started wondering what is going on. People don't know where they are any more, and both urban and rural dwellers seem to have lost their bearings. Morale is low. 'There's no atmosphere,' grumble the civil servants – some of whom, inciden-tally, are first-rate. They take refuge in apathy, showing more concern for their own and their family's wellbeing than for the national interest. What's the point, after all? They know that whatever they do the situation won't improve until a firm political will makes itself felt: 'Why tighten our belts when others are loosening theirs?'

Boys and girls who've been educated to secondary level are so disenchanted that they take refuge in cynicism and escape into vaguely Marxist daydreaming, or paranoia about 'the enemy'. Soon they'll be trying to swell the ranks of the parastatals, because there is no other choice open to them. The atmosphere doesn't encourage conscien-tiousness, but a 'get-rich-quick' attitude. To hell with the future. The Zambians are so frustrated at not being able to put the American dream into practice that they keep dwelling on plans that can never now be fulfilled, large-scale projects that can't be launched, plant and machinery the country can't afford. They never turn their thoughts to another type of development, because they see it as a backward step. And they're terrified they may have to go back to the bush!

Who will get Zambia back on her feet? The civil service still gives preferential treatment to the ruling class, who run the country in their own short-term interests. They do have to bear in mind the miners' unions, which enjoy certain privileges, but who cares about the poor living in the villages and shanty towns? Overall production figures have been either at a standstill or dropping since 1976, and the same goes for the level of productive investment. The education system is turning out frustrated and unproductive misfits who are doomed to unemployment by the economic system. Malnutrition is constantly on the increase, yet only the medical profession recognizes its existence, amid a widespread lack of concern.

As Zambia is a religious country, they pray for the miracle that will allow them, at long last, to start dreaming again. But no one dreams of changing matters. Except possibly President Kaunda, who admitted to us in shattered tones: 'When I see what's happened to this country, I have nightmares.' But what is there left for him to do at this stage? He is hamstrung by divergent interests and quarrels at home and abroad. It looks very much as though things have gone too far. His main concern now is to keep the country united and stable – which involves him in a dangerous chess game – and to contain urban discontent, which is more of a threat than rural discontent. Dissatisfied manual workers or unemployed shanty-town dwellers represent a greater threat to the government, which is concentrated in the towns (most members of parliament representing rural districts live in Lusaka, except when elections are being held), than the scattered and non-unionized peasants. And how would the sycophantic élites react if they were forced into giving up their privileges? After all, they're the ones who keep the government in power, taking advantage (unfair advantage) of its good reputation abroad and its honesty to line their own pockets. 'They say you're surrounded by crooks,' claimed one journalist in a television interview. 'You credit me with powers I haven't got,' was Kaunda's reply. 'If it was up to me . . .' 'If he had a good clean-up, he'd be left alone,' observers say.

3 How long will the privileged minorities stay in power?

1 *Who exactly are the privileged few?*

Foreigners to start with. They are still here in fairly large numbers and still living in considerable style. They play a dominant part in the mines and hold the top jobs in construction, roads and industry in general – and the more technologically sophisticated the factory the more foreigners it will employ. We came across them at all levels in secondary and university education, giving lessons and lectures imported from abroad, and felt that they were still far too much in evidence in many branches of the civil service, particularly in the capital, though the problem does arise elsewhere too. They still play a major part – and this goes for Indians as well as Europeans – in trade, and as advisers to the state-run import firms. Worse still, the tiny minority of commercial farmers supply the towns, and boast of doing so. They feed a high proportion of Zambian towns with produce from their 'California-style' farms (strawberries watered drop by drop, irrigated wheat and so on).

Another factor is the corrosive part played by advisers and experts who've come here to make their fortune, or the diplomats, who cling together in their round of elegant little dinner parties (using ingredients imported in the diplomatic bag), or the representatives of the international organizations, some of whom remark quite brazenly: 'Where else could we earn so much for doing so little?' The United Nations employees live in terror of a coup and are constantly drawing up evacuation plans. As Zambia officially counts as 'dangerous', they get two weeks' free holiday by the sea in Kenya to rest their shattered nerves (at the taxpayer's expense, needless to say). All these people enjoy an inordinately lavish lifestyle that exacerbates the envy and the longing for luxury experienced by the Africans who mix with them, or merely watch them. 'You'd have to be a millionaire to live like this back home,' admitted one ambassador.

All these white groups are the leading lights of the social scene, with

74

its Rotary Club and Lions' Club, ostentatiously charitable and condescendingly contemptuous. They organize gastronomic evenings and parties, but at the dinner dance we saw in Kitwe the only Africans present were armed and were standing guard over the entrance – they're clearly afraid.

The better-off Africans follow suit, or feel they must do so to prove their new-found equality, even if it means dipping into the state's coffers now and again, which they have to do anyway to satisfy both their own new taste for high living and the demands of their large families, who never fail to flock in from their villages as soon as one of their relatives has 'made it' in the big city. And as there's a fear of poison, or the vengeance of a traditional society with laws of its own, they're sure to be made welcome. One civil servant complained that he had twenty mouths to feed every day, on a salary that, although comfortable, was pretty pathetic compared to European salaries. Many of them have acquired such tastes abroad. What can you expect a man from the savannah to think when he comes back from a training course in California? At bottom some of them do feel rather uneasy in their new incarnation. They've been completely sold on the consumer society and make up for their feeling of insecurity by acquiring status symbols such as a Mercedes or a swimming pool, because they've so often been told that such things spell civilization. Their feeling of uprootedness is fostered and underlined by the country's pathetic television service, which is officially referred to as Zambian but is in fact made up of the worst American programmes. Colour television has even put in an appearance recently!

So a new class-ridden society has grown up that differs from the old colonial society only in the colour of people's skins – black is now the predominant colour. But the problem is that this time the privileged minority is much bigger, and costs the country a great deal more, which means that the poor are getting even poorer, and that the regime is moving in a very definite direction.

2 *The growth of privilege*

The main concern of the privileged minorities is to look after their own interests, so they take advantage of the system. For instance they can obtain loans worth thousands, or rather tens of thousands, of kwachas, and many will make sure never to pay them back. Although top civil servants live in the most luxurious government mansions, their rent is equivalent to only 12½ per cent of their salary. If they've bought their house they're given a housing allowance which was doubled in 1975 and now ranges from 40 kwachas a month for a small, unpretentious house to 150 kwachas for mansions worth over 30,000 kwachas. The more you have the more you get! Top management in the parastatals are even better off: 'Expensive houses built for the emergent élite swallow up the bulk of urban housing investments. Thus the construction of 1,710 high- and medium-cost dwellings and 1,307 servants' quarters absorbed 77·2 per cent of the amount spent on urban housing in 1974. Another 13·4 per cent went into the building of 1,266 low-cost units, 4·7 per cent into 2,000 houses on serviced plots, and the remaining 4·7 per cent into 9,905 shanty houses.'[1]

Another privilege is loaded justice, as witness two of the many cases that happened to be reported in the press during our visit. One wretched man, when asked by a civil servant to come back another day for some papers he badly needed, shyly proffered a 10-kwacha note in the hope of getting them immediately instead of having to make another expensive journey from his remote village. 'Bribery,' thundered the judge, 'is wreaking havoc on this country' and sentenced the man to three years in prison. A few days later an ambassador involved in the illegal diamond trade that loses the country tens of *millions* of kwachas was given a mere nine months in prison (and he didn't serve the full sentence either). Other managers charged with the theft of cattle being transported on the railway or of being involved in the soapworks scandal were merely 'suspended from duty'. Under English libel law you can't name the main culprits (which leads to the worst sort of gossip). You can't incriminate someone who hasn't been tried. The result is class justice – one law for the rich and one for the poor!

The land is in the public domain, but it is the powerful few who take over the estates abandoned by the whites, and only a handful farm them efficiently. Some sell off everything they can, and don't farm any of the land. Others (who may indeed include the first group) manage to get hold of grants, which they have no real intention of repaying, from the same banks or official bodies that are so short of capital that they've stopped lending money to peasant farmers. But apparently Party membership counts as collateral, and as they're influential, they won't be taken to court.

In a sermon preached in the cathedral on Independence Day 1979, with the president and all the country's bigwigs present (many of them get the odd fit of tactical piety), a clergyman spoke out against the Party leaders, referring to them as 'brigands in evening dress robbing the state and the people'. The following day the Party's secretary-general protested, but in the oddest terms, claiming that it wasn't just the leaders, everyone in the Party stole! With that sort of example, how can they expect the working classes to work themselves to death? Why should the peasants dig more land and ordinary men and women be prepared to make sacrifices?

Why bother about the rural areas? The white settlers supply food for the towns, accounting for an increasing percentage of the country's GNP. The figure rose from 2·6 per cent in 1965 to 5·6 per cent in 1976, whereas the peasants, referred to as the 'subsistence sector', produced only 8 per cent in 1976 compared to 11·1 per cent in 1965. If there isn't enough food, there's always overseas aid or imports, so the authorities don't see any need to help the peasant farmers and aren't pushed into doing so by force of circumstances. The peasants have to make do with the crumbs, but the national cake has shrunk and there are fewer and fewer crumbs in these times of greed. A member of the Central Committee we met at the Rotary Club reminded us, in an outburst of humanitarian rhetoric, that 'Zambia had put up with so many sacrifices' as a result of the Rhodesian offensives. Fair enough, but who actually made the sacrifices? During the crisis in autumn 1979, at the height of the Rhodesian offensive, foreigners visiting Lusaka might well have been amazed to see the city running smoothly, like the engines of all those Mercedes. But at the same time the rural areas were at a standstill, with shortages of every kind, and forgotten by the authorities. It takes a lot to kill off privileges.

3 *Protocol and prestige first*

The Zambians may be lukewarm on saving, but they're hot on protocol, and with protocol goes prestige. When the Commonwealth Conference was held in Lusaka in August 1979 the Queen and all those heads of state obviously had to be entertained in the most opulent manner, in spite of the economic difficulties and the problems along the borders, to prove that the country was taking the strain. The mansions set aside for vips, which are only used for a week every three or four years, were refurnished in the most sumptuous manner, the rocks and tree trunks lining the road to the airport were painted white, forty-five black Mercedes 250s were bought (there are forty-one states in the Commonwealth) and fifty cream-coloured Peugeot 504s were imported from France. The Pamodzi Hotel was completed at lightning speed, and a million kwachas' worth of wine, liqueurs, cheeses and fruit and other luxury produce was imported, virtually all of it from South Africa. The official figures put the total expenditure at 9 million kwachas, but the true figure was considerably higher. But that's a mere bagatelle to a poor country like Zambia when it comes to impressing world opinion! When will one of the so-called developing countries (Tanzania or Mozambique perhaps?) summon up the courage to admit: 'We're poor, so we entertain very simply'? Others might well follow their example.

On 8 December the Pamodzi Hotel was officially opened and boasted of being 'Zambia's one and only five-star hotel' (thank goodness it is the only one, though we have to admit that we ourselves were put up there). The comrade president had greeted us so warmly that we took the liberty of writing him a brief note: 'We beg you not to perform the opening ceremony at the Pamodzi yourself, when the poor have so much trouble getting food.' His answer was that the hotel provided jobs (which indeed it did, but at what a price!) and showed the world that Zambia refused to go under. After all, he's used to opening splendid buildings of this type, even though he disapproves of them. He did perform the opening ceremony, with the champagne flowing straight down the throats of the 'haves'. Meanwhile a couple of kilometres away in Karachi Road hundreds of poor people queued for at least five hours, and sometimes ten, for their 50-kilo sacks of maize flour.

The luxury tastes of the privileged few affect Zambia's development model, leading to the building of huge, centralized, imposing factories, an ultra-modern university and schools with academic curricula (for their own offspring), vast hospitals and so on. It's only fair to add that these tendencies are encouraged by all the foreigners who stand to gain by large-scale building projects and provide the necessary equipment.

4 *The prestige of a major hospital*

We were told that right from the start all the government's decisions
on health and education were influenced by foreigners. Although this
is most probably true, they did fit in well with a specific development
philosophy that is characteristic of privileged élites. Nothing was too
good for Zambia.

So a teaching hospital was built, a huge, rambling building that is
positively harmful for patients, with its corridors open to all weathers.
The staff waste time just going from place to place, but the hospital
must be up to the standards of London and New York. The same
applies to the doctors, who are trained there too. Needless to say
they're pretty ineffectual in a country whose major problem is
malnutrition, followed by all the usual diseases connected with
underdevelopment. Worse still, as Zambia is a non-aligned country,
its health model, too, is non-aligned. Its doctors return home from
overseas training with a wide range of different methods. The foreign
personnel too have very varying approaches (both ideological and
medical). The result is utter confusion, with each standing up for his
or her own school of thought.

But whether their outlook is Eastern or Western, all Zambia's
doctors do have one thing in common: they refuse to work in the rural
areas, where they'll never find either the modern equipment or the
type of cases they're used to. Why should doctors who've done at least
seven years' training be willing to bury themselves in the sticks?
Zambia isn't Cuba or China, and as in her profit-oriented society
there's no form of bonus or special privileges attached to working
there, they only ever envisage being in Lusaka. It even proved
impossible to force a surgeon to accept a job in Ndola, which is not
exactly the back of beyond – it's the major city in the Copperbelt, with
a population of three hundred thousand. 'As we can't count on either
the doctors or the nurses, we'll get by without them,' said one top civil
servant in the Health Ministry, no doubt exasperated by his knowledge of where the country's real needs lie. But in that case why spend
so much money training these people?

Zambia therefore finds itself saddled with a few large hospitals
which have to be made to operate somehow. Admittedly the Plan
does talk of increasing preventive medicine, but 45 per cent of the
budget is earmarked for the hospitals, 18 per cent of it for the teaching

hospital (a very small sum, it was pointed out, compared to teaching hospitals in the United States – the points of comparison used are symptomatic). This would merely be a lesser evil if the money were at least put to good use and the hospital was run efficiently. But it isn't, and it's been clearly shown that large-scale units of this kind simply don't work in an underdeveloped country, because of the shortages of equipment and spare parts, the shortcomings – and sometimes the sheer incompetence – of the staff, and so on. If they're to work properly they must be staffed by foreigners, which perpetuates the country's state of dependence. But the powers that be are anxious to have everything Zambianized. They want spectacular results, and while thousands of people in the rural areas are still dying of unnecessary diseases, city dwellers can be heard raving over 'the splendid operating theatre – just like London!' Yet although it was the privileged few who pushed the government into spending all that money, they aren't really satisfied with the hospital, which clearly isn't working properly. They want, needless to say, to see another one built. Meanwhile the white members of the privileged minority travel to South Africa for medical treatment, the black members to London. As they have the right contacts and can pull strings, they can get the Bank to hand over the foreign currency they need for the journey, even though it's in short supply.

The privileged minority refuse to see that there's a malnutrition problem, which seems pretty unimportant if you're well fed yourself. The United Nations tells us that a high proportion of the 1,500,000,000 people suffering from starvation and malnutrition are infants, pregnant women and nursing mothers. As long ago as 1937 the League of Nations in Geneva told us the same thing, and over the forty-five years since then the rate and degree of malnutrition have got steadily worse. Although the problem is now better understood in India, it's still very pronounced in tropical Africa. We might have expected better of Zambia, which used to be a rich country and still is relatively speaking, according to the criteria laid down by the World Bank, which refers to an annual income of $450 per head (1978 figures), compared to $190 in Tanzania, though it seemed to us that the peasant class in Zambia was less well fed. At any rate the country is certainly richer than its neighbours (Kenya, Tanzania, Malawi and Uganda).

Even in the rural areas people are undernourished, with 82 per cent of households below the poverty line. The privileged minority, who are completely sold on Western-style food (a major status symbol because it is associated with the whites), simply don't want to know. They can afford meat, fruit and vegetables, which the middle classes can't – their eating habits, too, have been adversely affected by contact with whites, but they're short of money. A study of the diet of the Copperbelt miners reveals that the poorest of them, who eat African-style, are not as undernourished as the 'medium poor', who often make do with white bread washed down with Coca-Cola.

The long and the short of it is that a good diet, clean water, preventive medicine and sanitation are much more important than medical treatment. If they existed throughout the country they would reduce both the need for treatment and the unnecessary sums spent on expensive medicines for children who are seriously undernourished. One pediatrician has calculated that half the sum allocated for medicine in the children's hospitals would be better spent on extra food for children under three. Prevention is cheaper than care.

The country's health system ought to be competely re-thought, or at any rate planned with regard to the true needs of the population as a whole. But this is essentially a political decision, and as one article tells us: 'In less than a generation politicians have genuinely forgotten the circumstances of life and death as experienced by the ordinary villagers that they, or at least their parents, had been.'[2] Here too personal or class interests are put before the national interest. The important point is that they and their children should be healthy and benefit from normal intellectual development. Privileges are transmitted through health, and through education too.

5 *Educational reforms are long overdue*

The whole of Zambia's education system is still a carbon copy of the Western model. It's difficult to get away from, though many African countries do still dream of doing so, but Zambia seems to have made no special effort to change. The preferences of the privileged minority are plainly visible. For instance the TNDP states: 'The planned goal of consolidating the physical plan of the primary school system was far from being achieved.' A little further on we find: 'The major part of the planned secondary school expansion programme has been completed.' It's a case of one law for the rich and one for the poor.

Yet it is at the primary school level that Zambia's problems start. As educational reforms are fashionable, the Zambians made a study of their own system. This cost a fortune, involving as it did special missions to various points on the globe, including Cuba and China. The initial report, drawn up in 1975 and published in 1976, gave priority to technical training, manual and farm labour, and crafts, which was precisely what the privileged few didn't want. They had no intention of seeing their children doing manual work – they cherished loftier ambitions. So the planned reforms were unpopular. As they couldn't be rejected out of hand, they had to be watered down and the final plan, published in 1977, was meek and inoffensive.

It's still sitting on a shelf somewhere, to be resurrected again whenever anyone starts criticizing the education system, as a sort of cure-all. According to officials, it covers every aspect of the problem. The provincial authorities scarcely ever give it a mention, and the same goes for the district authorities, except that they complain: 'They'll try it out in the towns, as usual, though it's us who need it so badly.' As soon as you travel outside Lusaka the civil servants seem more realistic. Village primary schoolteachers know about the report only from hearsay: 'Apparently the reforms will happen right at the start, when the school's being built.' Like so many things in Zambia, the reforms exist only on paper, and are unlikely ever to be put into practice, because the funds aren't available. The cost of implementing them was put at 360 million kwachas (1977 values), since modest budgets just don't happen in Zambia.

The plans call for nine years' compulsory schooling instead of seven, with technical training and practical work in the last two years, as a sort of pre-apprenticeship. But as many children can't even get into the first year of school, and a third of the others never get beyond the fourth year, we're entitled to wonder how Zambia will ever manage nine years' compulsory education for all. And in the end we begin to wonder whether compulsory schooling deserves such an overriding priority. Wouldn't it be better to start by getting rid of the malnutrition and poverty which place so crushing a burden on the peasants? On top of this, the government's whole policy ought to be changed so that it can absorb all these educated youngsters. What is the point of two extra years at school if they're sure to finish up unemployed? A necessary precondition for a reform of this kind would also be retraining the teaching staff, and introducing a different kind of teacher training altogether. And the most important precondition is a higher standard of living in the rural areas. Whether or not the planned reforms are ever implemented, primary school teachers won't find the thought of working in the rural areas any more attractive. The government would have to ensure that they can make a proper career for themselves by staying in the rural areas, with at least the same opportunities for promotion as in the towns, and the same facilities. No one's going to want to live in a village where there are no facilities at all.

If we were asked for some general recommendations, we'd start by letting the peasants build the schools they're clamouring for (they see school as a way out) with their own hands and where they are most needed, using local materials and thatched roofs. (The same applies, incidentally, to their houses – the inevitable corrugated iron makes their homes hot in summer and cold in winter, and during the rainy season the noise is unbearable, but they see it as 'modern'.) Repairs should be carried out to existing schools with whatever materials and equipment are available. The money saved in this way could be used for sending children living in shanty towns or remote rural areas to school, and for buying books and pencils for them all. From the fourth to the seventh year of school, pupils could do two hours' manual work per day, particularly in the fields, learning the relevant techniques and growing food for their canteens – an extra meal wouldn't be a bad thing, as many of the children get nothing to eat all day.

Our next suggestion would be to involve the local blacksmiths, carpenters, joiners, wheelwrights, brickmakers, masons and other available craftsmen by giving them work so that they can help to build schools, dispensaries, houses and furniture for teachers and nurses and so on. The necessary funds would be obtained by cutting back on major roads, luxury flats and houses and other superfluous urban expenditure. Village children would learn the rudiments of the basic trades and skills by helping the various tradesmen. Hundreds of volunteers could help to train these apprentices – there'd be no difficulty in finding them. The next step would be to set up hundreds of non-academic, practical schools, for children who've been through primary schooling and reached Grade 7 but failed to get into secondary school. Tens of thousands of such children could be trained every year, rather than the mere thousand provided for in the TNDP. The new regulations concerning public buildings would mean a saving on imported equipment, and therefore on foreign currency expenditure, and would give work to a far larger number of youngsters.

Zambia does admittedly need senior managers, but its need for engineers and technicians is far greater than for the law and arts graduates who are still in the majority. Respect for technical skills doesn't seem to be an African quality, as long as there is the prospect of going into the plush offices of the parastatals and settling cosily behind a civil servant's desk. Even the agricultural colleges are non-productive – all they do is turn out just enough experts to replace their predecessors who've abandoned the rural areas for an office job in the city. Yet what Zambia needs most today is the NCO of the labour army – the qualified skilled tradesman or craftsman – plus a professional and conscientious attitude on the part of manual workers and their foremen. The academic education based on book-learning that is a legacy of the colonial era will never train these skilled tradesmen, yet that is what is needed if the country is ever to emerge from underdevelopment.

This type of reform would no doubt come as a shock to the privileged few, who assess the country's level of development by the yardstick, first of their own luxurious lifestyle and, second, of the number, appearance and splendour of public buildings. 'If we change our economic model and go for a more modest form of development, how shall we ever be able to build the Champs-Elysées in Lusaka?' was the ingenuous question one minister put to us. And his view is less grandiose than that of many other people who think only in terms of the United States.

If no attempt is made to rehabilitate manual labour and to give all young people a proper trade so that they can subsequently all be put to productive use, how can the country ever escape from the present deadlock? Just think of the enormous amount of work that could be achieved by the young people who are now unemployed. That's virtually all Zambia needs.

But most important of all is the political will for change. It's only too easy to draw up plans on paper when you know there's no real will to implement them.

6 *The Third National Development Plan (*TNDP*): a catalogue of wishful thinking*

Zambia has already, in theory, implemented two Five-Year Plans. The first covered the period 1966–70 but was extended into 1971; the second was for 1972–6 but was extended to cover 1977 and 1978 as well. The Zambians never managed to see them through, and not only because of external problems. The Second Plan was supposed to create 100,000 new jobs in five years, yet it had very little effect, leading if anything to the loss of several thousand jobs.

The twenty-seven commissions drawing up the TNDP all consisted of urban dwellers, including one wealthy settler. There wasn't a single peasant among them. In fact as far as the authorities are concerned the peasants simply don't exist. The only people to be 'registered' are the farmers who buy fertilizers and sell their surplus produce; they and they alone are given grants, advice and assistance. The so-called Plan is really a mere 'catalogue' of projects put forward by the various ministers and by the country's eight regions; pieces of wishful thinking calling for foreign aid to back them and designed principally to satisfy well-off city dwellers. There's no attempt to set out clear-cut priorities within the framework of a firmly expressed national will. Considering how little money the nation saves, the TNDP relies substantially on external financing. And its main aim is to expand and develop activities inherited from the previous era which, as we have stressed, are frequently full of shortcomings.

It provides for an investment of 50 kwachas per house for improving rural housing, but between 400 and 20,000 kwachas per house (a huge range!) in urban districts. It earmarks 14 million kwachas over five years for rural dwellings (which house 60 per cent of the population) and 283 million, or twenty times more, for urban dwellings. What an example of discrimination! A thoroughly class-based policy, weighted against the peasants. It also provides for 147 million kwachas to be spent on the roads, but makes do with describing the vast potential for irrigation, without setting aside any specific funds.

An asphalt road has just been built between Mongu and Lumilunga, the Lozi chief's summer residence. It cost over a million kwachas, and is far too wide considering the amount of traffic it is expected to carry.

At the end of the nineteenth century the Lozi kingdom, in the western provinces, dug navigation and drainage channels in the flood plain and the adjacent valleys, but these are now partly silted up. The 1979 budget provided for funds totalling 100,000 kwachas for drainage in the whole of Zambia, but the 18 kilometres of roads referred to above cost ten or twelve times that sum. So most of the fertile and peaty soil, which is suitable for all types of rich crops, cannot be cultivated, and the peasants now have to make do with a diet based on cassava, the only plant that will grow on the poor sandy soil of Barotseland, which in turn has the only large acreages now available. In Northern Province the new road linking Mpika, Kasama and Mbala cost 50 million kwachas, yet it carries pathetically little traffic. It could have been built only half the width and the money saved would have rescued from isolation a large number of villages with no secondary road links. But the people in power only ever use the trunk roads, and they want them to be easy to drive on.

We could quote many other examples of the rural areas being neglected and abandoned. Yet the résumé of the TNDP reiterates even more strongly than the preceding Plans the need to give 'the highest priority' to rural development and to narrow the gap between urban and rural areas and reduce unemployment. As to the gap between rich and poor, it scarcely gets a mention. At any rate an effective way to start the TNDP would be to give absolute priority to putting back in working order everything that isn't working at all, or isn't working properly, because of a shortage of raw materials and particularly of spare parts – i.e. factories, workshops and transport vehicles. Also badly in need of overhauling are the country's repair facilities. The army's engineering department turns out to be incapable of providing proper and sufficiently speedy maintenance of public vehicles, of which incidentally there are far too many, because they are in a very poor state of repair and are far too often used for private travel. New projects should be given third priority, well behind making full use of the capital already invested. Putting young people to work ought to rank equal first on any list of national priorities and could be closely linked to genuine rural development.

To sum up: investment provided for in the TNDP is grouped under the main headings of transport, communications and industry. Agriculture (which covers stock rearing, forestry and fisheries, plus all the problems related to water supply, irrigation and drainage) is scheduled to receive a mere 12½ per cent of the overall investment figure. Now a good 50 per cent of the population are still involved in agriculture, and food affects the country's independence. We believe that agriculture deserves 40 per cent of the total. The next priority is housing, particularly in urban areas. The bare minimum has been allocated to education (with 3 per cent of planned investment) and health (1·3 per cent). Now at the moment these two areas are more off-beam than any of the others. It clearly wouldn't do merely to give them more money, just in order to perpetuate current mistakes. If 'another'* development is to be achieved, top priority will have to be given to helping the informal sector in towns and poor suburbs – all those humble tradesmen and craftsmen – to enable them to carry out more productive jobs and recruit more labour.

In particular the poor peasants ought to be properly organized, and be given real leadership, advice, supplies, funds, education and health care so that they can at long last live decently. That would encourage their children to stay in the villages. But if all that is to be achieved, far more funds will be needed to turn the underprivileged, the peasants and the unemployed into productive citizens than are provided for in the TNDP. Where are these funds to come from? The answer is to call a halt to expenditure on urban comforts, which is still very heavy, and to the tower blocks being built on Cairo Road for the parastatals; to the allocation of funds for any but small-scale housing, and essential public buildings; to stop building new roads designed for heavy traffic, and urban motorways, and instead improve communications with the villages, even those in remote areas; and to axe all plans for large-scale and overcentralized factories and encourage the growth of small rural industries instead.

Here are some other ideas. No loans to buy private cars for a period of two years, and no import licences for cars either; the money saved to be spent on buses for both urban and rural areas, lorries, small motorbikes and cycles, plus all the spare parts, tyres, inner tubes and pumps that are so badly needed. After the two-year period only *small* cars should be bought, and not many of them – no more Mercedes. Imports of luxury articles for the privileged few must stop, and imports of semi-luxury articles should be heavily taxed. It's absolutely essential for the country's political leaders to set an example here. So

---

* The report we submitted to President Kaunda is called *Towards another Development in Rural Zambia.*

far they've made do with haranguing the masses to tighten their belts, be public-spirited, work hard. But how are they going to react when the time comes for them to give up their Mercedes and other creature comforts? It doesn't take long to get used to privileges, and oddly enough, some observers point out that if ever the government were to be overthrown, the coup would most probably come from the privileged few on the right, who are greedy and want more and more, rather than from the despised masses living in the shanty towns or the forgotten villagers. At any rate the élite who enjoy so much ill-gotten power have no intention of handing any back to the peasants. It isn't in their interest to do so. On the other hand, they do have to eat.

7 Viable village units

The peasants aren't stupid and backward, as many town-dwellers think. They know their land and their soil, they know which plants are useful – for instance those that can be used to gauge the fertility of the soil. The chieftainries who used to oversee them in the old days made sure that certain traditional rules were respected, such as fallow periods to keep the soil fertile, and grazing discipline in the dry or rainy seasons. The colonial authorities curtailed the chiefs' powers, and post-independence governments have stepped up the process. As a result the peasants don't know where they are. Who's in charge? The Party, the district administrators or the chief? They'd like to think it was the chief, but they know that his power has been taken over by the Party, which incidentally has to approve the appointment of chiefs, or even put forward its own names. Instead of getting the peasants to rally round, the Party has effectively encouraged them to sit back, without attempting to organize them or to replace the structure initially demolished by the colonial authorities. In fact the peasants take very little notice of the Party. They know that it isn't really bothered about the villages, and they don't belong to it. It is still very much an external authority and has no real interest in organizing peasant structures or sharing its authority.

The schools bring together children from dozens of tiny hamlets. Their catchment area could perhaps be used as a basis for marking out 'village units' grouped round a central nucleus of development, which would be gradually strengthened. If they were to be viable these units would have to cover somewhere between a thousand and two thousand peasants, and their boundaries would be worked out with their agreement. They could therefore decide to join one centre or another and would discuss the ideal site. All this would take place with the agreement of the technical services outlined above, but all those technocrats would at last be putting themselves at the service of the whole of the country's peasant population, including their women-folk (who have never been consulted before), and not just of Party members. Now some recent decrees say that Party members should be entrusted with organizing the villages. But the Party, run as it is from the towns, can't represent the peasants properly. What's needed is peasant associations, run by peasants, as happens with women's and youth associations, trade unions and so on. The planters have their own department, but the small-scale peasants have nothing, either economically, socially, culturally or politically speaking. They are simply 'forgotten'.

The central authority of these future villages would organize a water supply next to the school. In due course it could supply some of the local hamlets. Other new services would be a dispensary and a shop (or cooperative store) supplying essential goods such as paraffin, salt, sugar, soap, matches, cheap fabrics (rather than expensive ready-made garments), oil and so on. The agricultural services, Namboard (the state marketing board) and the cooperatives could then organize a communal agricultural centre to supply the peasants with seeds (for both fields and gardens), fruit tree saplings (starting with the hardiest varieties – papaws and guavas in preference to citrus fruits), fertilizers, which should also be sold retail, and pesticides; machetes, hoes, axes, spare parts for carts, ploughs and harrows, and so on. The agricultural agent would collect the surplus crops put on sale and pay for them in cash. He would run an emergency granary from which families could buy back grain if they ran short, as they so often do between harvests. Each village would build its own communal granary for storing fertilizers, crops and so on.

With the help of an assistant, the centre's top extension officer would personally cultivate a demonstration field, with a balanced pattern of crop rotation, a garden and an orchard for his own needs, and later on a nursery for both fruit trees and forest trees. They would be run in close conjunction with the village council, a body elected by the peasants and responsible for protecting its own land. The state is the sole owner of the land, but it would hand over the right to use it in perpetuity to each of the village units as they were formed. Once the unit was aware that it really did possess the right to use it in perpetuity, it would soon understand that it must protect its land in the interest of future generations – a concept that has been completely forgotten in the present chaotic situation in the rural areas.

The village council could therefore regulate grazing rights, to ensure that there was no overgrazing, which does so much damage, especially in the south of the country. It could organize a cropping pattern so as to maintain and increase productivity and soil fertility. It could control tree felling, marking out the sectors where this was permitted. A village nursery would mean that reafforestation could at last take place, and would provide the women with firewood and building poles very close to the village. Later on communal carts could be used to transport timber to people's homes, which would leave the women more time for working in the fields.

The council could then give a helping hand to a whole series of skilled tradesmen and craftsmen, such as blacksmiths, joiners, carpenters, masons and brickmakers. They would be kept busy repairing farm tools and carts, and making school desks and all the furnishings and fittings needed for public buildings as well as for the peasants' own houses, which would at long last receive the same sort of subsidies as towndwellers. All the members of one family could use a communal maize sheller worked by hand or by foot, and store fruit and vegetables. A communal mill could be used to grind maize and other cereals, a press to extract oil from oilseeds and hand looms to weave cotton, which could be ginned and spun in the district factory. It could be like an Indian village, or a Chinese commune in the early days.

But it's no good continuing this scenario for the future. It's pretty well useless in the climate of the early eighties, where everything is done for the towns, where the capital is the only real source of inspiration, setting the only acceptable example, and where anything that comes from the villages is still looked down on by everyone, starting with the Minister of Agriculture, who is on the side of the commercial farmers and interested only in large and highly mechanized farms. He was educated in Sweden and his mind seems to be permanently in the United States, when he isn't attending international conferences, that is. It's easy to imagine how furious he was when we spoke highly of appropriate technologies and a return to simplicity, arguing that sophisticated methods had been a failure. He claimed that we wanted to see Zambia back in the Stone Age. His whole empire tottered round his ears, and we found ourselves labelled as 'sham progressives' in the local press. How can any dialogue be possible in such circumstances?

8 *Autumn 1979 in Lusaka*

The Zambian press loves a controversy. Day after day the papers delight in denouncing corruption and scandals left, right and centre, and publishing the abuse and insults uttered by the country's leaders, and the counter-insults too. They are more concerned with sensational stories than serious news, and foster a false atmosphere of 'freedom' ('show-down' would be nearer the mark), and eventually finish up depressing everybody. It's no good looking to the press to change the atmosphere, which is already oppressive and offensive.

Not surprisingly, our visit and our criticisms (which they lost no time in printing) were a welcome source of new copy, a row they did their best to fuel for weeks on end. We were only saying out loud what many people privately thought, but we apparently caught the authorities off guard, since they expect nothing but praise from abroad. Foreign visitors who hypocritically shower praise on Zambia are often the cause of the smugly complacent attitude of officials. Yet the country seems to be adept at avoiding proper discussion and sweeping problems under the carpet. We therefore acted as a sort of catalyst, and it wasn't long before 'pro' and 'anti' camps had formed. The 'pro' camp consisted of the poor and the ordinary men and women who never dare to speak out, but it also included a large number of agricultural technicians and provincial or district officials, the people who have to cope day in and day out with problems those in the capital don't even know about.

The 'anti' camp was made up, needless to say, of the 'élite' and others in privileged positions, plus a large number of expatriates who are staunch supporters of the country's development model (though they criticize the system in private, as it isn't sufficiently capitalist for them), including the white agronomists at the Mount Makulu research centre, who were put out at our questioning their usefulness and their Eurocentric attitude. It also included all those people who, for one reason or another, had placed all their hopes in a form of development imported from outside, and who blamed all setbacks solely on the Rhodesian raids. This group even included the Party secretary, who telephoned our friends to say: 'Get them to keep quiet. Let them prepare their report and then slip quietly away!' Meanwhile President Kaunda stood up for us both in private and in public and urged us to keep up the good work and not to worry about the privileged few.

Whereas we were always given a warm welcome by the various officials in the rural areas or in small towns, including the governors (even though they were in the Party), who were of exactly the same opinion as us, no one in Lusaka was prepared to accept a word of criticism. The people there seemed to speak a different language and live in a different world. There were two Zambias and two nations, in spite of the country's motto ('One Zambia, One Nation'). And then people wonder why the president has such difficulty keeping the nation united. But gradually some of our opponents did adopt a more moderate tone. We may have brought them down to earth with a jolt, but they did eventually concede that we weren't entirely in the wrong. The food situation was looking very serious. With disaffection in the rural areas, paralysis in the provinces, and a combination of low grain prices and drought, the 1979 maize harvest was well down. In fact it had been dropping steadily since 1976, when the figure was 8·3 million 90-kilo sacks, whereas in 1979 the figure for maize *marketed* was down to 3·6 million.

The planters, who, whatever they may claim, are in Zambia more in their own interest than in that of the nation, were so fed up with the very low price of maize that they turned to cattle, which pay very well but don't provide food for anyone but the privileged few. Queues for maize started getting worryingly long in the streets of Lusaka, Ndola and Kitwe. Zambia had to appeal to the world's generosity and gifts were soon coming in, even from little Malawi, once despised. But these gifts weren't enough to solve the problem, and they turned to the hereditary enemy, South Africa, to buy 200,000 tonnes of cheap maize. This deal had been made even more necessary when the Rhodesians blew up the bridges over the Chambeshi on 12 October, thus cutting off the road to the north and the railway line linking the country to the port of Dar es Salaam, preventing part of the expected maize from getting through. The only hope left was the road to the south, but at the beginning of November the Rhodesians lost no time in cutting that too, a symbolic gesture to demonstrate their refusal to let the South African maize through. The idea behind this was to force Zambia, faced as she was with the threat of famine, to put pressure on the guerrillas to agree to an armistice on the conditions laid down by the Conservative government in London.

In any other country people would have started panicking. But not the Zambians, who are used to disasters. 'It'll be all right in the end,' they said, or: 'They'll fly us in some maize.' Everything seems so straightforward in Lusaka, which floats in a sea of unreality. In fact the day after the blockade started the Minister for Agriculture was busy reassuring the nation: 'Our American friends★ are going to send us a hundred thousand tonnes of maize.' But who was going to pay the cost of transporting it by air – a full-scale airlift? No one seemed unduly bothered.

Except, that is, for the president, who flew to London urgently. The Front Line states held a large number of meetings between Dakar and Maputo. The Rhodesian commandos blew up another six bridges in an attempt to hurry things along, and on 17 December Mugabe and Nkomo agreed to sign. The blockade was lifted that same day, emphasizing the link between the two events.

So 'food power', or rather 'grain power', had proved to be an effective political weapon. Unable to feed itself, in spite of having such a large amount of very sparsely populated land, Zambia had to comply with the economic conditions laid down by the IMF, and subsequently with the political conditions set by London. As Africa gets increasingly heavily into debt, she can't afford to go on paying for growing cereal imports, for the old international economic order is strangling her – and now there is the oil weapon too.

In early November we had put forward some ways in which the Zambians themselves could try to improve their powers of negotiation and adopt a less passive stance. For instance they could have gone in for more short-cycle crops (beans, dwarf sorghum, etc.) and stepped up the rate of flour extraction. Our suggestions were met with widespread apathy. Some people did agree with us, but there was no political authority to take the decision, as the Agriculture Minister had just set off on a twenty-five-day trip to London and Rome – at the

---

★ The students were soon calling them 'imperialist dogs'.

height of the blockade and at the beginning of the rainy season, just when the next maize campaign should have been launched. When he got back and questions were asked in Parliament about his agricultural policy, he produced his shopping list, which covered the maize that had already arrived and the amounts he was hoping for. The politics of the begging bowl.

9 *A politically unacceptable report*

Our report was printed by the government by order of the president and given the seal of the Republic. On 28 November we handed it over to him in a ceremony covered by the press and the broadcasting media. Yet in spite of Kaunda's praise (or because of it), the report was destined to lie under lock and key in the security room at the Government Printer's. But then in the underdeveloped countries what looks like opposition may sometimes be nothing more sinister than bureaucratic inertia.

Our report may have been economically desirable, but it was politically unacceptable. Kaunda is – rightly – afraid of urban disturbances, and has to look for support to the clique of people round him, who take advantage of the so-called 'socialist' path that gives them a chance to acquire more class privileges and don't give a damn for social justice, which should be the cornerstone of socialism. They need Kaunda to maintain a degree of political stability and to keep the balance between the tribes. In defending solely their own short-term political interests, the regime's privileged few don't even realize that they're sawing through the branch they're sitting on. Yet how can the atmosphere and the attitude of the authorities be changed? For the problem really is one of attitude.

Although a revolution is unlikely, crime is becoming such a major problem that it may represent an effective threat. But only providing that it is generally accepted that it is linked to unemployment and to growing inequalities, which in the end present a threat to the present social order, unless it can adapt before it's too late. The élites deny this. As they see it, unemployment and a high crime rate are phenomena common to all countries. But what they forget is that Zambian society has changed too fast, and that part of the population has undergone so rapid a rise in social status that it has exacerbated the envy and frustration of the rest. Why should some people be 'haves' and others 'have-nots', when sixteen years ago they were all living on a more or less equal footing? And there's their famous copper, and the whole development model that goes with it. How can we expect young people who have once had a taste of industrial society to agree to return to the harsh life prevailing in the rural areas, when their heads are stuffed with images of 'modern living'? It looks as if it will be hard to put the clock back.

10 *A statement of bankruptcy*

Now it so happens that this copper of theirs is costing more. Copper prices did go up a bit during 1979 and 1980, but the cost of extracting it is so high that 60 per cent of the foreign currency Zambia earns goes on the equipment and materials needed by the mines, and another 30 per cent goes on paying off the interest on the country's ever-increasing borrowings. Prospecting for new deposits has been halted and the quality of the work done in the mines seems to be declining. Agricultural output is dropping and is becoming increasingly dependent on foreign countries. Oil prices keep going up every month, but it never occurs to anyone to introduce petrol rationing in the towns; the only people to go short, increasingly so, are in the rural areas.

Zambia is a sick country, economically and socially speaking. Even though she is paying a high price abroad for sticking to her principles, at home Zambian society seems to have no ideals other than immediate profits. Yet we did meet a large number of young people who are worried about the future of their country, public-spirited officials and peasants doing their utmost. But none of these groups receives any backing from the authorities, and it won't be long before they're swamped by the general apathy and depression. Even the privileged minority are confused and everyone drowns his sorrows in the beer that flows so freely, yet still can't keep the breweries out of the red. Alcoholism has become one of the country's major problems, and when it affects the poor it makes the problem of malnutrition even worse.

'Zambia is Africa's paradise,' say the expatriates, going into raptures in their snug enclave in the Copperbelt and Lusaka. They probably haven't ever visited the villages, or even the shanty towns;

haven't ever heard the furious peasants yelling after them: 'If you ever come back this way, we'll be dead!'; haven't ever felt their heart miss a beat at the sound of those forgotten creatures singing the national anthem, 'One Zambia, One Nation', and doing their best to believe it. The important thing as far as they're concerned is to keep leading the life they enjoyed in the good old colonial days. For instance some of the whites get a kick out of undermining the whole system, and their greed is matched only by their arrogance and their racist attitude – as witness this remark addressed to a surgeon during a smart whites-only party: 'Is it you who sew up all those terrorists again? You'd do much better to kill 'em off, it'd be cheaper.' South Africa isn't far away. No wonder the blacks feel humiliated. In Zambia you never come across people who're proud of being African, and the women (including those living in the shanty towns) persist in making their faces look paler by rubbing in those horrible creams that are on sale all over Zambia but are banned in the parts of Africa that are proud of being African. Zambia has cut adrift. How can a radical change be brought about?

After all none of this is true development. Yet there have been plenty of warnings, even from the most conventional bodies. The World Bank insists on the need for rural development. A very long International Labour Office report is called *Narrowing the Gaps: Planning for basic needs and productive employment in Zambia* (it was published in January 1977). It demonstrates the need to give top priority to the basic needs of the population as a whole before attempting to supply the rich with luxury goods, and to ensure that everyone has productive work to do. Needless to say this report is now gathering dust on a shelf somewhere, surrounded by others of the same type. The Zambians complain that any advice they get from abroad is always bad, but they always go for the advice that appeals to them and tells them what they want to hear. We mustn't forget that all this happens against a background of what passes for socialism, which is supposed, according to the president, to lead to humanism.

11 *Is there a political will for recovery?*

Humanism is the official philosophy propounded by Kaunda, who aims to achieve an egalitarian society with man at its centre. But his socialism hasn't been properly set out yet, and nor has a coherent economic policy. Since there is no clearly defined line, everyone takes advantage of this situation to follow his own preferred path. Kaunda is untiring in his attacks on colonialism, neocolonialism, racism and Zionism, denouncing man's exploitation of his fellow man and the exploiting ways of international capitalism.* But although he has made himself the champion of freedom abroad, at home inequalities are increasing.

At the end of 1979 he decided that Zambia had wasted too much time on politics and that it was time to turn to economics. But is the machinery at his disposal – machinery he himself set up – capable of righting the situation on its own?

The Party has a monopoly of power but no means of carrying out projects. Each member of the central committee has his own office, two or three secretaries, a couple of cars, but is unable to act. Meanwhile the government does have the necessary executive powers, covering all aspects of the administration, but has no political power. Daniel Lisulo is, in theory the prime minister, living in Lusaka, but he is soon to be superseded by a member of another tribe.

All power is concentrated in Kaunda, both in the sense of defining policy and of carrying it out, but he is too involved with minutiae to be really effective. The people round him have only to use a bit of passive resistance to sabotage his best ideas if they don't approve of them. Very few civil servants put in any real work. The rest are afraid of compromising themselves if they take an initiative that has political repercussions, so they adopt a laissez-faire policy.

Kenneth Kaunda is an enigmatic man, unaffected, with a warm and kindly manner, public-spirited and essentially upright, but a prisoner of impossible circumstances. He was expected to lose the last election, yet there he is back in power, showing renewed vigour. The people of Zambia have no illusions about a large number of Party men, but they do trust him on the whole. 'We can't afford to buy a Party card,' was the explanation some of the peasants gave us – though they might not have wanted one anyway – 'but you can tell the "old man" we're on his side.'

---

* He then goes on to praise the IMF for forcing him to adopt 'strict financial discipline'. We have pointed out (see chapter 2, section 10) the damage caused to Zambia's agriculture and economy by this 'discipline'.

In spite of his cheerful good nature, he is a lonely man who can't rely on anyone. In a speech he gave in January 1980 he urged the political leaders and other members of the élite to stop giving in to corruption, since it forced him to suspend them from duty and made his life unbearable. He even launched a violent attack on all those who use the Party as a springboard to set themselves up in business and get hold of funds, then proceed to leave the public sector for the private sector, and line their pockets in the most scandalous way, only to start criticizing the public sector. He subsequently admitted to us that corruption was becoming a nightmare and the report on the railways scandal was only the tip of the iceberg. He then added, clearly bewildered: 'State enterprises can exploit people just as much as the capitalists do. When you come down to it, it's always the poor and the peasants who suffer.' But he doesn't dismiss anyone; he just shifts them to other jobs. He is criticized for keeping people who are widely known to be corrupt in positions close to him, but he probably prefers to keep an eye on them so that he can limit the amount of damage they can do. He is an extremely astute politician who knows his chessboard inside out and manipulates his pawns. For eighteen years he has managed to keep tribal in-fighting under control, no doubt because he comes from a small tribe. But these political games take a lot out of a man, and in the long run he too may be debilitated by an atmosphere liable to mar even the best intentions. He can be highly emotional, and every now and then will carry out a major reshuffle, striking dread into those with a guilty conscience.

But the main impression Kaunda makes is that of a stubborn man. For years he's gone on talking about principles in a society that has few of them. He chose to be one of the 'Front Line states' against South Africa, and he will stick up for his principles to the bitter end, in spite of reported opposition from within the Party, and undoubtedly from a good many of his people. At a time when the word 'socialism' was highly unpopular, particularly in late 1979, when there were constant rumours of a political coup, he still had the courage to state his views. He sings the praises of Mozambique and Cuba and came back with a great admiration for Samora Machel and Fidel Castro. He also harbours a secret passion for China. 'It's a bit of a foible of mine,' he admitted with a modest smile. 'You can't disregard or forgive the excesses they've committed, but look at what they've done for China. When you think of the feudal situation they started out with!

Discipline and hard work . . .' An African head of state must dream of achieving these two qualities.

Soon he was introducing classes on Marxism at the Party school, to the fury of the Church (especially the Catholic Church), which was horrified at the very word socialism. Kaunda countered by accusing it of backing apartheid. At the height of the crisis, in November 1979, when opposition to him was very vocal, he invited all the students to State House. For some time they'd been sneering at both humanism and the president, but he managed to win them over temporarily★ with a fierce diatribe against *international* capitalism and in favour of socialism. That was the day when he became 'Comrade President' rather than 'His Excellency' as before.

It's hard to understand how a man who holds so much power and is a genuine head of state can have let the situation deteriorate so badly. We have seen the cliques at work and all the many pressures being put on him, but this doesn't seem to be the whole explanation. In the early days Kaunda used to follow President Nyerere in neighbouring Tanzania, albeit timidly and after an interval. As we shall see, Zambia isn't Tanzania. But Zambia's president has never had the courage to take immediate steps to wipe out privileges. And he hasn't had the will to break with the model inherited from the colonial past. We put forward the following tentative explanation for this.

Kaunda is the son of a pastor, and his religious upbringing has had a strong influence on him, conditioning his behaviour. He isn't a revolutionary but tends to favour constitutional change. He thought that by retaining the structures and development model already in place it would eventually be possible to achieve a humanist society, whereas in fact this imported system was based on individualism and exploitation. Another contradiction is his concept of the masses, which seems uncomfortably close to the Christian concept of it being a duty to offer charity to the poor. Until this view has been superseded it seems doubtful whether it will ever be possible to envisage genuine mobilization of the mass of the people. When Kaunda talks – and he is sincere in this – about wanting to organize them, you can still sense an underlying élitist attitude, a form of humanism 'from above'.

Yet we're bound to acknowledge his courage during our visit. He

---

★ Although the students protest about the multinationals, they don't seem very keen to give up their own privileges.

was very aware of the stir it was causing, but he was invariably on our side, however unpopular this made him. And when he had eventually given instructions that our report was to be published, he finished up with the words, accompanied by a weary smile but with a determined look in his eye: 'Only cowards are afraid of the truth.'

On the day when peace was signed in Zimbabwe and the road to the south was reopened, the delighted Zambians started talking about the return of that delicious Salisbury ice cream, and about South African butter, which would cost less than Irish butter.

Zambia offers, alas, a perfect example of an unprepared élite who have slavishly followed the colonial and Western model, one which is leading to urban pseudo-development and ensuring that the country remains dependent. High copper prices enabled sheer folly to be committed. African agriculture has been sacrificed and education for all has mainly turned out a generation of unemployed. These problems won't be solved by an upturn in the price of copper and in the terms of trade, however desirable that may be, unless the whole concept of development is challenged. And development can never be achieved if the rural half of the population is neglected and the peasants forgotten, so that they finish up in the shanty towns.

4 Tanzania – the Ujamaa dream

1 *Nyerere, his dream and ours*

'Tanzania is talked about a lot. . . . But when it comes down to it, you know, we're only interesting by contrast. Our neighbours haven't achieved much, so we create a good impression, that's all.' The modesty and lucidity of the small, frail, prematurely white-haired figure inspire respect, as he speaks without bitterness and apparently not weighed down by his responsibilities. He's wearing a short-sleeved sports shirt and sandals, and sits with one foot tucked up beneath him. Julius K. Nyerere is the strength behind Tanzania. He is the chief in the noble sense of the word, a charismatic figure, but he prefers to be called '*Mwalimu*', 'Teacher', an affectionate term used by everyone from the ministry offices to the depths of the rural areas. He is the enlightened guide of his people. For twenty-five years now, against all the odds, he has been pursuing his Ujamaa dream, a humanistic, almost personalistic, form of socialism that claims to be African and is intended to ensure that each individual's needs are satisfied and that he can realize his potential.

'It's just a point of contrast,' he repeats, lost in thought. 'You'll soon see that nothing much has changed. The huts are just as poor and the peasants just as destitute. It's a good thing you've come at harvest time – it's really impressive this year.'* A mood of youthful gaiety took hold of him: 'Just think, we've even managed to export some cereals.' But he admitted: 'Apart from that, we're not short of ideas here in Tanzania, but we're so poor we haven't got the means to put them into practice.' This preamble, right at the start of our visit, removed any illusions we might have had left. Back in Europe Nyerere's writings

---

* He was speaking to us on 14 April 1979. A year later many regions were suffering from famine and the harvest of May–June 1980 was disastrous. Transport has been deteriorating and stocks of produce that aren't properly stored are going to waste.

had filled us with enthusiasm. The trouble is that, stuck with our privileges as we are, we rely so heavily on others to keep our hopes alive and forget the difficulties involved. We're too preoccupied with seeing our dreams fulfilled in countries where the prime concern is sheer survival, and whose populations may not share the aspirations of us 'haves' in the so-called 'developed' nations.

Tanzania isn't Zambia. In fact they are very different. A degree of modesty seems to prevail here. The Tanzanians aren't always out to dazzle and impress. This applies first and foremost to the capital. Although later on we shall be criticizing some of the advantages granted to Dar es Salaam, we have to admit that it hasn't swallowed up overseas aid by putting up lavish buildings and imposing avenues. The rural areas are given priority and the peasants have pride of place. Mwalimu has set the tone, and all over the country people talk about the peasants, even when this preoccupation doesn't go further than fine words. The aim behind this general concern with getting the peasants organized is often to step up output come what may. But at any rate no one ignores the peasants, though many have rather forgotten the villages. In the streets and offices of Dar es Salaam you can sense the people's dignity and their pride in being Tanzanian. We never came across any cases of shame or embarrassment at being African. The atmosphere in Dar is relatively hard-working, all things considered. But we must never forget that this is an underdeveloped country.

Foreign residents are generally very discreet and don't behave as though they owned the place. They're accepted for what they are – people providing temporary assistance. Not that this stops them complaining about delays and shortages. There are still quite a lot of small shops, generally run by Indians (who often behave arrogantly), and offering essential goods for sale rather than non-necessities. There are no imported luxury articles. Tanzanian merchandise comes first and priority isn't given to cosmetics, luxury foods, whisky and the like when it comes to spending foreign exchange. The Tanzanians are serious about the need for belt-tightening. It's just too bad for the foreigners. They're in the same boat and find themselves having to queue like everyone else. Anyway Mwalimu announced recently that in these difficult times people would have to do without whisky, and if the foreign residents don't like it, they'll have to stay at home – or make do with Dodoma wine, which is incidentally excellent.

Dodoma, which is bang in the middle of the country, is to be the new capital by the late eighties. It's in a semi-arid region that has the reputation of being bleak. 'Priority is being given to the villages, so we'll all go off and live in a village,' was one minister's comment. Even though Dodoma isn't quite the back of beyond, it isn't exactly Dar either, and it's a far cry from the gentle climate of the Indian Ocean. But the former capital, looking outwards from its coastal site, can't control such a huge country with no major roads. The very fact of living there cuts the inhabitants off from the interior, and the people who live in the outlying areas end up feeling closer to the borders that are physically near them.

Yet unlike many African countries, Tanzania does display a degree of national unity – and a clearly nationalist outlook. Defending her borders means something, and during the war against General Amin the peasants readily gave 100,000 head of cattle for the soldiers at the front – they'd only been asked for 14,000. We came across these gift herds all round Lake Victoria, on their way to Kampala. Historically, Tanzania has had the questionable good fortune to be poor since time immemorial: '. . . the very fact that our country had experienced almost no economic development meant that there were no islands of wealth surrounded by vast areas of misery. . . . There were comparatively few citizen vested interests which had to be taken into account in determining policies . . .'.[1] As for the tribes, there were so many of them (and still are) that it wasn't easy for one group to dominate the rest. One important unifying factor is Swahili, the national language, which is understood and spoken from Lake Tanganyika to Mount Kilimanjaro, and right down to the borders with Malawi or Mozambique. Lastly, the whole country is united round one man, their leader, Nyerere. Whereas the sympathy and respect of the ordinary peasant for Nyerere are genuine – they see him as something of a father figure defending his children – his veneration by some of the élite groups may seem suspect and self-seeking, as with their adherence to the official Party line. But all of them, for a variety of reasons, need him, and he is never attacked personally, even if the system comes in for criticism. Anyway this distinction is justifiable in that it's important to be able to differentiate between ideology and praxis, which don't necessarily coincide. The only problem is that if the head of state allows himself to be too highly revered he runs the risk of cutting himself off from the people and from everyday life. This danger is particularly acute when it isn't in the interest of the people he deals with to reveal all the difficulties they come across. It sometimes seems as though Mwalimu Nyerere is very much alone – alone with his dream.

Yet over and above his persuasive writings and special ideology, Julius Nyerere is a man of action too, a politician who has managed to build up a strong Party and knows how to handle power. He's also an exceptionally broad-minded head of state when it comes to African and international problems. His position as the leader of the Front Line states fighting South Africa, his good standing with the various African and international organizations and the major part he played in the Food and Agriculture Organization in July 1979 may one day make him a candidate for the role of president of the non-aligned nations. His influence is felt well beyond Tanzania itself. It has been said of that other charismatic leader, Fidel Castro, that he became too big for his island. Perhaps Mwalimu has become too big for Tanzania – unless, that is, the countless internal difficulties tend to make him look increasingly outwards.

2 *Many different countries rolled into one*

Tanzania lies 150 kilometres south of the equator beside the Indian Ocean and is bounded by Kenya, Uganda, Rwanda, Burundi, Zaïre, Zambia, Malawi and Mozambique. Its 940,000 square kilometres house a population of 18 million (1980 figures), which is growing at an increasing rate (currently 3·3 per cent annually), with the birth rate stable but the death rate dropping. The country is like a vast amphitheatre open on one side to the ocean and surrounded by mountains, most of which have rich well-watered soil. The Tanzanians have developed the mountainous region round the mighty volcanoes in the north by planting coffee and banana groves (Bukoba, Arusha and Kilimanjaro), while on the plateaux south of Lake Victoria, which are peopled by the country's largest ethnic group, the Sukuma – there will soon be over two million of them – the staple crop is cotton. The mountains in the south were cut off from the rest of the country until recently and have not been developed to the same extent, but the new railway and road links to Zambia have opened them up, and they will no longer serve merely as a source of labour for the sisal plantations on the coast, which are shrinking rapidly. The semi-desert plateau in the centre of the country, with its poor soil, is subject to severe famines and there is danger that overgrazing by its overabundant herds of cattle will worsen erosion and even lead to desertification.

Tanzania therefore suffers from a lack of balance, with many parts of the north and centre overpopulated, while the south and west are heavily underpopulated. Yet the productive potential of the south and west is far greater than on the central plateau, and it may well have been a mistake to site the new capital there. It was important to get away from Dar es Salaam, but instead of picking Dodoma the Tanzanians could have gone further south, to Iringa for instance.

Tanzania is a many-faceted country, but taken as a whole a poor one, one of the poorest in Africa – for want of mineral resources – and therefore in the world. It was neglected by the colonial powers: although Tanzania was under British mandate from the end of the First World War, the British despised the country and showed more concern for Kenya, which they wanted to turn into a British Algeria. The history of Tanzania today represents a unique attempt to emerge from a state of underdevelopment in a world that gives no second chances to casualties – especially if they haven't got much to offer.

3 *The early neocolonialist days*

The Tanganyika African National Union, TANU, was founded in July 1954, and Julius Nyerere, who was then thirty-two and had been back from Edinburgh University for two years, became its president. He has held the post ever since, but the Party is now known as the Chama cha Mapinduzi (CCM) or Revolutionary Party after its merger with Zanzibar's Afro-Shirazi Party (ASP). The president has continued to dominate the country's political life to this day. Yet although he is the undisputed leader, the privileged minority who hold the many levers of power in the government and the Party govern along their own lines and in their own interests, their main concern being to hang on to power.

Shortly after the country became independent on 9 December 1961, Nyerere announced his resignation as prime minister, which had been prepared over a long period, in order to take over the presidency.

Speaking on 22 January 1962, he referred to the need to build a bridge between the people and the new government by demonstrating in practical terms the importance of the Party and helping the people to identify with the institutions of an independent nation. He forged a firmly based party by means of which he could govern the country. In his pamphlet, *Ujamaa*, published in 1962, he set out the political line he intended to give his country (although difficulties were encountered in putting it into practice). Socialism, like democracy, is an attitude of mind, Nyerere argued. The basis of African socialism must be the extended family. Ujamaa – which he translated as 'familyhood' – was opposed both to capitalism, built on the exploitation of man by man, and to doctrinaire socialism, which presupposed conflict between man and man. As early as 1963, during a meeting in Prague, the Communist states, whose greatest fear ever since Marx has been utopian socialism, 'excommunicated' Léopold Senghor of Senegal and Julius Nyerere – an odd combination that! – 'because they claim to be putting an African version of socialism into practice'. 'If they fail to understand that there's only one form of socialism, we shall reject them,' stipulated Khrushchev, speaking in Bucharest in May 1963 (though seventeen months later it was his turn to be 'rejected'). It's interesting to note that at the time the Communist states believed that the only African countries travelling along the road to the one and only 'scientific' form of socialism were Ghana under Nkrumah, Mali under Modibo Keita and Guinea under Sékou Touré. The first two were later to fail politically, and Ghana has been easily overtaken by the Ivory Coast. As for Sékou Touré, he was to fail from every possible point of view, but has hung on to power by means of assassination and torture – not exactly a socialist regime.

4 *The Arusha Declaration is a major source of hope for Africa*

In October 1966 a form of national service for students was organized, to put them in touch with ordinary work and with manual workers, whom they were already tending to look down on. They promptly staged protest demonstrations, marching behind banners boldly proclaiming: 'Colonialism was better!' Nyerere had just read my book *False Start in Africa* and was making his ministers and senior civil servants read it too. He toured the country again, visiting the villages, and was reminded of the fact that the gulf between urban and rural areas was constantly widening, resulting in increasing rural discontent. He considered the problem and decided to act: on 5 February 1967 the famous Arusha Declaration came as a bombshell:

It is as if we have said, 'Money is the basis of development. Without money there can be no development.' . . . It is stupid to rely on money as the major instrument of development when we know only too well that our country is poor. . . . The largest proportion of the loans will be spent in, or for, the urban areas, but the largest proportion of the repayment will be made through the efforts of the farmers. . . . If we are not careful we might get to the position where the real exploitation in Tanzania is that of the town dwellers exploiting the peasants. . . . Agriculture is the basis of development. . . . In order to maintain our independence and our people's freedom we ought to be self-reliant in every possible way. . . . in the villages the women work very hard. At times they work for 12 or 14 hours a day. They even work on Sundays and public holidays. . . . But the men who live in villages (and some of the women in towns) are on leave for half of their life. The energies . . . at present wasted in gossip, dancing and drinking, are a great treasure. . . . In our country work should be something to be proud of, and laziness, drunkenness and idleness should be things to be ashamed of . . . nobody should be allowed to loiter in towns or villages.*[2]

Part Five quotes the Arusha Resolution from the National Executive Committee, which begins:

1. Every TANU and Government leader must be either a Peasant or a Worker, and should in no way be associated with the practices of Capitalism or Feudalism.
2. No TANU or government leader should hold shares in any Company.
3. No TANU or Government leader should hold Directorships in any privately-owned enterprises.

---

* These phrases are still true today.

4. No TANU or Government leader should receive two or more salaries.

5. No TANU or Government leader should own houses which he rents to others.[3]

Immediately after the declaration Nyerere and TANU nationalized the country's twenty-seven 'big factories', the insurance companies and the banks, in return for compensation. The British banks refused to negotiate and recalled all their expatriate employees in an attempt to torpedo the experiment, leaving Indian middle-ranking managerial staff to keep them going until reinforcements came. But here too the parastatals that took over from the private factories have not proved very satisfactory.

Not all the privileged few gave up their privileges willingly. Oscar Kambona, one of Nyerere's companions during the early struggles for independence, and the plump Bibi Titi, head of the Union of Women of Tanzania (UWT), resigned with a flourish, and Kambona has since been trying to attack the regime from outside. On the other hand young people throughout the country organized long marches in support of the new policy, and the peasants were by no means the least enthusiastic.

The international repercussions were enormous. By then the 'scientific socialists' of West Africa were already compromised – Kwame Nkrumah had actually been overthrown – while the so-called 'African' forms of socialism, of the type practised by Léopold Senghor, were clearly getting bogged down in neocolonialism. Socialists in Scandinavia were wildly enthusiastic, thinking even at this early stage that their own dreams were being put into practice in a historical, sociological and economic context that is after all very different from their own. They forgot – or underestimated – the primary problem of underdevelopment, the bureaucracy it necessitates, and the inevitable formation of a state bourgeoisie.

Now fully in his stride, the eloquent Nyerere explained his policy to the country's students on 5 August 1967. He told them that his Arusha Declaration was a commitment to a specific quality of life, to a fully accepted form of Africanhood; they were trying to bring about a 'telescoped' development of the nation's economy and society, so that they would reach the same level of affluence as in Britain or the United

States, but at a much faster pace (alas!). While it took 40,000 shillings*
to create a new job in a highly mechanized industry, 130 shillings'
worth of fertilizer and insecticides would increase the yield from a
1-acre field of cotton (cotton again!) by 100 per cent, and a plough
costing 250 shillings would enable a peasant to double the size of the
acreage he could cultivate. It would therefore be a mistake to cover
Tanzania with mechanized farms using tractors and combine harves-
ters.

The next pamphlet by Nyerere to appear was *Education for
Self-reliance*, in March 1967. It put forward an education policy based
on the needs of the villages and on letting pupils be involved in manual
work, particularly farm work. Lastly, in September 1967, came the
text that was to have the greatest significance for Tanzania's villagers.
Indeed its effects are still being felt.

5 *The Ujamaa philosophy*

In his pamphlet *Socialism and Rural Development*, Nyerere salutes
traditional Tanzanian society but admits that it gave women an
inferior status and that poverty resulted from ignorance and from the
small size of peasant farms. He reminds his readers that 'there has been
a general acceptance of the social attitudes and ideas of our colonial
masters' and that 'there is an almost universal belief that life in the
towns is more comfortable and more secure . . . and that people in the
rural parts of the country are condemned to poverty and insecurity for
their whole lives.' He points out that if cotton farmers increase their
acreage by taking on extra labour apart from the family, 'we shall find
ourselves with a farmers' class and a labourers' class'. He then stands
up for 'cooperative societies which are owned and governed by the
farmers themselves', but admits that they may eventually 'replace the
exploitation of man by man by the exploitation of inefficiency and
bureaucratic dishonesty'.[4]

He then puts forward the idea of 'rural *economic and social communities
where people live together and work together for the good of all*' (his italics).
He speaks of villages made up of thirty or forty families. If it had been

---

* The Tanzanian shilling was originally worth the same as a British shilling
(5p). By 1980 it was worth only 2½p.

possible to stick to a small unit of this type many difficulties would have been avoided. He specifies that 'socialist communities cannot be established by compulsion'; and that 'the task of leadership and of Government is not to try and force this kind of development, but to explain, encourage, and participate'. He points out that progress may be quite slow at first in setting up communal plots: 'the people would keep their individual plots'. These would be chiefly restricted to food crops ('These socialist villages must grow from an application of the principle of self-reliance') and 'within easy reach of the area where the houses will be'. 'Promises of miracles, even promises of great Government help, will only lead to disaster.'

His conclusion – and this short sentence was to govern rural policy in Tanzania for many years – was that: 'the most important thing is . . . that within its resources [the Government] should *give priority to requests which are received from villages where the people are living together and working together for the good of all*' (our italics). He also points out: 'Nonetheless, the experience of existing Ujamaa villages, such as those now operating within the Ruvuma Development Association, could be helpful.' Ruvuma is the only example he gives, but it didn't bring luck to these pioneers of Ujamaa. At any rate, in spite of all his comments about the need to proceed by slow stages and with caution, he is clearly referring to a form of socialism that is thought out from above. What do the great majority of the peasants know about socialism, even if it goes by the name of Ujamaa? They do clearly want to improve their situation, and most of all they want better food and clothing – and to drink their *pombe* with their friends as often as possible.

6 *The joys and sorrows of the Ruvuma Development Association*

Even before the country had become independent, as early as 1960, nine young activists started collectively cultivating a small cashew nut plantation in Ruvuma region in southern Tanzania. The Ruvuma Development Association (RDA) was set up, with three villages and seventy families, in 1963; during the period 1967–9 it embraced seventeen villages and over four hundred families. The accent was on collective output as the basis of development. Mixed cropping was practised, and yields increased, enabling them to set up small-scale industries and to carry out improvements in housing, health services and education. A self-financing boarding school perfected new teaching methods. Gradually a successful method of achieving rural development, that highly complex and difficult process, could be seen emerging. Which of course explains why Nyerere referred to it. During one visit to the area (which incidentally the senior civil servants didn't like visiting), he even presented one of the RDA communities with a truck. The Association managed to acquire a sawmill and a maize mill that were a great deal more efficient and economic than the ones run by the authorities, but it refused to accept handouts from the authorities.

At that point the RDA was a highly democratic body, following Nyerere's directives to the letter (which isn't the case elsewhere) when he said: 'Ujamaa villages will . . . be created by the village people themselves, and maintained by them. It must be done from their own resources.'[5] But it did make sure to have Party and regional officials on its committee, alongside representatives of the village. These officials, and particularly the top man, the regional commissioner, had well-paid and high-status jobs, but they could be summarily dismissed, so they had little job security. Ralph Ibbott, the Englishman who acted as their adviser, living with them and leading a very simple life, told us that of the five people who held the job at various times between 1963 and 1969, four subsequently lost their official status entirely. This means that these senior civil servants feel they must please the powers that be in every particular.

The Italian economist Bruno Musti di Gennaro[6] believes that the RDA represented a highly developed form of peasant struggle, with the peasants trying to win back control over the surplus created by the rural areas. These peasant communities put the stress on food crops that could improve their health and productivity and make them less dependent on the cash economy. They would invest their surpluses on the spot and thus gain direct benefit from them.

This didn't suit the state at all, or its various organs, both political (the Party) and administrative. They encouraged the peasants – as they still do – to go in for export crops, because then they can control the surplus value realized on the world market, in particular by means of export duties, and it can be diverted to urban consumption or investment – i.e. away from the peasants' control, and mainly for the benefit of the privileged few in positions of power. When, in 1969,

TANU went in for a policy of setting up Ujamaa villages all over the country, the first important action performed by its central committee was to abolish the RDA. That was on 24 September. The following day the Minister for Rural Development and a few members of the committee turned up in Songea in an official plane to explain to the peasants why they had decided to disband the association. They claimed it had been 'plotting against the Party' and that the Party must 'control every stage in the development of the villages'.

According to Musti, there was a clear-cut ideological conflict between the élitist concept that expects the people passively to receive directives handed down from on high, and the grass roots of the RDA, the poor peasants, helped by progressive elements from the lower middle classes. Many peasants in this poor part of the country had to emigrate to the sisal plantations or the mines of South Africa, and thus become members of the proletariat.

This decision reveals a consequence of the Arusha Declaration that hasn't been fully appreciated: the state bourgeoisie has acquired a new form of power as a result of the state's increased involvement in the economic sphere – prematurely referred to as socialism! The main beneficiaries of the farm cooperatives were the Tanzanian equivalent of the kulaks, but the new authorities, which are getting stronger all the time, have used the (valid) excuse of their inefficiency and corruption to replace them with 'crop authorities' – parastatal bodies that soon turned out to be just as inefficient and just as corrupt! This time the presence of corruption worked to the advantage of the state bourgeoisie, who thus acquired, alongside their undisputed political powers, an increase in economic power that strengthened their own interests.

7 The Ujamaa period (1969–73) gets off to a bad start

Once this decision had been taken, the Party and district and regional officials used every means at their disposal to encourage the setting up of Ujamaa villages that were initially supposed to be voluntary, and founded by charismatic leaders. But they soon proved a failure, frequently because enthusiasm was missing, or the site chosen was unsuitable, and sometimes because of fear of witchcraft. The villages were often too small to make it worth piping in water and installing a school and a dispensary. The next step was to implement Presidential Circular no. 1 (1969), which stated:

> It is to the building of Ujamaa villages that Government must turn its attention. We have to organize our party and government machinery to assist their establishment; we have to give them priority in all our credit, servicing and extension services – at the expense of the individual producer.

This time the message was quite clear: the idea was to speed up the semi-collectivization of the rural areas. But the criteria for deciding whether or not a village was a true Ujamaa village, and therefore deserved to be given priority in these many different areas, were never clearly set out. There had to be a 'certain proportion' of communal crops, but no figure was ever laid down. Roadside placards proudly pointed down side-tracks leading to self-styled Ujamaa villages, so called because that was what the authorities wanted, and it was therefore the best way of getting hold of government handouts. Once they had been officially recognized as Ujamaa villages they would be given gifts or loans (few of which would ever be repaid) in the form of seeds, fertilizers, insecticides – even tractors. Yet the tractors put a stop to the spread of ox-drawn vehicles – a vital need because this is the only self-sufficient method.

The Scandinavian authors of a book they have called *Ujamaa, Socialism from Above* point out that:

> Regional leaders in government and in TANU felt themselves under especially great pressure to show results, where at the same time they enjoyed a large degree of freedom with regard to the ways and means to achieve them – and with regard to their actual content. . . . Incentives to establish Ujamaa villages ranged from ideological commitment and understanding by the villagers themselves over different degrees of persuasion and coercion by administrative and political officials, to material rewards in the form of expanded services and direct support from the government.[7]

The majority of these measures are totally at variance with the directives Nyerere laid down in 1967: '. . . socialist communities cannot be established by compulsion. . . . Viable socialist communities can only be established by willing members. . . . promises of great Government help will only lead to disaster.'[8] Even with this 'great Government help' many Tanzanian peasants, who became deeply individualistic as a result of colonial rule, failed to understand the principle underlying the Ujamaa villages, or in some cases actually rejected it. A surfeit of subsidies is never a recipe for economic success. Admittedly one or two Ujamaa groups or villages, often consisting of twenty to thirty families and set up by young people with no land (the idea being to acquire some), have been a success. We saw some that had survived. The local authorities like to be able to show their superiors and visiting foreigners a model village, even if it doesn't pay its way. But such cases are exceptional, and meanwhile the great majority of the peasants had no Ujamaa status as yet and weren't receiving any assistance at all. This situation affected the country's agricultural output, which had been increasing nicely down to 1966. The decline was later put down to the effects of the drought, which was certainly severe in central Tanzania, but it wasn't the only reason.

A mini-bureaucracy of Party officials, agricultural officers and community development officers had settled into the Ujamaa villages. They were paid far more than the peasants, and lived apart from the villagers – their only contacts were with other bureaucrats at district level. These privileged bureaucrats despised manual labour and were too remote from the peasants in every sense of the word to be able to encourage local efforts, as in China, or to make full use of the country's indigenous resources to foster genuine development. It's true that communal activities involving human investment did result in the development of services such as water supplies, schools and health care, but they were never geared to developing the whole area, particularly in the two fields that have proved such a success in China – water control and reafforestation. The origins, traditions and history of the Tanzanian peasant are completely different from those of his counterpart in China. In 1973 it was eventually recognized – and not before time – that the Ujamaa villages had been a failure. The authorities then decided to move on to a different policy.

8 'Villagization' is carried out in too authoritarian a manner

At the end of 1973 the 'exorbitant' privileges bestowed on self-styled

Ujamaa villages were therefore halted, but on 7 November 1973 the *Daily News* (which is virtually the official government newspaper) told its readers that as a result of a TANU decision it was now compulsory to live in villages, and that this order was to be carried out within the next three years. Whereas it had long been said that the maximum population of a village should be 250 families, in 1973 this was being given as a minimum figure; the optimum figure was now 500 families, the maximum 600.

In fact this 'villagization' policy was only a new version of Nyerere's long-cherished dream. He was obsessed with the idea of grouping the whole peasant population in villages, so that the government could give them assistance and provide them with basic services, but at the same time organize and supervise output. Ever since 1961 he had been trying out various methods of achieving this aim, but each attempt had resulted in failure. It looks as though he became fed up with the length of time it was taking and decided to use compulsion.

Up to this point most Tanzanian peasants had been living in scattered settlements,* on isolated farms or in small hamlets, tilling the fields very close to where they lived and able to practise shifting cultivation, with the natural vegetation on the land lying fallow producing humus to restock the soil. If the land became infertile they would move on – anyway, the standard form of housing, with a thatched roof built over poles and mud walls, didn't last more than eight to ten years. The order to 'villagize' started off with 'Operation Dodoma', which involved grouping together very poor subsistence farmers, many of them half-starved, beside the main roads so that they could also be supplied with water. Some of them held out against this enforced move, but the army stepped in, burning down old houses in some cases.

When it was Kigoma's turn the authorities had learnt their lesson and the operation was better planned. From then on they swept all before them – half of Mwanza, a huge and densely populated area, had to move in July 1974, the other half in August. The authorities, all of them city-dwellers, didn't always appreciate the enormous amount of

---

* This was not always the case. Sumbawanga and Mtwara already had villages grouped together. The houses in the overpopulated Chagga zones (Kilimanjaro) were pretty close together.

work involved. Nobody wanted to look as if they were dragging their feet, Shinyanga and the other regions followed on too quickly, and there was no time for the studies that were an essential preliminary to selecting the right site for the new villages.

Sylvain Urfer has written several books that come out strongly in favour of the Tanzanian experiment. Yet in his book *Une Afrique socialiste: la Tanzanie*, he comments:

> Between August and November 1974 it was as if a tidal wave had washed over the country, with millions of people being moved in a dictatorial manner, sometimes overnight, on to waste land that they were expected to turn into villages and fields. In many places the army was called in to bring anyone who was reluctant to heel and move them *manu militari*. During the month of October the country seemed to be emerging from some national disaster, with mean huts made from branches and foliage stretching in untidy rows beside the roads.[9]

And in October the *Daily News* gave accounts of populations being moved *en masse* with no attempt to work out how they could organize themselves on their new land. It painted a picture of people uprooted from their villages and abandoned in the bush, where they were supposed to find planned villages.

In fact it would be fair to say that the operation took place without any planning at all, what with the bureaucrats giving orders and 'villagizing' on paper with no knowledge whatsoever of the regions affected, plus the local leaders' zeal to act quickly and demonstrate their diligence by cramming in the maximum number of people. In some cases the peasants came forward voluntarily to attach themselves to an Ujamaa group that was working well, hoping to take advantage of the communal work done by the other members at little cost to themselves. If it's got to be socialism . . .

Bernard Joinet emphasizes that when the British forbade peasants to settle in areas infected with sleeping sickness, everyone talked about the West's civilizing role, whereas 'when Tanzania moves her peasants to combat famine some foreign observers talk about totalitarian violence.'[10] Yet the real point is whether this was the best way to combat famine.

Urfer comments that the movement started when Nyerere was

abroad. (At any rate Tanzania is such a huge country, and communications are so poor, that he would have had great difficulty checking that the operation was proceeding smoothly in all the various districts at once.) The fact that the villagization policy was carried out in too authoritarian a manner could have been the work of antisocialist elements exceeding their orders in order to discredit the Ujamaa philosophy; or perhaps Marxists cutting corners in the race towards their own brand of scientific socialism. Whatever the reason, during this period of villagization running from 1974 to 1976, output of export crops was at a standstill and there was a drop in food crops. Here too the situation was blamed wholly on the drought, whereas villagization was also to blame. In 1974 Tanzania had to import 384,000 tonnnes (and another 521,000 in 1975) of wheat, rice and particularly maize, in which it is normally self-sufficient, and this at a time when the price of oil was going up and up. The country's foreign exchange reserves collapsed and its indebtedness – which, we must remember, was the result of our paying too little for its export crops, and of unequal terms of trade – was constantly increasing. Since then the economic situation has been continually difficult.

9 *A basic mistake – the villages were too big*

Here too the Minister of Agriculture hardly ever conceived of agricultural modernization except in terms of an injection of external inputs, chiefly fertilizers and tractors. He liked the idea of communal fields because they made the use of tractors easier. The peasants were reluctant, so the minister fell back on what are known as 'block farms'. These consist of rows of individual plots, often 1–2 acres per family, all of them devoted to the same crop, either maize or cotton. This meant that the acreage cultivated by each peasant could be controlled, competition encouraged – and the tractor often put to good use.

So when the authorities urged the peasants to group themselves into large villages the Agriculture Minister didn't object – 'his' tractors could easily be deployed there. But not every village had a tractor, and even now, in 1982, no one can say when, or even if, it will be possible to see them all over the country. We went to one village housing 600 families in Songea district in Ruvuma region. One of the women told us that she had to make forty journeys to bring back 1,200 kilos of cobs from her 1-acre maize field, which was five miles away. For each homeward journey she would be carrying a load weighing 30 kilos on her head, and she covered a total of 400 miles on foot all told. No one seems to have given any thought to this problem, but she bitterly resented it, and she wasn't the only one.

Besides, short of a mass exodus from the rural areas, the population in these villages will have doubled in twenty-five years. Now the first field starts just beyond the last house. Where are they going to put the new young couples? They'll have to live even further away. To ensure that the distance between the fields and the village doesn't become even greater, permanent cultivation round the villages is the order of the day, with none of the land lying fallow. The soil in the highlands has a high humus content and is unaffected by this, but in the case of many poor soils, such as that at Ismani round Iringa, the drop in fertility caused by permanent cultivation occurs swiftly and has catastrophic results.

The village of Bashay, near Karatu and the famous Ngorongoro crater, consisted of eighty families in early 1974, but this figure had risen to 450 by the end of the year, and by 1979 it was over 520 families. Their land covered 1,855 hectares, including 700 hectares of waste land and grazing land, much of it already laid bare by erosion. The density of animals was so high that it resulted in overgrazing, and this in turn made the erosion worse, leading to 'ravines several metres deep, patches of hillside stripped of any form of vegetation and of their layer of arable soil.'[11] One thing is certain: the 1,130 hectares of ploughed land, with extensive use of the village's thirteen tractors, weren't enough to keep its 874 working people (with 1,280 children between them!) fully employed. Crop yields were falling because the land is never left to lie fallow, and because there is no manure. Yet Tanzania is not an overpopulated country.

Many of the former settlements that the peasants had to leave were surrounded by papaw and citrus trees, guavas, coconut palms in coastal areas, and banana trees. The soil in their gardens (known as *bustani*) was enriched with humus – an immense capital asset that is left unused. In the south, in Mtwara region, the settlements have been sited further away from the cashew nut plantations and output has dropped a great deal as a result. The authorities like to have easy access to the villages they are in charge of, so they can often be seen lining the country's main roads, such as the Iringa–Mbeya road, like soldiers on parade. But the roads were mapped out to link one town to another, and often avoid the more fertile valleys. In other cases villages have been sited on semi-marshland, and are flooded at regular intervals during each rainy season! Some villages have been moved twice, and the bewildered peasants are afraid they'll have to move yet again – scarcely an incentive to increase output.

Having said this, it is not the actual principle of villagization that we would criticize, but the fact that it has been implemented too hastily and with no proper planning. Not a single serious study has been carried out. What ought to happen is *rationalized* villagization, for it is easy to see why a country with such a sparse and scattered population should want to group people together. Otherwise it is very difficult to supply the inhabitants with the social services crucial to their survival – clean water, dispensaries and so on.

Tanzania does clearly want to improve the lot of its villagers, but although the government has promised all sorts of social benefits it isn't in a position to fulfil its promises throughout the country. So the peasants feel indignant: 'They told us to get together in villages, and here we are. But where's the clean water? Where's the dispensary? Why didn't the fertilizers get here in time?' The government have therefore aroused expectations they can't meet straight away. And even if the necessary equipment has been provided, it doesn't always work. Tanzania is a poor country, communications are difficult and roads are often impassable (especially during the rainy season). This means that lorries have a short life, and the cost of replacing them is going up and up. And the price of petrol – when there is any – is another problem. All this leads to difficulties with distribution, which are heightened by too much red tape.

10 *In the village*

Villagization may have been too authoritarian at times, but it certainly hasn't been uniform. Tanzania has 9,000 villages and it would be fair to say that each one is different. They vary in the type of economy practised, in the region's potential, in their traditions, in the temperament of the villagers – and in the civil servants whose job it is to organize them. The Ujamaa spirit also varies from one village to another.

On the slopes of Mount Kilimanjaro or Mount Meru, which are covered with coffee shrubs shaded by banana trees, there is little of the Ujamaa spirit. The peasants living here have always been individualists and the rich ones see no need to share their wealth. Yet these favoured regions do suffer from a hidden form of unemployment, in that there are too many people trying to share in their blessings. In these parts of the country, villagization has involved not so much physical changes as the marking out of boundaries. The peasants living on the arid Dodoma plateau, who are chronically in need of aid in the form of food, embarked enthusiastically on setting up collective fields (even if this meant neglecting their private fields). Their enthusiasm was increased by the offer of aid and a supply of 'miracle' cereal crops – lulo and serena sorghum, short-cycle dwarf sorghums that are hardier in times of drought. But they don't keep well and the peasants don't like the taste. They often sell off their harvests – and then ask for aid. At which point the Chaggas, a hard-working and enterprising people from the Kilimanjaro region, grumble: 'If that's what you call socialism . . .'

The coastal villages tend to be easy-going. They've never had a strong tradition of hard work, since it's possible to survive there without much of an effort. But in the remote highlands the peasants are hard-working, because they're used to relying on nothing but their own efforts. The climate is harsh and communications are poor. In Kigoma region, near the Burundi highlands, the former sisal cutters have returned and go in for intensive cultivation; they have kept the energetic qualities characteristic of mountain peoples and immigrants, while the people of Sumbawanga (southeast of Lake Tanganyika) have suddenly realized that they're very backward and have decided to change this state of affairs by a collective effort. As for the nomads,★ they are presumably unwilling to join a village. They often reject a type of development because they suspect that it would force them to go in for farming, which they hate.

The situation also varies within a single region or district, depending on the traditions, interests or commitment of the people living there. We were often to see villages very close together, one of them working while the other was a failure. In extreme cases, such as Mareu (Arusha), a very Ujamaa-minded group has managed to survive in a

---

★ See chapter 5, section 1, for a discussion of the Masai.

village where 'kulaks' predominate. As a general rule the authorities favour and help those who are well organized and productive. The others tend to be neglected.

Tanzania's villages can't be visited (which is a great pity for the young Europeans who are keen to study the 'Ujamaa spirit'), and don't like being disturbed. Since they've had their own government even the regional and district officials have to make an appointment before coming. One regional development director (RDD), the administrative head of the region, commented: 'Now we've handed power over to them, we have to observe protocol.' As we shall be seeing later, this power is somewhat ambiguous. But we were the president's guests and the authorities in charge of the fourteen regions we visited greeted us warmly before handing us on to the district authorities, who in turn took us into the villages they'd selected as being 'representative'. The term was ambiguous and we often had to insist on seeing ordinary villages, not just the ones most popular with the powers that be, those which won prizes and were rewarded for their efforts on the national holiday or Saba Saba on 7 July, which is also Peasants' Day – Tanzania is the only country to honour its peasantry in this way.

At any rate we were warned as soon as we got there that there is no such thing as an Ujamaa village nowadays. The current term is 'development village'. All over the country groups were waiting for us, with the local bigwigs out in front; they greeted us with a degree of ceremony that reflected how interested they were. In some cases children from the local school would welcome us with dancing and singing (the traditional dances and songs are being carefully preserved). But there would always be two separate camps. There would be the officials travelling with us, the village chairman and his twenty-five-member council, all of them elected by the village assembly. Then came the *katibu* or secretary, a young and often dynamic man who'd been chosen on the spot by the Party. He was in theory the party's ideologist and watchdog, in a village where he was aware of everything that went on, even private matters. In some cases there was also a village manager, a type of coordinator sent there and paid by the prime minister's office. This could be an excellent new idea, but it was implemented too hastily, and the office was often forced into picking the first person who came along. The managers vary enormously in their qualifications and in the extent to which they share in the life of the village, but the average manager is pretty low-grade, whereas the job requires technical abilities, a highly enterprising approach and a degree of ingenuity in finding your feet and striking the right balance between all the different authorities who intermingle at village level. But where could a whole set of such rare creatures be found? It's always the same problem in this country that tends to act over-hastily – there's a shortage of executives.

The peasants would stand together, keeping at a respectful distance from our group and watching and listening rather than joining in our discussions, with the women huddled in a corner even farther away from us. In spite of their new rights an exaggerated respect for authority is still common in Tanzania – a legacy from precolonial and colonial traditions. Yet in a few cases you do sense that the villagers are used to taking part in meetings and discussions, whereas elsewhere they wait passively to be told what to do. Some of them are quite outspoken, and the members of the opposition would often take advantage of our visit to criticize the experiments made by the district or the inappropriate advice given by a *bwana shamba* (agricultural adviser) fresh out of some agricultural college.

The so-called 'backward' or 'conservative' peasants often knew perfectly well that the directives and instructions issued from on high were nonsensical. For instance in once case they refused to plant cotton on marginal land where, to make matters worse, they weren't getting any insecticides. And when we were talking to them we ended up wondering who were the real ignoramuses. They'd even ask us about agricultural achievements elsewhere, in China or West Africa! But in the stock-rearing areas everyone's eyes would light up when we started talking cattle, their favourite subject, particularly when it came to working out who had the largest herd in the village. They'd start counting on their fingers, with a half smile. When a visitor was talking learnedly about cattle-rearing and veterinary medicine they'd feel they had to point out: 'We don't breed our cattle for economic reasons, you know.'

After the various tales of fertilizers not arriving in time, seeds that hadn't germinated and loans that hadn't always been repaid, and their dreams of tractors, we'd hear about their everyday concerns. There was the school that needed enlarging; the dispensary – they were all ready to build it but they needed nails and cement and both were unobtainable; suplies of salt and soap were sporadic; there was no clothing in the village shop, which wasn't always properly stocked by the Regional Trading Corporation (RTC), a government body that sometimes prefers to sell to the Indian traders first. And then they'd talk in general terms about all the difficulties in the way of transport, organization and distribution. Medicines in particular fail to turn up; this dampens the nurse's enthusiasm and is a major cause of concern to the villagers, who are very aware of all these health-care problems. Here too the emphasis is officially on prevention, but the lion's share of the budget is swallowed up by three monsters – the three hospitals at Moshi, Mwanza and Dar, which are in theory consultant hospitals for the whole country but in fact, because of transport difficulties, give priority to the towns. And in spite of Mwalimu's declarations, another is to be built at Mbeya; it's a gift from the British, but maintenance costs will obviously have to be met by Tanzania. When we told the government that chloroquine could increase yields faster than fertilizers in a country where malaria causes havoc, the Agriculture Minister was highly indignant. But the peasants have a different set of priorities.

Having said that, although the peasants don't show overmuch enthusiasm for collective farming, they do seem to be very pleased with the social services – where they're provided, that is – and at any rate happy to be living together. This is particularly true of the women: 'Now when we need help we can call on our next-door neighbour.' The young people are happy too. They organize football and dancing clubs and find it easier to escape from under their family's thumb than in isolated hamlets. Villagization has enabled them to have a social life, even though it does inevitably lead to clashes between one group and another. But the main activity is still farming.

11 *In the fields*

It was harvest time and the villagers took us off into the fields, their readiness to do so depending on the state of their crops. We were still thinking in Ujamaa terms and our top priority was to see the communal plot. Nowadays it goes under the name of 'village development field' and everyone has to put in a fixed minimum of work there to enable the community to obtain resources. The money acquired in this way can be invested in building a school, a warehouse or a dispensary, or is sometimes used to buy a lorry, a mill or a tractor (a quarter of the price has to be paid cash-down). But some villages have no economic expertise and don't know how to get the best use out of their money. The village manager is supposed to help them draw up plans, but their ideas can't always be put into practice and the mills or lorries they hanker after may be unobtainable. In some cases the money will be used to increase the capital of the communal shop. Apparently all these activities bring in more than working in the fields. The general rule is that transport or trade always pay better than farming.

Many a peasant complains of not knowing where the resulting earnings go. Then again, attitudes towards the communal plot vary a great deal, depending on the traditions and wealth of the peasants concerned; and in some cases the authorities threaten to impose heavy fines on slackers. Some villages keep the best land for private cultivation and use whatever is left over as the communal plot, even if it has poor soil and is well away from the village, to keep in with the authorities; in other cases the communal plots are a model of good farming – but they are the exception, because as a rule crop yields on private land are much higher.

'So you think my field's better,' said one elderly peasant in Tanga, bursting with pride. 'The thing is, of course, I sow it before the other one. And,' he added with a cunning smile, 'I buy my seeds privately.' So even private seeds are better, or thought to be so, because the peasants distrust collective schemes and many of them send their womenfolk to work in the communal plots, which after all they haven't chosen for themselves. The same applies to the 'block farms' or rows of private fields that have been compulsorily grouped together, and the fact that the size and site of the plots have been decided over their heads increases their suspicion. Sometimes they don't even bother to keep the field weeded, or even to harvest the crops. The block farms make it easier to use insecticides (and also for the authorities to check up on them) and are supposed to encourage healthy competition, but many peasants don't like people looking at their fields and keeping such a close eye on them.

Anyway, when you get down to it, why should the peasants work on the communal plot if there are no incentives for doing so? Some of them don't bring in anything at all, and others only earn money for the collective unit. In some highly prosperous villages we saw poverty-stricken peasants going short of salt, suffering from undernourishment and soothing their frustrations by staring at the gleaming communal truck, the Party offices or the well-stocked shop – whose goods they couldn't afford to buy. What Dar es Salaam, or the regional and district officials, deem to be in the general interest may not be seen in the same light by the ordinary man or woman. But it's impossible to generalize, because the way the profits from the communal plots are shared out varies widely; and we shall be emphasizing later on that some remarkable work has been done.

In too many cases the peasants don't fully understand what is expected of them, because the projects aren't explained properly, or the explanations are too hurried. It rather looks as if some people enjoy causing confusion. Everyone has his own pet theory, and it isn't always based on Mwalimu's doctrines. Ujamaa activities (especially the plots) are badly planned and badly organized, and the peasants, who have their doubts from the outset, are soon put off by low crop yields and promptly associate Ujamaa with poverty. When they've spent a whole year working without any concrete results it's doubtful whether they'll be prepared to start again the following year. They'll feel more inclined to work harder on their own fields, which is very understandable. To make matters worse, hard-working peasants are put off by their lazy neighbours, and it's hard to build socialism without socialists. If the peasants are to abandon their individualism, they must be given convincing proof that communal work is advantageous. Although they're said to be conservative and backward, they aren't fools, especially when, as happens in some cases, they realize that the only people to get anything out of their work are the village chairman and the *katibu*. It would be wrong to generalize, but it's easy to see that this is a danger.

In Sumbawanga we saw well-organized plots producing high yields and peasants who were well pleased. They were building houses and buying mills with what they earned from the communal plot; having been poor since time immemorial, they were now improving their standard of living. But maize monoculture as favoured by the World Bank is liable to lead to falling yields. Some Ujamaa groups working solely on a collective basis are achieving much higher yields than the peasants round about, but they are hard-working, highly motivated, well organized and disciplined, with leaders who are genuine administrators, and they have good accountants. All these different ingredients of success can't be present in nine thousand villages.

This is a great pity, since the village has to shoulder a large number of responsibilities, starting with marketing, in which it acts as agent for the crop authorities in return for a commission which is a major source of income. In 1976 the marketing cooperatives, together with their associations and unions, were suddenly disbanded. It had been decided that the villages automatically constituted a basic cooperative in charge of collecting produce for the national marketing boards. But a large number of villages aren't in a position to take on this marketing function effectively, because they haven't got any godowns or accountants, and because the service offered by the marketing boards leaves a lot to be desired. Many peasants value these new facilities, because in the old days they couldn't get rid of their produce, but those who have an opportunity to sell on the open market, to private customers, prefer to do so, like the rice growers of Usangu along the Zambia road, offering their produce for sale at the top price (especially in times of scarcity, such as the 1980 famine). In one of these villages they were boasting about a high paddy yield, yet the commission paid to the village was ludicrously low. What had happened to the rice? The district authorities were upset by our arguments and told us firmly that 'open' selling was illegal. What can they do?

This marketing function does have some drawbacks, however. It can lead to malnutrition, for instance. Traditionally the head of the family was duty-bound to see that his granary was full. Nowadays he's more likely to sell off too high a proportion of his crops, and the family granary is shrinking rapidly. The villagers assume that they'll always be able to buy back some flour, but this is often impossible.

As a result the village economy is increasingly cash-based, and this involves heavy expenditure on storage, transport and distribution. If a farming economy doesn't step up its output, this increased marketing role represents a new burden on it, and one that is hard to bear. And the reserves that used to enable them to survive in the lean years are now disappearing.* The village granary could include a communal

---

* In southern Morocco there used to be a really good harvest every five years, and it would be carefully stored because it would be followed by two mediocre harvests and another two that were virtually non-existent. In 1923 a road was built, lorries appeared, and so did imported goods; the peasants succumbed to temptation, sold off their reserves – and in due course very nearly starved to death.

silo, with each family supplying a set amount of grain, which they would be entitled to have back again to tide them over between harvests. But who will pay for this?

At the moment the silo is merely a stage in the marketing process, but an essential one if storage losses are to be avoided. The prime minister emphasized that he would very much like to see Tanzanians showing the same enthusiasm for building godowns as for new stadia, especially when we told him that some villages were giving priority to building Party offices – more prestige for the local bigwigs.

12 *Power to the village*

'Power to the peasants' is a long-standing dream of Nyerere's (and our dream too). The villagization policy of 1975 did give power to the villagers – on paper, that is – but it isn't as straightforward or as easy as that. The ideology of the system is self-governing, and so is the village structure. But the outcome is less so, because the human element has to be taken into account. This point shouldn't be underestimated, as Mwalimu admits in *Socialism and Rural Development*: '. . . no social organization should be based on the expectation that all members will be angels.'[12] And power isn't something people much like sharing, even in socialist countries.

The village is a democratic association, so the village assembly elects its chairman and the twenty-five members of the village council. We saw chairmen of every shape and size, young and old, running the full gamut of ideologies. In some cases a former chief was elected; in others a wise old body who wouldn't rock the boat. That's a built-in hazard of democracy. In cattle regions like Mara, on the shores of Lake Victoria, no one would dream of picking a man without cattle and therefore without prestige. Nyerere comes from there and in the early days the people in his village were amazed: 'What on earth is a president doing without any cattle? Funny sort of a leader that is . . .'

Also, the Party has a say in selecting a candidate, because the chairman will have to represent the Party too. In Hanang region the villagers had their favourite, an excellent candidate, but the Party rejected him because he contravened the 'leadership code'. The point is that selection is a negative process, the key criteria being what a person must not be rather than what he ought to be. Possession of a tractor doesn't rule out loyalty or administrative abilities; the chairman ought to be capable of running a village both from the economic and the social points of view. As a result many 'kulaks'* prefer to stay on the sidelines and pull the strings.

It was decided that to prevent villages being overrun by red tape the chairman would represent both the village and the Party. So there is no counterbalancing power, except in theory for the secretary, although, for convenience's sake he works with the chairman. As the secretary is a political appointee it's harder to give him the sack, because it means going right to the top, and the procedure laid down for getting rid of a secretary can drag on for two years, during which the man who's been accused can do plenty of damage and get his own back on his critics.

Sometimes the chairman and secretary are so intoxicated with their own power that they start laying down the law in their village and take unfair advantage of their posts. They'll drive off in the lorry for a trip to town, at the village's expense, and as in many cases they're the only adults able to read and write properly, and, most important of all to calculate, they can fiddle the surpluses and the commissions paid. In some villages no figure had ever been publicly announced for the commission. In theory the council are entitled to have their say, but they often take the leaders' side and are afraid of criticizing them. Meanwhile the manager – who is an outsider to all this, and not very welcome – is well advised to watch his step and keep well out of it. The village assembly meets once a year, but this is a mere formality. Officially it holds all the power, but as the leaders are disinclined to help it to exercise this power, it scarcely ever takes advantage of its status, let alone abuses it. This situation reflects an exaggerated respect for authority.

That really is the crux of the matter. Who's going to explain the villagers' rights to them, and, more important, teach them how to use them? It isn't really in anyone's interest to do so – certainly not the elected leaders who've acquired a taste for power; or the cunning 'kulaks' who join the Party and talk in Ujamaa terms to pull the wool over the eyes of both the authorities and the peasants, meanwhile grabbing any power that's going; or the district officials who like foisting their views on others and wouldn't be exactly overjoyed to be

---

* This term isn't really appropriate. It would be better to talk of peasant entrepreneurs who have a small amount of capital at their disposal.

criticized by people they think of as their inferiors. Village chairmen and secretaries are now paid a salary of Shs. 500 per month, which is liable to encourage them to seek election, but doesn't necessarily make them more committed. They are gradually cutting themselves off from the ordinary villagers and instinctively moving over to join the civil servants and district authorities, whom they indeed represent and for whom they act as interpreters. When all of them, albeit to a varying extent, have had great difficulty in acquiring power, why should they start giving it away to the common peasants?

This is no doubt a simplistic way of looking at things, but it's obvious that with so many leaders attached to both the Party and the civil service the peasants don't get much of a look-in. And if they are ever to seize power they must first have the will to do so, which can't always be taken for granted. Centuries of submissiveness, old traditions, reluctance to shoulder responsibility, and even fear of witchcraft, take their toll. Some people believe that giving them a political education would do the trick – what faith in the power of words! But you'd first have to consult the peasants themselves and look into their basic needs and interests; and, most of all, free them from all that red tape.

The Zambian peasants we met complained of too few visitors, but their counterparts in Tanzania could complain of too many. So many people come to the villages to give them such a range of directives, orders and advice that they don't know where to start. All these Plans and new ventures are devised by the district or even regional authorities, whose word is law when it comes to funding. And directives at national level are distorted in the oddest way by the bureaucrats. For instance when the prime minister referred to 'two acres of food crops and one acre of cash crops per adult', by the time this reached Mwanza it came out as two acres of maize and one of cotton – and this was compulsory, no matter what the local conditions were, and even if the peasants knew perfectly well that their land was unsuitable. Bureaucrats like keeping things simple. If a peasant lives in an area selected for a 'large-scale' development project, he also has to take account of directives from abroad! And hardly any of these educated gentlemen bother to consult him; they are only too delighted to have got away from village life, and often adopt a contemptuous or paternalistic attitude when they come back.

Whereas elsewhere the pace is slow, in Tanzania it tends to be too fast. The bewildered peasants see all these people turning up one after another, some of them well-meaning but with little in the way of technical training, and presenting them with new ideas. They simply can't keep up. So many people are eager to see them 'developed' – after all, it's the government's only source of income.

One political leader publicly admitted in our presence: 'The peasants can't act or show any initiative because they're smothered by red tape, and we aren't doing anything to encourage them to be enterprising. If we'd taken people into our confidence they'd have told us about their problems, but we've behaved in much the same way as the colonial powers. The people sent into the villages adopt a very "big city" attitude and the peasants hardly talk to us at all because they identify us with the authorities and the government. We force so many schemes on them that they prefer to ignore the lot – it's the only way they can keep going. Attitudes will have to change on both sides.'

We should take off our hats to this senior civil servant for his honesty and courage.

'We have to run while others walk,' Nyerere would say. But some people mutter: 'In trying to run too fast we're liable to fall flat on our faces.' If you're too keen for democracy you end up with bureaucracy. And if ordinary people don't genuinely have a share in power, you're back with the mistakes made by dogmatic socialists. Dialogue is crucial. But we must be clear what this means. 'Talking with the people' is all very well, but 'is the purpose behind this to help them to take decisions or merely to persuade them into accepting decisions taken at a higher level?'[13] Needless to say, a strong Party will be inclined to go for the second definition.

Our no doubt justified grumbles about red tape tend to make us fall into the trap of goodies-and-baddies – the good peasant *v.* wicked civil servant. Unfortunately this is an oversimplification. It's pretty obvious that individuals on both sides of the fence will try to turn the system to their own advantage. There are wily and cunning peasants just as there are go-getting civil servants. We're oddly intolerant abroad about things that we find easy to accept at home. At both district and regional level we found public-spirited civil servants, Party men who travelled the rural districts on foot, and regional administrators who were familiar with all the fields in the area. The people we refer to, somewhat over-hastily, as the privileged few often live in difficult and uncomfortable circumstances, suffering from the lack of transport facilities and of experienced technicians to rely on. Underdevelopment is enough to put off even those with the best intentions. In the highlands close to the border with Burundi, in the back of beyond, we came across a highly capable governor. He'd been dumped there, miles from anywhere, after five years with the UN in New York. He had no electricity, no beer, no radio, virtually no contact with the outside world, except via an appalling road. Yet he didn't complain and he knew his villages inside-out, spending a great deal of time there. And we met many others like him.

Inside the villages all these authorities that seem, when viewed from the outside, to be smothering the peasants, in fact have to reach a compromise in which all the various parties gain some sort of advantage – a state of peaceful coexistence. The compromises reached don't always fit in with the Ujamaa spirit. In Bashay, for instance, everyone eventually derived some benefit – the kulaks stripped of their lands, the landless peasants, the tradesmen, and the authorities, who were pleased to be able to show off a nice big Ujamaa field – everyone except the Ujamaa group, who mourned their thwarted dreams. People have to make a living, though uncompromising intellectuals don't always grasp this. Meanwhile we, who really are privileged, can afford the luxury of indulging in idealism and sacrifice – theoretical sacrifice, that is.

But don't let's be too disillusioned. A small number of purely African experiments, carried out without overseas aid, are clear enough evidence that in exceptional conditions the dream can come true.

13 *Successful Ujamaa villages*

An Ujamaa group was started up in 1971 in Mareu, on the eastern lower slope of Mount Meru, between Arusha and Moshi and below the coffee and banana complex. It consists of a hundred or so families in a village of five hundred families all told, with an anti-Ujamaa mayor. The group's chairman is an illiterate peasant, but bright enough to be able, without a second's hesitation, to quote figures covering crops, acreages, yields and the number of members for the whole of the eight years the group had been in existence. Their maize fields, on which tractors are used, were producing yields three times higher than the average for the area; they had their own butcher's, their own carpenter's workshop, their own general store; and they were developing dairy cattle on artificial fodder. There was just one obstacle in their path: they were short of land, because too many families had been assembled in one village. The main reason behind the group's economic success is the organizing abilities of its chairman, a true African peasant. Whereas the RDA had been given unpaid help by an expatriate, and financial support by various charitable organizations, Mareu's success is 100 per cent African. And it isn't the only one.

In the highlands in the south of the country, west of Mbeya, is an Ujamaa group at Isanza that has continued after villagization. Its leader is the son of a chief and was formerly a member of Parliament and district officer, but he chose to return with a much less grandiose title and 'develop' his village. The founding members sold off their modest possessions to raise a small amount of initial capital; everything is owned jointly and they are very hard-working. They get very high yields (over 5 tonnes of maize per hectare) and also breed dairy cattle; their shop is well stocked, and a henhouse has been turned into a hotel that's used on market days. The children have their own field and start working in it at the age of five so as to get used to the idea of communal labour, each child's work depending on his or her strength. The coffee plantation is due for improvements; attractive seven-roomed houses are being built for members, there is a lorry to take care of transport, and so on.

Although not all the villagers belong to the Ujamaa group, since membership is deliberately restricted and you have to prove yourself worthy of it, all of them benefit from the communal services provided (school, shop, transport, etc). Here too the success of the group is due to the quality of the leadership, and also to the discipline that each member accepts.

Lulanzi, in the highlands south of Iringa, could perhaps be called a 'semi-Ujamaa village'. The communal sector is very highly developed, with a cowshed, piggery, mill and a large field of maize. Lumber and the sawmill are highly profitable and the village has made exceptional progress with reafforestation. The chairman, who keeps a very firm hand on the tiller, is a real peasant entrepreneur, good at handling both figures and people. Tanzania could do with several thousands of people of the same calibre, one per village.

Yet even in this highly prosperous village the women seemed very timid, and although we saw a large number of carts lying idle, they still performed the never-ending drudgery of carrying wood and water containers on their heads. Power may have been given to the villages (in theory), and some people may have managed to benefit from this, but one category of people has been completely forgotten – the women, as usual. . . .

14 *No one remembers the peasant women*

There's no secret about the fact that Tanzanian agriculture is entirely dependent on the female population. (Incidentally the same applies to many of their sisters in tropical Africa.) Even in a country that is making a real effort to improve the lot of the peasants, the women still lose out. So just think how those in other countries must suffer! In China the revolution has radically altered women's lives and status, though there are still some inequalities. But Tanzania hasn't gone in for a violent revolution.

Before we start talking about slavery we should beware of our Western attitudes, which tend to disregard the complicated mechanisms that operate within each ethnic group. But this doesn't alter the fact that only too often the lot of the women is scarcely enviable, and that they are still thought of as free labour. Mwalimu has recognized that they 'still do more than their fair share of the work in the fields and in the homes',[14] and that 'Women who work in the villages work harder than anybody else'.[15] Now no would-be socialist system can disregard inequality on such a scale within rural society. Yet in Dar es Salaam middle-class ladies will tell you that the government has taken steps and that everything's fine now. On paper, that is. Yet again, what extraordinary faith they have in words!

Peasant women are early risers so that they can go about all their various household and kitchen tasks – popularly known as 'women's work'. Then every day they must cope with the drudgery of fetching wood and water. On the Makonde plateau we saw women who walked twenty kilometres there and back to fetch the *one* bucket of water that the family used for their daily needs. The girls weren't as timid as their mothers and complained of backache! They have to take the children to the dispensary, which may be some way away, and look after the kitchen garden surrounding their house, which is crucial for feeding their family. In their spare time they'll be pounding away at the maize if there isn't a grinding machine, though some of them prefer to walk up to eight kilometres to the nearest mill, with 30 kilos of maize on their heads.

But most of their time is spent working in the fields. At the height of the farm year they'll be out there at dawn and will spend nine or ten hours digging, hoeing, planting, weeding and harvesting. As they're usually the only means of transport available, they'll also bring the crops back to the village. We've already referred to the woman who was doing a total of 640 kilometres or 400 miles to bring back an acre's worth of crops. The distance won't always be as great, but the weight of the load is always considerable. This image of ageless women, bowed down under their load, their babies perched on their backs, endlessly treading the paths of Africa in their bare feet, has become so common that no one takes any notice of them now. But we couldn't help feeling unutterably ashamed when we came face to face with these exhausted creatures, knowing perfectly well that we were incapable of doing a quarter of what they did. They hardly ever complain and somehow find time to smile. When we held meetings we'd make them sit in the front row, much to the annoyance of the villagers and their leaders. They seemed surprised that we could possibly want to ask them questions and take an interest in their problems. Anyway there was always some man or other ready to speak for them, even when it was a question of strictly female matters.

They are mere beasts of burden. In Gogoland the men were horrified at the idea of 'punishing' their cattle by putting them to work, but they were quite happy to let their womenfolk wear themselves out. Tucked quietly away in a corner, the women would tell us confidingly: 'What we'd like is . . .' And when we were talking about potential improvements the men would call for tractors and other machinery, but no one would think of mentioning carts. That's women's work. The proud Masai have donkeys, which are treated with great respect (they are never eaten), but they carry 90-kilo loads.

In the precolonial era African women shared many rights with their menfolk in predominantly farming communities. The colonial administrators put the stress on developing cash crops, which became a male prerogative, while the women were relegated to subsistence farming. They were generally ignored by the colonial authorities. In many African countries the same attitude prevailed after independence. The women work to feed the family, the men work for money – and keep it for themselves.

But Tanzania has tried to change matters, and in the new-style village 'democracy' the women do in theory have the same rights as the men. Yet in practice we never came across a village council with more than six women out of the total of twenty-five members. Apparently the average is one or two. There's no doubt that if a man and a woman are equally capable, the village will always vote for the man. This applies to the women too. One very dynamic, capable and committed woman had been elected chairman of a village near Iringa. She didn't seem to have any trouble making people treat her with respect, but she had to be a highly remarkable woman to have got herself accepted in the first place. There must be other women like her in Tanzania.

Even if women are voted on to the council they hardly ever have time to attend meetings, as they have so many chores to do. The men talk while the women work. If they are brave enough to speak, their word doesn't carry any weight: 'We don't like having women at our meetings; they just sit around saying nothing . . .' The men's attitude clearly isn't going to change things. And the same attitude is found elsewhere. The bureaucrats laughed derisively when we brought up the subject and we met the same sneering attitude during ministerial meetings, at gatherings in the universities, and even in the Party college. On that particular day we reminded the 'future leaders' (as they are fond of calling themselves) at Kivukoni that the foreign exchange needed to pay for their Land-Rovers was earned by the exertions of the peasant women they despised. Among the audience we noticed girls with short memories sneering in unison, no doubt delighted to have escaped from the backwoods and dreaming of jobs in international organizations.

The Party has accepted that there is such a thing as 'the women's problem' and has set up a special organization called the Union of Women of Tanzania (UWT). The UWT has published a very attractive and well-meaning little booklet, but the men remark condescendingly: 'They just pass a lot of resolutions. But when it comes to implementing them . . .' These women are cut off from the reality of village life (though many of them come from the villages) and sit in their city offices planning activities designed to lead to the 'liberation of the rural areas'. Near the border with Kenya we saw a project that had been devised at regional level. Women from six different villages would come together to work on a large communal field – any collective enterprise must be on a spectacular scale. They were obviously enthusiastic, and there was singing and music and so on. But thanks to bad choice of soil, poor tractor ploughing, low-quality seeds and a total lack of discipline and organization in their work, it was easy to predict the outcome – yields almost nonexistent. What a shame to put off people who are so willing.

In fact Tanzanian women seem to have more of an Ujamaa spirit than the men. Because they are an oppressed group *par excellence* they are used to hard work, dedication, and receiving orders. They probably hope to make a new life for themselves in this way, especially if they're paid for the work they do, which is better than wearing themselves out for their husbands. But as one UWT woman remarked: 'What's the use of their earning their share, considering they'll only hand it over to their husbands?' What we think of as liberation is often merely another form of alienation, since these women are busy slaving away on the village plot, the block farm and their own private plot. And 'liberating' them, means putting them to work on the women's field!

There's a danger that they won't live to enjoy the benefits of their exhausting labours. These peasant women who are worn out by so many different forms of drudgery are generally suffering from malnutrition; they are constantly either pregnant or nursing a child, and are anaemic and weak. They are worn out by too frequent child-bearing, with too little medical attention; and the maternity leave referred to by the ladies in the towns is a far-off dream for women who have to struggle to keep their families alive. The government has therefore set up mother and child health clinics (MCH), but not all women have the time to attend regularly. In some cases the point of these centres hasn't been properly explained to the village women, and they are suspicious of 'those dispensaries which give you advice instead of medicines'! They are strongly encouraged to space out their children, but we were told that 'the men see this as an insult to their virility and go off to look for another woman who hasn't been so contaminated by modern ideas . . .' Yet the idea of the centres does seem gradually to be proving popular, and more and more women are attending them. Some of them are even starting to have their babies there, and then they're sent home a few hours later. That should make European women think . . .

There is so much dedication, so much patient suffering, so much unproductive labour, so much time wasted without any visible result. If only a little attention were paid to these women, output would go up. The time saved in this way could be of value to the community. Modernization doesn't always help the women. As an oppressed class they don't necessarily benefit from technological progress. When a tractor is given it always goes to the men. Acreages are increased, but this means more work in the way of weeding and harvesting; and weeding becomes an even bigger job with the use of chemical fertilizers, which help the weeds to grow too. Ox-drawn weeding and hoeing machines are unknown. And the amounts of grains that have to be carried on the women's heads are even greater. Even in the wealthy villages, the women still do the fetching and carrying of wood and water. In one place thirty women will be transporting water to make bricks for the new shed, when a single cart could do the same amount of work. Yet there are carts in the villages, and oxen trained to draw them. In Lulanzi the communal carts are used for three weeks per year to transport manure and bring in the harvest, but every single day of the year fifty or so women and little girls can be seen bowed beneath the weight of bundles of wood that have to come from further and further away because the village is spreading.

Technical progress is primarily and solely of benefit to the men. On top of this, the extension services always concentrate on the men, whereas the women often need their help. But one extension officer told us: 'In the African tradition we're supposed to address the head of the family. If we talk to the women, what will the men think . . .?'

Traditions are always blamed. But all these leaders and bureaucrats who are so nervous about upsetting traditions forget that they've been getting upset in the villages of Tanzania for quite some time. Some traditions aren't sacrosanct, others are. All this will take time, they kept telling us. But it's important to accept that there is a serious problem here and to buckle down to doing something about it. Now the point is that time isn't on their side. Since 1977 primary schooling has been compulsory for all children and is free. And almost all the girls do go to school. It's most unusual in a poor country in tropical Africa to have no discrimination against girls. Admittedly some fathers do still try to marry off their daughters young (this is an offence carrying a prison sentence), but on the whole schools have as many girl pupils as boys.

The problem is that if there isn't a radical change in the life peasant women have to live and in the attitude towards them, will these educated girls be willing to stay in the villages and lead the same life as their mothers? Will they be willing to act as slaves, when they're entitled to hanker after an office job in town? Even if they'll finish up unemployed, there'll be no holding them. And it's hard to imagine a village with no women in it.

Now the women simply don't exist as far as the authorities, the villagers, or the experts are concerned. They ought to be the first to benefit from appropriate technologies, which ought to bring them some relief. Otherwise education will produce exactly the opposite of the intended goal of encouraging young people to live in villages and of halting or slowing down the rush to the towns.

15 *UPE or Universal Primary Education*

This is probably Tanzania's biggest success story. 'Universal Primary Education' was scheduled to be completed in 1989 but was already a reality, at least in theory, in 1977! The country took the huge gamble of giving education to all children, thus making a clean break with the colonial era, and trying to make the young people stay in their villages.

As early as 1967 Nyerere was writing, in *Education for Self-Reliance*: '. . . we have never really stopped to consider why we want education – what its purpose is.'[16] And he offers a lucid analysis of the role played by the type of school inherited from the colonial era, which 'emphasized and encouraged the individualistic instincts of mankind, instead of his co-operative instincts' and 'induced attitudes of human inequality'.[17]

He is aware that education is liable to cut young people off from the real world, because it is often 'inadequate' and 'inappropriate' for a poor and newly independent African nation. If a new society is to be built up a different type of education must emerge. Nyerere starts by defining the type of society they want to achieve: '. . . a socialist society which is based on three principles: equality and respect for human dignity; sharing of the resources which are produced by our efforts; work by everyone and exploitation by none.'[18] Tanzania is:

a rural society where improvement will depend largely upon the efforts of the people in agriculture and in village development. This does not mean that education in Tanzania should be designed just to produce passive agricultural workers . . . who simply carry out plans or directions received from above. It must produce good farmers; it has also to prepare people for their responsibilities as free workers and citizens. . . . They have to be able to think for themselves, to make judgements on all the issues affecting them. . . .[19]

This text seems crucial now that power has been given (in theory) to the villages. Nyerere the teacher believes that the schools must be the starting point for a change in society, but this was written in 1967, at a time when he considerably underestimated the difficulties that would arise in all spheres.

Tanzania therefore embarked on an extraordinary programme to get all its children to school – and promptly came up against underdevelopment. Schools had to be built, and most of the peasants tackled the job with great enthusiasm. But teachers still had to be found and, more important, trained; and at the same time the syllabus had to be changed. Here too there was a shortage of executives, though enthusiasm was never lacking. In two years the syllabus was ready and every village had its own school, even if some of them were a bit flimsy, where the village's resources were limited; it also had its own teachers, some more competent than others. Forty thousand young villagers who had done well at school were recruited and hastily trained, spending a few days per week in the district and a few days on in-service training. They were known as 'assistants' and after three years would become fully-fledged teachers. Those at a lower level received further training, sometimes in the form of correspondence courses. Yet all this willingness may not have been enough, since the standard of teaching depends largely on the training the teachers have been given.

There is talk now of modifying the syllabus, of devising a form of education that is geared more to village life, of the 'open-door school' type. Until experiments in this area can be extended to the whole country, manual work is being encouraged and the pupils work in their own field. The results vary considerably. We saw some excellent fields, near Mbeya or Sumbawanga, but others weren't always properly cultivated and this is liable to dishearten the children and put them off farming. Another idea is to encourage craft skills and train up craftsmen and tradesmen, but there is a shortage of ordinary technicians capable of teaching woodwork, metalwork, the various building trades and making farm equipment. Volunteers could be asked to help train master craftsmen.

The school can also play a vital part in village organization. As we have seen, the villages are often overwhelmed by a whole series of matters that uneducated peasants have difficulty dealing with. If the young people were trained to run the affairs of villages there would be much less danger of the leaders abusing their power, and the gap between the authorities and the ordinary peasant would be narrower. But the big question mark hanging over Tanzania is whether the young people will agree to stay in the villages. Will it win its gamble when the rest of tropical Africa has failed?

The fact of giving education to everyone – or at any rate getting everyone to attend school – does of course limit the dream of getting a full-time job in the public sector or the modern sector with nothing more than the basic school leaving certificate, though some parents and teachers cling to the old attitude of seeing school as a passport allowing pupils to make their escape to the towns. It takes time to change an outlook that was the legacy of the colonial era – after all, only a few decades ago the same outlook prevailed in the developed countries. Yet at the moment only a very small percentage of primary school pupils get in to secondary school, and even those who have been through the first stage of secondary education, or the first and second stages, can't always get a paid job at the end of it.

Im October 1979 there were 800,000 new primary school pupils, but this was an abnormally high figure because the schools agreed to take children of varying ages who hadn't been able to go to school before. The 103 secondary schools now in existence can't take more than 11,000 pupils per year. Even if we assume that more schools will be opened, what's going to happen to all those primary school leavers who won't be able to continue their education? Most of them will have to stay in their villages. But at the same time it's vital to make radical improvements to village life, to make it attractive and to attempt to involve young people in rural development.

The whole approach underlying secondary education may even have to be rethought. In spite of Nyerere's exhortations only very few secondary schools are self-reliant. One agricultural college that we visited cultivated its land so badly that we're entitled to wonder what sort of teaching it can give. Meanwhile the technical institutes think primarily in terms of tractors; and the totally inadequate instruction they give in economics means that the students aren't capable of making a proper analysis of the profitability or otherwise of the improvements to peasant or collective farms suggested by the technicians.

As a general rule there isn't a high enough proportion of technicians yet, and the lack of qualified technicians is holding up the country's economic development. One highly symptomatic example of this can be seen at Morogoro, where there are two institutes side by side, one covering agriculture, animal husbandry and forestry, the other teaching development administration. The former has had great difficulty mustering 140 pupils over four years, the latter, which chiefly trains bureaucrats, has 940 students. This is a hangover from the old colonial tradition, which took care of 'law and order' but didn't bother much about modernization. Since in those days the schools were training grounds for civil servants and people going into business firms, these fields have remained status symbols, particularly since Africans have taken over from the British. The civil service and the parastatal bodies have now become the main vehicle for anyone who wants to climb the social ladder. But a political career is even more highly coveted, since it enables people to 'get on' without having any particular ability or skill. This being so, why should young people go in for technical careers? The only reason would be if they were offered tempting salaries, which would certainly be justified, since no amount of political speechifying is ever going to extricate Tanzania from underdevelopment. And what's the good of all those managers and civil servants when the machine seizes up because there aren't any technicians? The country does of course need both, but yet again it's a question of priorities.

But then we mustn't ever forget that in 1961 Tanzania had just one engineer and thirty university graduates.

5 The difficulties facing Tanzanian socialism

1 *The Masai, lords of the steppe**

As soon as you leave Arusha you find that every now and then splashes of ochre will appear suddenly amid the yellow of the steppe, signalling the presence of groups of Masai warriors, spears in hand, their proud faces raised to the sky and the winds. Sometimes a huge boy will appear at a bend in the road, his ochre-coloured hair twisted in a plait and using a shield to protect himself. Or you may come across a solitary figure wrapped in a blanket and urging on a few cows; he'll be carrying the staff used by cattle minders, who are thought of as the élite. And they'll always bestow a dazzling and open-hearted smile on all who pass by, with no ulterior motive. The Masai are not an envious people.

On the Monduli Juu road we saw a group of lovely girls on their way to the Sunday market amid peals of laughter. With their shaven heads and heavy red or blue robes, their arms loaded with bracelets and their ears stretched downwards by a series of interlocking rings, while their necks emerged from the enormous plate-like neck ornaments they wear for special occasions, they were going to market more to be seen than to buy, though they do buy lengths of wire and beads to make more ornaments, or the white cloth for dyeing with the natural ochre from the mountains.

We Westerners, filled with nostalgia beneath the tropical sun, admire their great dignity and gape at all this 'folklore', idealizing this celebrated ethnic group which is desperately clinging to its way of life and its traditions, these Nilotic peoples who were once respected lords and masters and are now mere survivors from a very different past. Yet we often forget that these steppe peoples lead a very hard life and go hungry for six months in every year, when their cows don't give

---

* Lazaro Parkipuny and Finn Kjaerby helped us a great deal in understanding the Masai.

enough milk. Their diet is based on milk, topped up in the old days by cows' blood. Nowadays they're eating increasing amounts of maize, which they either grow themselves or buy. Thanks to their milk consumption they, and especially their children, enjoy good health, but during the dry season they are dependent on maize and sometimes have trouble getting hold of it.

As they have difficulty finding enough grazing land they have to cover enormous distances, and there's nothing very romantic about their kraals, groups of low-roofed huts made by the women from cow dung and arranged in circles round the cattle pen, which attracts flies – the children are covered with them. The official government policy is to discourage this attitude, but the technocrats are so keen to see everything standardized that they've gone too far. There's no denying that the Masai are first and foremost a pastoral, cattle-rearing people.

Some official or other in Arusha decreed one day that before any aid was given to the Masai they must be properly dressed – puritanical old maids on safari had been shocked by the sight of their muscular bodies! So these 'savages' couldn't go into the shops unless they were wearing shirts and trousers. This measure was a failure, no doubt because the 'savages' didn't feel that a pair of trousers was a particularly African garment, so a new idea was tried: instead of cattle rearing they would go in for farming. Now the Masai have a history of being driven out of their grazing land by encroaching cultivation. They started off on the fertile and well-watered slopes of Mount Kilimanjaro but subsequently found themselves on the arid steppe where no one else wanted to go. They didn't raise any protest – after all it was better than dying of maize fever. Even the prime minister, who is a member of the Masai tribe and comes from Monduli, admitted to us: 'We hate farming. You've seen my house – it's got nothing round it but grass and cows.'

The Masai, who've always been highly suspicious of governments ever since the colonial era, now withdrew into themselves. They were so terrified at the thought of being condemned to farming, and having a form of development forced on them that would deny their culture, that they decided it was better to refuse everything offered to them, including schools, which they believed would alienate their children. They rejected any attempts to change their hard lives, even when it would have been in their own interest.

They did enjoy a degree of prosperity in the nineteenth century.

They would occasionally make off with their neighbours' cattle, but never sold their neighbours to the slave merchants. Their society was one of the most democratic in tropical Africa. Their head or spokesman was elected by a very large gathering and all adult males were entitled to express their views publicly. This didn't of course apply to the women, who were considered to be puny creatures, not very different from children. To be chosen as the Masai leader was an honour, but it also involved sacrifice, since leaders didn't receive any form of payment. Members were compelled to conform to the group's rules solely by the weight of public opinion. Today's Masai find all this business of village councils very hard to understand: 'In the old days,' they say, 'people only got together in little groups if they had something to hide. Otherwise everything was decided out in the open, with everyone looking on.'

The British colonial authorities started off by trying to protect the Masai lands from encroachment by agriculture. The issuing in 1935 of a Native Authority ordinance made this a punishable offence. But then in about 1947 they started handing over land for growing export crops. At the same time they tried to step up the number of head of cattle available for sale by installing wells and setting up checks by vets. Dennis Branagan, who was a district veterinary officer in the late fifties, pointed out that the grazing systems forced on the Masai were totally unsuitable for the type of land they had. The use of dykes made it possible to build reservoirs, but they soon silted up with the mud brought by the flood waters.

Dipping the cattle at regular intervals did get rid of the ticks that transmit the deadly East Coast fever, but once the beasts have been treated they are more susceptible to the disease, and the traditional migrations during the dry season took them out of reach of the cattle dips. The Americans weren't shrewd enough to take warning from this failure, even though the first man they sent to investigate had stressed that it was essential to educate the people, to show them what to do and give them health care for themselves, so that they would feel the need for the progress the authorities hoped for and implement it *themselves*, with the authorities playing a purely advisory role.

The United States programme, which was set out in 1970, didn't go beyond the technocratic aspect and set specific production targets – output *must* go up by over 100 per cent in ten years! This was to be achieved by stepping up calving rates and the weight and proportion of cattle slaughtered, and lowering the death rate. This programme didn't involve any proper awareness of the problems faced by the Masai, of their traditions and of the life they were leading; it took no account of the problem of overgrazing, which is a threat to future production, and made no reference to the threat posed by regular periods of drought, which encourage the Masai to keep more cattle than would seem necessary.

Since on top of all this the programme was not based on any sociological or political data, it was bound to fail, and in 1979 production had simply fallen. In one area in which six reservoirs had been built it had been decreed that only the local stockbreeders could use them for their cattle, so as to avoid contamination. The planners had forgotten that in times of drought a Masai may not forbid access to his water supply to cattle belonging to a 'brother'.

The American experts, who believe they are omniscient, did not take past failures into account. Like the colonial authorities and some so-called 'modern' Tanzanians, they think that nothing much can be expected of these pastoral peoples from a bygone era, and don't bother to encourage local initiative. What they forget is that the true experts are still these people who may not be able to count up their cattle, but who know each beast by its name, even if they've got a couple of thousand of them, who know how to move through tsetse fly-infested areas without harming their cattle (by moving at night), and so on. The American experts may be effective in their own western states, where breeding is the only problem; they don't know anything about the steppe, where the life led by the people can't be dissociated from that of their cattle.

One resigned but dignified group of Masai told us about their problems. When we asked what had changed in their lives since independence, their reply was scathing and they burst out laughing: 'Nothing. Just look at that dam. It's all worked out for our beasts, but what about us? What are we supposed to drink – mud?' And they went back to their beer, which is invariably delivered even to shops in the middle of nowhere on the Masai steppe. (As indeed it is to the Indian reservations in North America.) Beer that tastes of frustration, of rejection by contemptuous people who won't accept you until they've assimilated you, body and soul.

2 *The so-called 'experts'*

The failure of this attempt to 'develop' the Masai is a good example of the West's attitude to development problems. These supposedly 'qualified' experts received high salaries, and needless to say they lived in Arusha, Tanzania's most attractive city, with its comfortable hotels, fine-looking houses and every facility. They monopolized the jeeps attached to the programme and spent a fortune in petrol getting to the villages, some of which were three hundred kilometres away. The Tanzanian technicians depended on them for transport, and in the end found it easier to stay in the district offices too. They had been trained in the United States and had come back with a very American outlook that wasn't much use for tackling the Masai and their problems. The one and only expert who did settle in the district, visiting the villages and talking to the local people, was assessed by USAID as 'being too biased towards Tanzania and the Masai', and his contract wasn't renewed. When the others drove back and forth across the steppe in vehicles they thought of as their own property, the Masai believed they were holidaymakers out hunting or looking for semi-precious stones – not exactly the best basis for a fruitful dialogue!

Tanzania had to pay out $2 million for this operation, which achieved nothing except to damage the land and degrade its people. The other $3 million were a gift, to pay for the vehicles, the petrol and the salaries paid to the experts. So all that aid, allegedly for the poor, devoured itself!

As if that weren't enough for the Masai, they're now having their land taken away. Since food production is the order of the day, the land has been allocated for growing seed beans, by people who probably don't think of either milk or meat as food. Big Dutch bean-exporting companies and private farmers ask the village authorities to give them land. If the authorities agree, the request is referred to the district land officer, who gives his approval. Why should the villages give up part of the grazing land they need so badly without any form of compensation? No doubt the higher-ups have a finger in the pie. A villager near Nabarera, where 3,000 hectares had just been handed over to a big firm, told us that no one had been consulted. 'When they told us it was too late, the land had already been handed over, and we didn't realize how much grazing land we were losing until they started ploughing it up. We don't like it, but what can we do?'

These deals become even more shady when the regional authorities turn up in the village to talk in highly convincing terms about the benefits of big farms. One Masai landowner remarked in disgust: 'We know it's only a question of time. All our land is going to be used for crop-growing. If they're going to massacre it they might as well give us tractors and we'll do it for them, now things have gone this far . . .' His steady voice held all the despair of a people who know they've no hope of surviving unless they conform.

Only a few years ago this land that's now being sold off cheap to all and sundry was officially proclaimed to be 'uncultivable' (except for a small bit of it). Now all of a sudden it has become arable, even where the soil is too thin, or where the slopes are vulnerable to erosion – even on bare rock. All of a sudden everyone is clearing land left, right and centre, and uprooting trees, taking no precautions whatsoever, not even digging contour ridges or bunds, with the result that it doesn't take long for the land to be destroyed by erosion. What is claimed to be development is actually destroying the nation's heritage.

The government is now planning for herdsmen's villages of 150 families (100 would be a better figure), with 400 hectares of grazing land per family. The idea is for *bomas* (fenced enclosures) containing the cattle belonging to three to five families to spread out round a circle of 3–4 kilometres radius, with the school, the water supply, cattle dip, dispensary, vet and so on all sited in the middle of the circle. This is yet another technocratic scheme with not a hope of success unless it has first been discussed, modified and eventually agreed by the local people. At that point a few crops could be added to the scheme – maize and beans, say – and later on there could be an orchard. The most urgent need is to talk to the people concerned, rather than merely dreaming up new ideas. Any scheme worked out without them, without even consulting them, and dependent solely on outside finance, so that there's no hope of getting the people themselves involved, is bound to fail. The Party is town-based. It shows little interest in farming and has never managed to get the Masai to accept it, because they think of it as belonging to a handful of leaders who claim to be in charge of everything. The whole structure of Masai society has been undermined; their way of life and their traditions are still intact, but their power structures have been destroyed.

When the forgotten Masai living on the steppe visit the show village of Monduli they don't go into raptures about the various facilities offered or the attractive modern houses made of brick and sheet iron.* Their first reaction is: 'They've got some fine cows here!' Their second: 'There's too much farming.' Monduli is the prime minister's village and has been showered with funds. An improved breed of dairy cattle has been introduced here; they can do well because Monduli enjoys a highland climate with a fair amount of rainfall. A communal cowshed big enough for four hundred head of cattle has been organized, with a vet to keep an eye on them. Regular milk collections are made and the milk is sold in the neighbouring towns. The authorities behave with great circumspection and take care not to offend the Masai, who simply take their cows and clear off if they aren't happy. Each family grows an acre of maize and beans, which again do well here. The Masai women seem to be very pleased with their new life; instead of being compelled to carry their milk to market and barter it for maize, they grow their own. They also love the idea of having a modern house, because they won't have to build it themselves – the new houses are men's work. Everything seems terribly easy, with the government's generous grants. Yet the Masai are used to having their savings in cows and aren't familiar with the idea of loans, often confusing loans with gifts. They don't understand that loans have to be repaid, and accept willingly but passively any government aid that's going.

The authorities again want to keep in with them and have encouraged this passive attitude. For instance they've rounded up all the district's lorries to transport materials, instead of encouraging the Masai to buy or build more carts. Had they continued with the type of education offered by Monduli's technical college, the village would now have all the craftsmen it needed. Once again the authorities are distorting the politicians' instructions, for the prime minister's idea was that his village should be developed primarily by the work of its own villagers, properly organized. If too many facilities are available, initiative is stifled and artificial needs are created that are too expensive

---

* These houses represent the third stage in the development process. The first stage has the standard huts made from cow dung, while the second offers a Tanzanian structure built by the women with local materials – timber, mud walls and thatched roofs.

to be met at this stage. The villages round about are struggling, and overgrazing is starting to cause erosion there.

The Masai are an extreme case in Tanzania, but their situation provides a good illustration of the fact that if traditions are not respected the result is bound to be failure. Also, if they go on being stripped of their lands they'll finish up as a new proletariat, like the Masai of Kenya, increasingly turned into a tourist attraction. This is neither more nor less than 'ethnocide'.

3 Overgrazing and desertification, deforestation, floods and erosion

As with Zambia, but even more so, virtually the only way Tanzania has managed to step up its agricultural output is by increasing the acreage under crops; yields have hardly gone up at all. The peasants try to clear new land so as to tap the fertility accumulated by leaf mould. But if, as for instance in Ismani, to the north of Iringa, they practise permanent maize cultivation instead of shifting cultivation alternating with fallow periods, which used to produce organic matter, their yields may drop very rapidly. The land really has been murdered in such cases.[1] Round Kigoma and other fairly densely populated highland areas the steep hillsides are being cleared so as to obtain the maximum benefit from the very fertile virgin soil, but it isn't long before it's carried off by erosion!

Fosbrooke[2] tells us that central Tanzania, which has a semi-arid climate, is in danger of being eroded to the point where the right word is desertification. This will get worse if population growth keeps soaring (the local people plant more and more crops instead of allowing the land to lie fallow at intervals), in step with deforestation (which is equally reckless here), and increased numbers of livestock (especially cattle). Overgrazing has become a national danger, assuming alarming proportions in arid areas and in times of drought, since the bare soil is a prey to erosion. In the Mara valley in northern Tanzania the grazing land had been cropped too close in early May, immediately after the rainy season. What on earth would it be like at the end of the dry season? The authorities have realized what is happening, and as early as 1975 the Party decreed that the number of cattle was to be reduced by 10 per cent.

This type of measure should not take the form of a blanket

instruction, however, because large areas in the south and west of the country, with plenty of rainfall and good grazing land, have either no cattle, or not enough. What is needed is a better distribution of cattle throughout the country, though this is easier said than done. In the endangered areas, especially in times of drought, the figure of 10 per cent is nowhere near high enough. Anyway, this destocking policy has hardly ever been implemented, because it affects the country's most deeply rooted social structures. The country's cattle are very unevenly distributed, and most of the peasants have none at all. Some have large or very large herds, and they exploit the natural forage resources which belong to the nation as a whole for their own personal benefit.

When their misuse of the land sparks off erosion they even destroy this national property at times. We placed a great deal of emphasis on the seriousness of the situation in our various reports and notes, but this brought little reaction.* We got the feeling that the cattle owners' lobby – those with large herds, that is, farming in Mara or Dodoma and many other regions – was hand in glove with the Party leaders and with the upper ranks of the civil service; in both of these privileged groups rich, cattle-owning families predominate. And as a rule the authorities, like their counterparts in the Sahel, don't realize the extreme gravity of the ecological threat hanging over them. What mainly concerns them is increased output.

Yet the danger was underlined in May 1979 by the unprecedented floods (particularly in the whole of the Rufiji basin) that destroyed tens of kilometres of the Tan–Zam railway line and hundreds of kilometres of roads, plus tens of thousands of hectares of good alluvial soil that was either carried off by the flood waters or, in the case of the low-lying valleys, covered with infertile sand, as we saw when we went to Dar es Salaam's beaches. Measurements of the Rufiji flooding show that its extent depends on the soil conservation policies adopted. For instance the level went down in the 1930s as a result of good protection measures. Here again the post-independence government

---

* However, shortly afterwards there was a ban on *all* cattle in the Kondoa area, which has suffered very badly from erosion. This seems to us to be going too far. If the area was restricted to draught animals and dairy and breeding cows this would put a stop to overgrazing, except in the most heavily eroded areas.

has proved incapable of repeating these measures, and the 1979 floods reached a higher level than any previous ones. Yet the cost of conservation measures would be far lower than that of repairing the flood damage!

In Mlinga district near Lake Nyasa, in the Southern Highlands, the Ngoro have for centuries been practising a form of intensive agriculture on the steep hillsides that ensures that there is no erosion and no loss of humus. They dig what are known as 'Matengo pits', which are like squares on a chessboard measuring two metres square, and pile the earth they've dug on the edges of the square, where they plant maize. Rainwater flowing down the hillsides is caught in the pits and soaks into the soil. When the harvest is over, maize stalks and weeds are piled up in the pits, and then other pits are dug on different squares of the chessboard and the first set of pits, now enriched with humus, are filled in. Now this is a system of intensive farming for a tropical climate, with no fallow periods, which has remained productive for centuries, though it does certainly require a great deal of hard work. So not all Africans are busy destroying their environment, as many expatriates still claim.

However, throughout Tanzania deforestation is becoming a major problem. The peasant women are going further and further away to fetch the wood they need for cooking, when the drudgery this involves would be better expended on the crops. The deforested hillsides are at the mercy of erosion, which is getting worse all the time. Faced with this threat, the forestry services state in their report that they've produced millions of eucalyptus, pine and cassia saplings and distributed them among the peasants. In the villages only a few tiny plots have been reafforested. The forestry people blame the peasants and the peasants answer their accusations by saying that the saplings turned up too late. Meanwhile, the whole of tropical Africa is being stripped dangerously bare, to the point where its future is in jeopardy.

4 *Agricultural modernization primarily based on external inputs*

Faced with the overall deficit in the country's agricultural output, largely resulting from precipitate Ujamaa or villagization measures,

Tanzania's Agriculture Minister thinks almost exclusively in terms of current output, in this year's or next year's campaign. The politicians are all for collective farming, but most of the communal plots we visited had virtually no food crops except maize, whereas what is needed is crop rotation, with legumes grown every three or four years (groundnuts or beans). We were told that they meant to look into this later on, but a third or a quarter of the crops should have been set aside for this from the very first. In India the 'green revolution' with its rice and wheat has led to a drop in legumes, forage crops and oilseeds, and thus to a lowering of the level of nutrition. In Tanzania too the green revolution based on maize is lowering the quality of the peasants' diet, which used to be more varied.

In the outsize villages the fields under crops can't be too far away, so permanent cultivation is already being practised in the area round these built-up zones. It's thought that the use of plenty of fertilizers will keep up fertility, but there can be shortages. And although this method of cultivation may perhaps be successful on the best highland soils, it isn't to be recommended throughout the country. 'Kilimo', the Agriculture Minister, thinks purely in terms of tractors and fertilizers and is over-hasty in his blanket condemnation of traditional techniques, such as shifting cultivation and fallow periods. He's always preaching the virtues of permanent cultivation, without first assessing the true potential of the land in question, and therefore the risks involved. Kilimo plugged the Ujamaa system in the hope that this would result in large fields suitable for tractors. He therefore committed the error, which I find hard to forgive, of not warning the country's political leaders of the dangers inherent in over-large villages, where work can't usually be done with tractors. It's the women who suffer, and the men in power aren't really bothered.

The oil crisis, which was after all easily predictable (I warned my readers about it in my book *Utopia or Else* . . . in June 1973, before the crisis in October that year), is now producing an increasingly difficult situation for Tanzania's agriculture, which is already way off-beam. We saw many 'block farms' that had been badly ploughed with tractors and planted too late, with reduced seed density; elsewhere the seeds had gone in too deep because the seed drills weren't properly adjusted, and so it went on. On top of this a hefty dose of chemical fertilizers would be used, with no preliminary calculations of the economically and technically optimum formula for the local circumstances – the biggest dose isn't usually the best. Many peasants who've used fertilizer on cotton don't then receive the insecticides in time, so the whole crop is ruined.

A system of agriculture based on external inputs must be capable of supplying them at regular intervals, but this is becoming increasingly rare. In August and September 1979 Arusha region, which is the most highly mechanized region in Tanzania, ran out of fuel oil for its tractors bang in the middle of the bean and wheat harvest. Unfortunately the same shortage is liable to occur again. It had been thought that production problems could be rectified by these external inputs, but the planners forgot that they are only profitable if all the necessary preconditions for successful farming apply – the right choice of fields, organic manure, good seedbed preparation, the right seed density, careful hoeing and so on.

After the problem years of 1974 and 1975, when grain imports were very expensive, the World Bank financed a National Maize Programme that started at the end of 1975 and was expected to raise the annual incomes of 380,000 families by 42 dollars (a much higher figure than their current money income); these families were living in 950 villages belonging to the thirteen regions that already had the largest maize acreages! The result was a series of failures, because the seeds weren't always of good quality and hybrid maize monoculture wasn't suitable for all regional conditions (rainfall, altitude, soil type). The fertilizers weren't distributed properly and didn't always turn up in time; some peasants didn't have enough, while others got far too much and couldn't store it because the planned sheds hadn't been built. So a great deal was wasted. The blanket recommendations for the amount of fertilizer to be used were hardly ever best-suited to the many different sets of circumstances. And they weren't always economic.

The programme overestimated the technical capabilities of the administrative staff at all levels, from the regional officials down to the villagers. And to make matters worse these various bodies were constantly being shaken up by new schemes – first decentralization, then villagization, then the sudden decision to disband the cooperatives. There's too great a tendency to think that a new system will automatically be better, whereas the process of adapting to a new system starts off by wasting time, and often efficiency too. Lastly, the World Bank, which claims to be giving aid to the rural poor, squanders its funds and finishes up slowing down a region's true potential for development because it fails to understand the problems involved – 'they' don't often visit the villages.

5 *State farms or an upgraded peasantry?*

There's a rice shortage in Dar es Salaam because consumption is rising all the time and there isn't enough foreign exchange. As no one trusts the peasants sufficiently and the extension services are generally inadequate, with virtually nothing being done to encourage animal-drawn implements, there is a ready tendency to rely on the state farms, without any attempt to assess how much they cost the economy. (The then Finance Minister, Edwin Mtei, was amazed when we told him how expensive they were.) Mbarali state farm in Mbeya region, which concentrates on irrigated rice, is probably one of the best, obtaining excellent yields (over 7 tonnes of paddy per hectare). But no one was able to tell us what it cost. The figure is bound to be very high, as a walk round the fields will show. The extensive irrigation network, which is based on a well-built dam across the river, the long channels and the expensive business of levelling the plots must all have cost a great deal more than merely improving the existing peasant irrigation systems.

Although Mbarali is run by an efficient Chinese team it seems more like an American farm, but it has far more equipment to the hectare than any private farm could afford. There is a large caterpillar tractor, two wheel tractors, a combine harvester etc for every 100 hectares of land (the whole farm covers 2,400 hectares). The capital tied up in machinery alone is out of all proportion, particularly when it's in foreign exchange, considering that it produces 700 tonnes of paddy per annum. Just think of the cost of the equipment, plus the spare parts, all of them using oil at a rate of knots.

Very close to here are the Usangu Flats, where the rice yield is only 2·5 tonnes per hectare, a third of the Mbarali figure; but it doesn't require any foreign exchange. It would be perfectly possible to develop and improve the irrigation channels here and thus increase output; as in China, this work could be done during the slack season on the farms, when there is serious under-employment. The rice straw can be used as fodder here, whereas in Mbarali it's burnt. You could admittedly bring forward the date for ploughing the hardest clay soils by using a few wheeled tractors, but that would cost, per tonne of rice produced, less than a tenth of the foreign exchange swallowed up by the state farm. But the authorities like the fact that all Mbarali's rice is delivered immediately to the official channels and goes straight off to the capital, where it is snapped up straight away in these times of shortages, and hence of high rice prices on the open market.

If this peasant system is to be made productive sooner, intelligent extension work is needed, plus a few grants and, most important of all, considerable involvement on the part of the peasants, who need to be *mobilized* into action. But for this to work they must be trusted and treated as fully-fledged citizens, on a par with towndwellers and civil servants. The district officials and village council must stop treating them as underlings whose role is merely to obey orders from the authorities. This type of attitude rejects out of hand the huge amount of practical know-how amassed by the peasants over the generations. Their advisers should start by studying this – they have so much to learn before they start teaching. But they don't 'learn how to learn' in school. This is one of the key factors connected with rural development in Africa, and therefore with development in general.

A similar comparison can be made in northern Tanzania, at Utegi state farm between Musoma, on the shores of Lake Victoria, and Tarime. It is a fine and well-run dairy farm, producing milk from high-yield Dutch cows. We couldn't see any major technical errors being committed there. Yet even with a large amount of starting capital (Shs. 5 million), the technical director told us: 'For every two shillings we bank from selling our milk we've spent three shillings.' The director, a Dutchman, held out little hope of ever making up all these losses. Here too the cost is very high in terms of foreign exchange, particularly when they have to pay for hundreds of pedigree heifers imported from New Zealand.

The local peasants, using local cows, produce milk that brings them in a small profit, and costs virtually nothing in foreign exchange. Their output could be improved at little cost using artificial insemination with just two imported bulls. This would result in hybrid cows, which are less demanding than the thoroughbreds imported at vast expense. But if this type of 'modern peasant farming' is to flourish, it is once again essential to help the farmers, encourage them,* and be efficient about collecting all the milk they produce. The peasants need to be given advice, but the most important thing is to help them to get organized, leaving them to take the initiative and eventually make their own choice of what type of modernization they want. To go on referring to them as 'backward' is a glaring blunder on the part of ill-educated technocrats. Nyerere has never said such a thing.

6 *Maize and beans, or cotton to buy cars with?*

Ever since the Ruvuma Development Association was disbanded the question of cash or export crops versus food crops has been argued over and over again. All the authorities and all the privileged few are very much in favour of cash crops, which bring in the foreign exchange they need so badly if they want a Western lifestyle and Western technology. Meanwhile malnutrition is still rife in the rural areas in Tanzania, especially in places where the main crop is cassava, such as Mtwara in the south.

If malnutrition is to be lessened, more cereals must be grown, and preferably eaten unrefined. In March 1980 there was a maize and bread shortage all over the country, but no one thought of increasing available supplies by stepping up the level of flour extraction to at least 85 per cent, though 100 per cent would be better still. There should also be more fruit and vegetables in their diet; more beans, groundnuts and other legumes; more milk and fish, which are more economical animal proteins than meat; and so on. Now let's take the case of Sengerema to the south of Lake Victoria in Sukumaland. What do the district authorities' 'orders' say? They're very straightforward in fact: each peasant family has been told to grow three acres of cotton, another three of cassava and another three of maize, no matter what their circumstances. Here the Geita-Sengerema cotton project has again been funded by the World Bank, which has – yet again – underestimated the difficulties in implementing it and shows little interest in either the real possibilities or what the peasants think about it.

---

* Derek Bryceson, a former Minister of Agriculture, told us that the state cattle farms keep very much to themselves. They could encourage the peasants to improve their animal husbandry, but they don't do a thing.

In fact a study of the soil in this part of the country has shown that the peasants can distinguish a whole series of different types of soil – at least a dozen – with varying potentials. They even have a specific vernacular term for each of them. Here again their knowledge is ignored. Cotton isn't suitable for soil that is too moist, and rice is in short supply, yet the people in charge have asked the peasants to plough up some of their *mbugas*, which are eminently suitable for rice-growing. This is sheer waste. Maize is less suitable than sorghum in the southern part of the district, which is more subject to drought; it is often a better form of insurance to grow both types of cereals. Incidentally the peasants have done their sums and worked out that in many cases the return on cotton, with an average yield of half a tonne of seed cotton per hectare, is far too low in view of the two hundred days of work, including sorting, it may require per hectare. Only the best farmers can make a profit out of it.

In order to buy a single ordinary car,* which cost Shs. 60,000 in 1979, Tanzania had to sell 5 tonnes of lint cotton, which are the equivalent of 15 tonnes of seed cotton, and therefore of 30 hectares of land with an average crop. This means that a peasant is required to work for 6,000 days, for very little pay, to enable a bureaucrat (who may be a mere parasite) to avoid using public transport – in which case public transport ought to be improved.

As in Kasulu district, many of the peasants prefer beans, which are an improvement to their diet and sell better too; but the Party prosecutes anyone who rebels against this form of forced farm labour – for which the old colonial regulations have been reinstated! Fines or even a prison sentence rain down on them. Party officials drive out in their cars to egg them on, but take good care not to dirty their hands by working alongside them. We begin to discern the outline of the major contradiction that Tanzanian socialism hasn't yet managed to resolve. For here too the gulf between urban and rural areas, bureaucrats and peasants, is still very marked, even if it isn't as bad as in Zambia. It is still the main obstacle in the path of endogenous

---

* Apparently an import licence is sometimes granted in return for a payment of Shs. 10,000 at the right moment and to the right person. There's a shortage of lorries to transport sisal hemp, but Dar has too many cars – and huge traffic jams. There was no corruption here down to 1969, and there is still less of it than in Zambia, but repeated shortages have opened the door.

development based first and foremost on the country's 'hidden productive resources'.

We must, however, acknowledge that since the 1974 food shortages, food crops – which Nyerere refers to as a matter of life or death – have again been given priority, at the expense of cotton (though not quite always).

7 *Correcting the errors of villagization*

The first task is to recognize the mistakes that have been made, as Nyerere willingly admits. But the people responsible in the Party and civil service won't be whole-hearted about it. Some villages have been sited on land that wasn't sufficiently fertile or had no water nearby, or was subject to periodic flooding, or to other problems. Such villages have got to be moved, no matter what the cost and the difficulties involved. But this time their new sites really must be chosen with great care, and not merely by the various teams of urban technocrats. There has to be constant collaboration with the peasants and their representatives, and not solely with the elected village leaders, or even with all the men in the village; the women must be involved too, and at long last be given a chance to express their views. After all, the longest and toughest work falls on their shoulders.

The optimum size of the new villages deserves to be thought out more carefully. We feel that the absolute maximum should be 250 families – after all, if migration from the rural areas is overcome the population may easily have doubled in a single generation. A drop in work productivity has already been noticed in the oversized villages, because a great deal more time is wasted getting to the fields, transporting the fertilizers and bringing in the harvest. And a drop in the productivity of the land is also beginning to be noticed, because of the permanent cultivation that is being practised there, without organic manure and usually without fertilizers either. If something isn't done soon, these semi-urban areas will soon be surrounded by ruined land, and in arid zones by semi-desert. This twofold drop in productivity is the basic cause of the farming losses and food shortages, which worsened in 1980.

In the case of the villages that are to stay where they are, a compromise must be found between two possibilities, both of them desirable – the provision of services (water, a school and a dispensary), and fields sown with crops. One idea would be to set up satellite villages round the oversized villages, about three or four kilometres away, and in three or four different places. The children could easily cover this distance morning and evening on their way to and from school, and all the fields would be that much nearer. Water presents a more serious problem, since it involves daily drudgery of the most unpleasant kind. It would therefore be a desirable objective to have all the satellite villages supplied with water in due course. The distance of the water supply is at least as important as that of the fields, since more water has to be transported. All this requires study, deliberation, and lengthy consultations with those concerned – discussions that really do take the form of dialogues.

These villages could be more carefully thought out if alongside the standard agencies – assemblies, councils, committees – there were also peasant unions within the Party, with genuine grassroots involvement. Up to now the Party's village branches have been run by higher authorities at regional and district level, and have been completely dominated by the privileged few who exploit the peasants' labour. Genuine grassroots power at all levels, including the Party (which is 'supreme'), would mean that an endogenous mode of development could be worked out in each village. The first move would be to satisfy the village's specific basic needs, in the way of food or skilled labour, relying chiefly on local resources and using them to the full. Cash and export crops wouldn't be allowed to squeeze out food crops, as they still do now only too often, partly to meet the luxury demands of the privileged few. But if this is to work the villages really would have to be self-governing, at any rate as far as their own needs are concerned.

8 Stock-farming – oxen versus tractors

Too many writers have argued that the traditional African method of stock farming was 'sentimental' or a means of acquiring social status. It's true that stock breeders are attached to their animals and that they act as a status symbol. But there is also a question of insurance: if they have more animals, even elderly cows, that means that more will survive if an epidemic occurs, and it will therefore take less time to build up the herd again. In a dry year, if there is a grain shortage, the stock farmer can easily get by by selling one or two of his animals. The same applies whenever he has to meet some unexpected expense, in the case of illness, taxes and so on.

Also, cattle form the basis of the Africans' social obligations. For instance they are needed as a dowry for the sons of the family, and to increase the social influence exercised by their owner. Breeders with large herds will lend some of their stock to families who have no cattle at all, so that they can have the benefits of their milk, of part of their increase in weight, perhaps even the manure. This means that the stock breeder can rely on his group of clients, made up of families dependent on him, who will ensure that he plays a prominent part in the village assembly. Admittedly some of the people with no cattle of their own did tell us that the 'big breeders' overgrazed the communal pastures at the expense of the smaller herds. But they wouldn't go as far as to suggest that the cattle should be redistributed or that there should be restrictions on the size of the large herds that enable the rich to keep their private fortunes at the expense of the common land. The people in charge haven't yet really grasped the fact that the nation's heritage is being dissipated, a process which can't be alleviated by national decrees or Party orders. But if the poor peasants, those who come into the 'less than 10 head of cattle' category, were politically organized, they would be in a position to demand their fair share of their life interest in the common pasture land.

It is nevertheless true that Tanzania's huge number of cattle – it has over 12 million head of cattle, the second largest number in tropical Africa, after Ethiopia – are very much under-used. The country still produces very little meat and even less milk (with a few local exceptions), and the herds provide virtually no labour at all – as we have seen, the women bear the heavy burden of fetching and carrying, while the animals do nothing at all.

So modernization in agriculture, which started in 1945 for colonial farmers and at independence for African farmers, has been based on tractors. This was the easy option – there was money available, tractors didn't cost too much and fuel oil was abnormally cheap. But this is no longer true, and French agronomists working in Bashay have shown that tractors now cost a great deal more than using draught animals. In 1979 a tractor owner was charging Shs. 140 for ploughing 40 acres, compared with Shs. 40–80 for hiring oxen. For carting bricks the difference was Shs. 100 compared to Shs. 30. And when oxen are hired the money stays in the village and costs nothing in the way of foreign exchange. It also means that the livestock capital is being fully used. Also, animal traction is always reliable, which can no longer be said of tractors; only too often spare parts are unobtainable, and more recently there have been fuel oil shortages.

The use of draught animals is much less common in Tanzania than in southern Zambia, though it does occur to a limited extent round Sumbawanga, Igunga and in some other places, but only for ploughs, hardly ever for carts. The extension services have hardly encouraged it at all, and the grants given for tractors have never been available for buying ploughs, carts, harrows and other animal-drawn implements, which have anyway hardly ever been obtainable. When land is ploughed, whether with a tractor or with an ox-plough, the work of harrowing increases enormously, and it is hard to keep up. Priority ought therefore to be given to animal-drawn harrowing and weeding machines, which are completely unknown. In July 1979 some Mbeya farmers complained in the press that the Tampu* in Arusha still hadn't delivered the carts they'd paid for four years earlier. The carts had eventually been built, but the railway couldn't transport them!

9 *Priority for appropriate technologies*

A branch of Tampu at Igunga near Tabora used to send to Arusha for the timber it needed for making carts and other implements, when all the requisite types of tree were available in the nearby forests. Each district – there are a hundred-odd districts in Tanzania – should have a workshop capable of making implements of this kind. (Zanzibar has been using and making carts drawn by a single ox for several generations. Cartwrights from Zanzibar could teach this trade to their colleagues in Tanzania.) The workshops should also be able to make maize shellers (good prototypes are available in both Arusha and Mbeya), plus harrows, seed drills, hoes, winnowers and so on. Draught animals and a thriving artisan class must go together. The

---

* This farm equipment workshop is inside an army camp, which makes it hard to get at.

lack of this crucial transport link is being increasingly felt in Tanzania, and the survival of the villages is dependent on it.

All these implements, plus many others, represent a type of technology that has so far been treated with considerable contempt by Africans. Yet we feel that in the present circumstances it is an essential stage in the continent's progress, if that progress is to affect the whole of Africa's peasantry. In Bashay, said the agronomists, tractors 'enable the rich to lay the foundations of their economic and political strength and leave the poor to their extreme poverty'; the same applies to lorries.

The Arusha Alternative Technology Project has begun to study the most urgent needs of the villagers and to help them to make the most useful implements, such as hand pumps, which one village is making for the neighbouring villages as well. Imported metal wind pumps are too expensive, but they can be made in the villages using bamboo towers and cotton sails, which can easily be folded if there's a tornado and are cheap to replace. Serious study should be given to all this; and the necessary funds and raw materials allocated.

It's true that there is an organization called SIDO* in existence whose function is to develop small-scale industries. But the projects it has undertaken (e.g. a sugar works) have looked into what we should refer to as medium-sized industries, all of them highly mechanized. The country's major effort should be to develop craft industries working in iron and wood, local manufacture of carts and ploughs, locally built mills, canneries, oil mills and so on, with technical advice available, plus grants for craftsmen to buy the necessary equipment.

As Ignacy Sachs has recently reminded us,[3] there is no question of sticking merely to what the British always used to call intermediate technologies. Tanzania does also need modern industries, providing they aren't too expensive in terms of foreign exchange and don't use too little semi-skilled labour. When they are calculating the economics of their schemes the technocrats forget that when there's a shortage of foreign exchange, Sh. 1 spent abroad is worth three or four times as much as Sh. 1 at home; this is confirmed by the dollar exchange rate on the black market – in May 1979 it fetched Shs. 8 at the official rate but Shs. 16 on the black market; and by March 1980 the figure was Shs. 22.

---

* Société pour le developpement des petites industries.

10 *First things first: the two agricultural revolutions*

The use of draught animals started very early in Europe, and it wasn't until much later that fodder crops and ley-farming became widespread, thus making it possible to intensify their use and at the same time step up the output of meat, milk and manure. This first agricultural revolution, which took place from the sixteenth century to the nineteenth century, and strengthened the association of crop-growing and animal husbandry, made it possible to build up better soils, worked more deeply and enriched with humus. It wasn't until the nineteenth century, and more generally the twentieth, that the second agricultural revolution led to the common use of chemical fertilizers and other chemicals. Subsequently draught horses, oxen and cows were superseded by tractors, thus breaking up the association between crop-growing and animal husbandry, and often eliminating the use of organic manure. This 'revolution' is now a threat to the future of our countryside.

It is this *second* agricultural revolution that tropical Africa is now embarking on, long before the first has been generally implemented. As a result the continent is building a form of agriculture that is too heavily dependent on outside help, and that is already endangering a great many of her soils, which are more fragile than in a temperate climate. It ought to be basing the modernization of its agriculture on its own resources, particularly on close links between cultivation and animal husbandry. The crop-growing sector can provide the byproducts of the crops grown, fodder and improved pasture, so that more livestock could be better fed. The stock breeding sector in its turn can provide labour and animal manure, plus much more meat and milk, not to mention leather and wool. The result would be a closed cycle of improvements in soils, animals and diet.

Growing fodder crops for the present overproduction of meat would not be profitable. But it could become so if there were a high milk output, and also if the oxen that finish up as meat had meanwhile provided labour. They can be used not merely for ploughing, for which they have to be retrained every year, but for other tasks such as harrowing and particularly for second dressing, which requires too much manual labour when the use of an ox-drawn plough results in increased acreages. Most important of all, they can be used as a means of transport, for as we have seen, you can't expect the girls to do too much drudgery if you want them to continue working in the fields.

Draught oxen and dairy cattle will soon become almost members of the family; they will therefore be better looked after and will repay the work of growing fodder crops. If they are stall fed, as they are now on the slopes of the big volcanoes, this would enable their owners to collect large quantities of manure. If the manure is kept in a shady spot and sprayed with water it will be more valuable, and it can be carted to the fields. In places where there are still only a few carts, sledges can be used; a pair of oxen can transport loads of 200 kilos on these sledges, or even 300 kilos if the runners are better shaped to lessen friction. The only economic way to step up output on the cotton estates in Sukumaland, where over-use of ammonia sulphate has acidified soil that already tended to be over-acid, is to use organic manure and much less fertilizer. This is the key to agricultural progress in tropical Africa, but it isn't an easy thing to accomplish. It took us two or three hundred years before organic manure was widely used in Europe, but whereas we could take our time because our population growth was only slight, the Africans will have to move faster if they are to remain independent.

11 *Small-scale stock rearing*

It's true that cattle are the chief status symbol for tribes that often have pastoral origins, but goats and sheep breed faster. Goats increase the value of fodder on fallow land or in undergrowth, and graze on foliage and shrubs and bushes; they must therefore be kept away from orchards and gardens and reafforested land, rather than being left to roam wild as they are in Zambia. On the crowded islands in Lake Victoria both cows and goats are tethered and the stakes are moved at regular intervals so that they do controlled rotational grazing. This disciplined form of grazing could be adopted all over the country.

Many Tanzanian children go short of milk, yet three goats, which eat less than a single cow, could keep a child in milk throughout the year. It's true that the local breeds don't give much milk, but this is because no attempt has been made to use selective breeding to produce better milkers. Better feeding would also help here, and cross-breeding with exotic breeds, which is now being tried in Zanzibar, would increase milk yields. Care would have to be taken with brucellosis, which is liable to transmit Malta fever to humans.

In the densely populated highlands – in the south for instance – children shiver on their way to school in the early morning because they wear light cotton clothes in temperatures close to zero centigrade – it can even freeze at times. Wool-bearing sheep are virtually unknown in Tanzania, yet they can be bred successfully, as we can see from the results achieved on the high Kitulo plateaux east of Mbeya (where incidentally six thousand high-yield dairy cows may soon be established). Developing a whole range of wool-based crafts and trades could eventually make a contribution to the country's exports, as in the Andes of South America.

Pigs reared on concentrated factory-produced fodder, such as those we saw near Arusha, are far too costly. In Kasulu district official grants have been used to build a piggery in which the pigs are housed better – and at far greater cost – than the peasants! Their food costs more too, since the concentrates were costing Sh. 1.70 per kilo in 1979, at a time when the peasants were eating maize costing Sh. 1 per kilo. And this doesn't take into account the cost of transport, which is staggering in the highlands. On the other hand the Lulanzi piggery is run very economically, with the pigs eating locally grown pumpkins and maize bran. As a result they look healthier than the local youngsters, who are fed on flour that is too white and has lost its most valuable components (amino-acids, vitamins, mineral salts). Piggeries are worth bothering with only if they are based chiefly on the use of local produce. For instance sweet potatoes and lupin, which does well near Mbeya, can provide a balanced local feed.

This also applies to poultry rearing, both for eggs and for broilers, which is mainly being developed on the outskirts of towns where there is a ready market for them. Before letting rich urban dwellers stuff themselves with pork products and chickens the Tanzanians ought to see whether enough of the grains and pulses fed to the pigs and chickens is reaching the peasants and other poor groups. Genuine agricultural development is a matter not just of output but of distribution; in the end, yet again, it's a matter of politics too.

Lastly we shouldn't forget about donkeys. These docile and hard-working animals don't cost much to feed and can carry the same load on pack saddles as three women; they can draw light carts with loads of 500 kilos. Here too improvements could be made by breeding.

12 *Priority for small-scale irrigation*

Tanzania can't go on depending on the good will of Allah the
Rainmaker for her crops. The authorities are therefore tending to give
top priority to irrigation, forgetting that large-scale irrigation is
generally the most expensive way of stepping up agricultural output
and should therefore be the last step to be taken. But as the necessary
studies take a long time and pilot projects have to be carried out,
the work should be started now. Meanwhile a large number of small-
scale schemes can pay their way; they should therefore be given
priority.

Small-scale irrigation of this type has been known in Tanzania for a
long time, and water channels were dug on the sides of the biggest
volcanoes long before the colonial era. With very porous soils, too
much irrigation, much of it not properly controlled, leads to leaching
and even erosion. The water could be used more profitably on the best
piedmont soils, where it rains much less. The peasants dug irrigation
channels there 'when the Germans were here' without asking for any
form of government aid – which anyway they wouldn't have been
given. Nowadays they rely too much on the state. They are still
willing to transport the necessary sand and stones and to provide
labour, but their contribution could be bigger, even in money terms.
If a mood of peasant 'mobilization' could be created they could be
asked to cover all the costs, paying some of them in instalments.

This type of small-scale irrigation often costs five to ten times less
per hectare irrigated than large-scale projects, and should therefore be
undertaken first. But the World Bank, as I've pointed out elsewhere in
the case of Sri Lanka,[4] prefers to fund large-scale projects that make fat
profits for major public works firms, and for the banks financing
them.

At any rate, the first priority is better use of water. Near Moshi, in
the Kahe irrigation scheme, there are orange groves and paddy fields
side by side, watered by the same irrigation channel. If the rice is to get
enough water the orange trees are going to get too much, and this will
harm them. Discipline is crucial if the water is to be fully used and the
future of the soil safeguarded. The best way to obtain the necessary
discipline is to base the irrigation tax on the actual volume of water
used, rather than the number of hectares irrigated. This would
encourage everyone to be sparing with water and would result in

better crops (they are harmed by overwatering) and less damage to soils liable to leaching and erosion.

Before embarking on expensive large-scale schemes it would be advisable to compile a list of all existing irrigation channels, so that for a start they can be used to maximum advantage. As well as water being wasted on a large scale, some existing systems have been quite simply overlooked. We saw an example of this at Mlali, near Morogoro, where a dam and its channels were in good condition and capable of irrigating 300 hectares of fertile soil. A mere four hectares were being irrigated! The Mwanapuli dam near Igunga was built in 1970 and could irrigate 640 hectares; ten years later the irrigation channels still hadn't been built, 'for lack of funds'. Yet the Arusha Declaration points out very clearly in several places that development will be achieved with hard work rather than money.

But Tanzania isn't China, and although peasant mobilization and voluntary labour can be achieved for services such as building a school, a dispensary or a godown, or providing a water supply, it has proved virtually impossible so far to steer this voluntary effort in the direction of the productive investment that we, in common with the Chinese, would regard as the top priority. Over the ten years that have already gone by, part of the reservoir has silted up, so its capacity is now smaller. In China the peasants would have taken the initiative and dug the channels themselves, but then China, which receives no aid in the way of foodstuffs, relies first and foremost on its own resources. We can't reiterate this too often.

A huge dam is already planned for Stiegler's Gorge on the river Rufiji. It will be able to produce eight times the amount of electricity Tanzania now needs! Like the Aswan Dam in Egypt it will hold back all the silt that fertilizes the low-lying valley and all the spawning grounds for the fish and shellfish in the mangrove swamps and coastal waters, jeopardizing the future of the fishing grounds and the potential for fish farming. It would cost a great deal less to set up a series of small dams as they are needed; these would let a lot of silt through, provide the right amount of electricity for each stage of development, and enable small irrigation systems to be developed. But the building firms claim to be powerful enough to get hold of the necessary funds from the World Bank. This time I have my doubts – the Bank won't fund a scheme to produce electricity that the country doesn't need now.

13 *An extremely difficult financial situation*

In spring 1980 Tanzania was facing some major difficulties: many regions were suffering from serious shortages, maize was in short supply, the bakeries were closing down, and rice had been unobtainable for a long time. Yet 30,000 tonnes of maize were lost in Arusha through rotting and insect damage for lack of proper storage. During the winter of 1979/80 the rains failed yet again, and although the peasants sowed more than usual, almost half of the crops withered and were ruined. It was a depressing sight, though not an uncommon one in Tanzania.

Taken as a whole, agricultural output can barely keep pace with population growth. With the present birth rate – which has remained stable for the last thirty years – if the death rate goes on falling Tanzania will have a population of 36 million by the end of the century and 87 million by 2025. It must therefore start paying greater attention to this problem, if only to improve the peasant women's 'quality of life'. It must not come to depend on the 'food weapon' wielded by the United States. Recurring droughts – a phenomenon that occurs only too regularly – find a country that has made no provision for emergency stores, and malnutrition is still too widespread.

The country's cash crops for export are levelling off or falling. Cotton remains well below its 1966 peak. Sisal is selling much better now, but there's a shortage of cutters, since the work is very hard and rates of pay are too low. The villagization policy has resulted in a fall in cashew nut output, and too many shelling plants have been built. The price of coffee, which saved the country's balance of payments in the period 1975–7, has dropped again, and production is at a standstill. Unlike the Ivory Coast, Tanzania hasn't got land as favourable or as vast, or immigrant labour so hard-working and poorly paid as the Mossi of Upper Volta. The only crops whose output is going up are tobacco and tea, but even they could do better. At 100,000 tonnes, sugar production in 1978 was 30,000 tonnes less than expected.

Tanzania's peasant population haven't inherited the tradition of hard work familiar to their counterparts in China. Circumstances have never forced them into working hard, with the exception of the immigrant workers on the sisal plantations. They like their time off, and although their womenfolk work hard all year, many of the men work on the land for only 100–120 days a year, if that, i.e. 800–900 hours. If they're asked to make more of an effort they weigh up what they'll get out of it, and compare it to the pleasure they get from their free time, chatting with their friends over a calabash of local beer or *pombe*. Mtei, the Finance Minister, also complained about the deteriorating labour discipline and common overmanning that is characteristic of the parastatals, and which leads to steadily falling output.

An even more important factor is the disastrous decision to adopt a Western form of modernization that relies chiefly on excessively expensive plant and equipment and requires extensive imports of raw materials. Both equipment and materials are in short supply, so the factories can't work at full capacity, and lorries and tractors grind to a halt because just one spare part is unobtainable when there's a shortage of foreign exchange. Import substituting industries are 'protected', yet many of them produce very little in the way of added value. As a result industrialists raise their selling prices, exaggerate their expenditure on raw materials and equipment, and put the difference into their Swiss bank accounts. Multinational companies are quite willing to be nationalized if they're allowed to go on with operations so advantageous to their parent firm. The parastatals often maintain links with the hydras of multinational capitalism, and their top executives can be paid for doing so.

Many a lorry that set off for the front never came back, more because of the bad state of the roads and erratic driving than because of the war. It is easier to supply Dar es Salaam with American maize arriving by sea than with locally produced maize; and because there's no way of transporting the local produce, large stocks are left to rot in the remote areas of the country such as Songea. Since independence virtually no thought has been given to any form of transport other than roads. The old railway network built by the Germans had been very badly maintained and there still aren't any diesel engines. The preliminary studies for the Tan-Zam Railway didn't allow for the 'unusual' floods that occurred in May 1979, washing away lengthy sections of the line. It's better to be safe than sorry in this type of area.

The peasants may not produce much, but then there's virtually nothing for them to buy. This is partly because of the lack of transport, and also because there has been a sharp cutback in the private sector, while the public sector hasn't always been capable of providing an effective substitute. It's true there's a shortage of lorries, but many of them travel empty because there's no proper coordination. When the loads to be transported are fairly light it would be a good idea if ox-drawn carts picked them up from local branch depots, to which they've been transported by lorry, and took them on to the various villages. Tanzania can no longer afford the waste involved when a large lorry is used to transport a mere 20 litres of oil. The peasants have been asked to work harder so as to earn the country more foreign exchange. But the people who earn it get virtually no benefit from it. As Nyerere said in the Arusha Declaration, foreign exchange is earned by the rural areas and spent by the towns – and this is still true today.

14 *Nyerere acknowledges the problems*

The French army has been ready to fight to uphold established governments, no matter how corrupt, to prevent 'destabilization' in areas where French interests were involved; but it made no move – and nor did any other army – when Idi Amin invaded the Kagera triangle in Tanzania in October 1978 and allowed his troops to go in for looting, rape and massacres. At the end of this expensive 'war of liberation' (it cost at least 500 million dollars, including a high proportion of foreign exchange), Tanzania appealed for aid to 'friendly' countries, asking specifically for foreign exchange. But its so-called 'friends' merely thanked it warmly for overthrowing the dictator Amin – and hearty handshakes don't cost much (the United States offer of 8 million dollars was for the following year, when what was needed was not 8 but 500 million).

The Tanzanians therefore had to appeal yet again to the good old GP who looks after ailing treasuries – the IMF. The Fund appeared on the scene with its little black bag, its portable dispensary proffering the same old pills no matter what the ailment – 'flu or malaria', as one minister of state, Kighoma Malima, put it. It insisted on spending cuts, though we've seen how harmful this has been in the case of Zambia. In Tanzania, too, the schools are short of books and exercise books and the dispensaries need more medicines. The devaluation it put forward as a remedy would make imports more expensive and wouldn't lead to an increase in exports, since it takes five years for sisal, coffee or cashew nuts to reach the production stage. And removal of exchange and price controls would make the flight of capital abroad easier, and swell black market profits. It's true that, as we have shown, many economic shortcomings can be corrected, if the country's leaders show the necessary humility. Yet *Self-Reliant Rural Development in Tanzania*, the report we handed to the prime minister, Edward Sokoine, after four months of research, during which we were given a great deal of very willing help, has never been seen by anyone other than a handful of secretary-generals and ministers.

Mtei, the Minister for Finance, who was allegedly pro-American, might perhaps have agreed to the conditions laid down by the IMF, but Nyerere decided to replace him with our friend Amir Jamal, who held the same post in 1967 and was recently a member of the Brandt Commission.

How was Tanzania going to get out of this predicament? The first step was to recognize the problems it faced, and on many occasions Nyerere has had the courage to do this, most importantly on the tenth anniversary of the Arusha Declaration in 1977. He warned:

> It is arrogance, and slackness, among leaders which we have to guard against . . . in practice leaders at all levels seem to delight in saying 'no' in response to even the most reasonable requests . . . Leaders are not Gods . . . A person who can admit a fault, and strive to do better, is both more worthy of trust, and more likely to be trusted, than one who pretends to be infallible . . . There is still a tendency for all levels of Government to act as if the peasants were of no account . . .

He recalled that during villagization some people were moved from an area with water to an area which is permanently dry, and that some new villages were too large for the amount of land available. He claims that the parastatals aren't making enough profit to finance new investment, management costs are often too high, with too many managers not doing their jobs properly and failing to order spare parts and raw materials in time. This was still true in 1979 in the case of the Tanga fertilizer factory, which suffered from a shortage of phosphate, sulphuric acid and items of equipment at various times.

Zanzibar's sugar cane harvest starts in June, but when we were there in August 1979 the factory, which had already been out of action during part of the previous season, couldn't go on stream because the

Chinese hadn't sent the necessary spare parts. A private factory would have rushed a representative to China to bring back the spares and prevent it going bankrupt. A state-run factory can't go bankrupt, but instead the whole of the population (except the leaders) suffers. The cane was eventually sent to a distillery.

15 *Dealing with underdevelopment*

The South African press likes drawing comparisons between what it refers to as the 'failure of socialism' in Tanzania and the 'success of capitalism' in Kenya, claiming that Kenya's annual growth rate is 7 per cent, while Tanzania's is only half this figure, at 3.5 per cent. The IMF gives a figure of 4·7 per cent for Tanzania, and the many difficulties experienced by Kenya, which were eventually recognized in 1980, cast doubt on the figure of 7 per cent. We visited Nairobi's slums and saw nothing anywhere near as horrific in Dar es Salaam, where constant (if not always successful) efforts are being made to lessen inequalities which Kenya accepts as a fact of life. Kenya too is short of maize* and transport facilities, and suffers from a greater housing shortage and very poor rural health. And this in spite of the fact that the British had built up a prosperous agricultural sector and an advanced industrial sector, with all the necessary infrastructure.

Let's return to Tanzania's situation after 1971. In that year Idi Amin seized power in Uganda, posing a new threat to the north of Tanzania, which had already been badly shaken in the south by Mozambique (then Portuguese) and South Africa. During 1972 a decentralization policy was implemented, giving more powers to the regions, but where was the staff to carry this through? At that time the State Trading Corporation was split up into six separate bodies, but the finishing touches needed to be put to all this. The price of oil has been going up since 1973: whereas in 1972 the 800,000 tonnes that Tanzania imported used up 10 per cent of the total value of her exports, by 1980

---

* But the United States are more willing to give the Kenyans maize because their battleships can use the facilities of Mombasa harbour, which isn't far from Arab and Iranian oil. Yet in March 1980 contraband maize was selling at five or six times higher prices on the border of Tanzania and Kenya than in Dar, stressing the existence of worse shortages in Kenya.

the figure was 60 per cent, even though consumption had dropped to 750,000 tonnes.

Major difficulties have continued since 1977, when the East African Community (Kenya, Uganda and Tanzania) was disbanded, necessitating expensive reorganization, particularly in the case of the railways, the ports and civil aviation. From October 1978 to May 1979 there was the war with Uganda, and no one gives credit in the arms business. We witnessed the serious floods in May 1979, and when Edward Sokoine, the prime minister, said to us: 'They're going to strangle us', the latest blow from the unequal terms of trade had come in the form of another rise in the price of petrol – and there's no reason why this rise should slow down.

Tanzania was granted independence in 1961, earlier than today's leaders would have liked. It could have continued with the economic system it inherited, within a neocolonial framework, but we know that such a system soon shows its limitations. Tanzania, with its severely limited resources, therefore decided to work out a different economic system in which the state would play the dominant role: inevitably the capitalists were concerned first and foremost with commercial profits, and were indifferent to the public interest. But the decision to opt for a new system, the first time this had happened anywhere in the world, slowed down growth by forcing the Tanzanians to tackle a large number of difficulties that result more from underdevelopment than from socialism. (The same could be said, incidentally, of Cuba. In my book about Cuba I tended to blame socialism for many difficulties that were in fact the result of underdevelopment, as Marie-France Mottin has shown.)[5]

16 *Socialism or bureaucracy?*

Scandinavia's social democrats criticize Tanzanian socialism for coming 'from above', from the president. They have also stressed, with greater justification, the question of bureaucrats versus peasants, though they make fewer references to the crucial question of men versus women. Socialism seems to be present in Mwalimu's speeches, full of intelligence and eloquence. In July 1979, when he gave the opening address at the FAO's congress on Agrarian Reform and Rural Development, he insisted with great vehemence on the need to give power to the people and to the peasants. But even at that stage we were entitled to wonder whether he had really given power to his own people in the rural areas, and indeed whether they really wanted it.

In making the transition from talking to doing, you come up against harsh reality. Mwalimu may make the speeches, but it's the Party that gives the orders (by word of mouth in many cases, which leaves no written record) and the government that carries them out. Both the Party and the government stick to their own point of view and often merely pay lip-service to the official ideology (though there are a few committed exceptions). Mwalimu has built up a strongly based Party and he governs via its bureaucracy, which in theory is drawn from the people, though in practice bureaucrats are much more likely to come from influential families and from parts of the country where compulsory education was soonest implemented. This bureaucracy forms a social group apart, which could be referred to as a class or a state bourgeoisie. Throughout the underdeveloped Third World, as well as in the countries that claim to be socialist, power is essentially in the hands of the bureaucracy. And it still has a large share of power in the capitalist world. It must therefore be recognized as a de facto reality, a necessary evil. Rather than automatically condemning it we would do better to recognize that it can take many forms and is highly complex, and to look into its social origins, its psychology and its propensities, some of which can be used to the nation's advantage.

In sixteen years Tanzania has managed to build up a structure. It doesn't always work well,* or at any rate not always as we should like to see it work, and improvements and corrections are needed, but at least it is there, whereas in Zambia nothing has been built up and

---

* The prime minister, with Mwalimu's agreement, gave us quite exceptional facilities to enable us to carry out our investigations, calling on all the country's officials to help us and even hiring special planes for us. He asked René Dumont to set out our views and arguments to the people responsible for rural development, and later to the ministers and secretary-generals, and to put forward urgent measures to be taken in the medium and long term. Yet when we had our last meeting with Mr Sokoine there was someone else (a Party official perhaps?) present and the tone had changed. 'Everything's fine,' he said. Our report only ever reached the secretary-generals, whereas the original idea was to have it translated into Swahili so that it could reach a wider audience. We got the impression that a Party and civil service mafia who were not amenable to criticism of any kind were trying to use our work to damage the prime minister, who was too honest for their liking.

recommendations disappear into a vacuum because the country has no coherent structures. The peasants do have some rights, even though, as Bernard Joinet pointed out, freedom isn't something that's given, it's something you have to take.

'All that Ujamaa business is Utopian socialism, just what Marx was right to condemn,' was the view expressed to us by a 'genuine' Marxist in Mozambique. But the three 'genuine' socialist regimes regognized as such in Prague in 1963, Ghana, Guinea and Mali, have all been total failures. Tanzania's 'Utopian socialism' – and we don't see this Utopianism as a stigma since we believe that Saint-Simon, Fourier and Proudhon didn't write in vain[6] – although surrounded by so many difficulties, has managed to build a nation to which its citizens see themselves as belonging, and of which they are on the whole proud. This is no small achievement, particularly in view of the fact that – and we mustn't be afraid to reiterate this – underdevelopment was caused by plundering the Third World, by unequal terms of trade, and is continuing because of these same factors.

If coffee, cotton, sisal, tobacco, tea and pyrethrum were paid for at their true value, Tanzania's balance of trade would be clearly positive. The country would even be able to make rapid strides in developing its infrastructure, plant and machinery, industry and public services (water supply, education, health and roads), particularly if it was helped to sell its agricultural output by greater value added. Instant coffee is already being produced in Bukoba and this industry could be improved (freeze-drying) and expanded. Instead of selling bales of raw cotton Tanzania could export it in the form of lengths of fabric dyed and printed locally (though competition from the Asian countries and the protectionist policies of the developed countries would be a problem). Virtually the whole of its sisal output could be exported in the form of ropes, mats, bags and fabrics, unless, that is, the oligopolistic cartel of European sisal processors made a concerted effort to prevent it. Tea could be sold in carefully devised blends packaged in small packets, if Brooke Bond and their like in London didn't have a virtual monopoly on this process, which is the only really profitable way of selling tea. Tobacco could be sold in the form of cigarettes or packets of pipe tobacco, if only the big boys involved in this processing industry weren't so powerful.

Yet it is not in Europe's interest to ruin Africa, or to cause difficulties for her or let difficulties develop of their own accord, such as local or civil wars or coups. It is of course true that all these difficulties enable France to sell more arms to the Africans, and therefore to squander the larger amounts of oil that these various incidents enable it to acquire. People like talking about Euro-Africa, but the time has come to treat the continent in quite a different light. As one of Tanzania's ministers said to us, the new international economic order is something people are fond of talking about, but no one is making any serious effort to promote it.

To sum up, Tanzania represents an attempt to set up a socialist system, but the country is having to face the difficulties of under-development. It is no longer a question of making dreams of African socialism come true, but, more prosaically, of helping peasant men and women to survive by allowing them to develop under their own steam, in a manner based on their own needs; and of giving them real powers so that they can effectively combat the bureaucrats who are still exploiting them in the name of socialism – a socialism that has been warped by the Party. The botched and authoritarian attempt at villagization was designed to serve the peasants, but also to control them; in the end it caused agricultural output to drop.

The Air France Boeing 747 that brought us back from Dar es Salaam to Paris burned up 55 tonnes of kerosene during the journey. Meanwhile in Sumbawanga the peasant women didn't have a drop of paraffin for their little Pigeon lamps – and nor did the bureaucrats.

6 West Africa – expanding desert; creeping neocolonialism

The élites speak like us in France – often better than us in fact – and think, live and eat *à la française*. In the street we would come across people just like our dustman in Paris, the man who sweeps the Métro, or our cleaning lady. In other words this is more familiar ground for French readers. Even though French West Africa is now officially just plain West Africa, there is still something of a French flavour. It's perhaps a bit like looking into a distorting mirror that throws back not just a caricature of ourselves but an image of our guilty conscience. We felt less innocent than in English-speaking Africa, more implicated. We were the guilty party this time. France still hasn't given up its famous 'presence in Africa', and nor have the Africans. You can still occasionally hear someone say: 'France is my country', and in spite of nationalist protests, the umbilical cord has never been truly severed. Dakar tries to be a small-scale Paris, while Abidjan hovers between Manhattan and Hollywood, only dubbed in French. Africa has lost its bearings here.

West Africa also includes the Sahel, our interest in which is periodically revived by famines. This interest is highly ambiguous and some people have already started asking: 'Who's growing fat on the Sahel's famines?' While the Sahara is gaining ground everywhere, moving both northwards and southwards, the rich countries go on importing the raw groundnuts and cotton that are ruining the soil, and exporting their industrial products, machinery and grain surpluses. And the place is swarming with experts, commissions and international agencies, all of them travelling at vast expense with suitcases bulging with charms, knick-knacks, grandiose miracle schemes and other forms of eyewash. All these different bureaucracies live off the Third World and would find themselves out of work if underdevelopment came to an end. Meanwhile the local ruling bourgeoisie have acquired a taste for power and hang on to it for dear life – their main concern being to ensure that they are there for their own good rather than their country's development. They look for satisfaction in the short term and are encouraged in this by foreign interests who egg them on to sell off the natural wealth of their country for next to nothing, and at the same time promote a Western development model that brings them in a good profit.

These various forms of strangulation are matched by the effect of the climate. The Sahel suffers from much worse natural conditions, particularly from the point of view of the climate, than the two East African countries we've been discussing so far. And as we shall see, the alleged 'Ivory Coast miracle', which is partly based on the disappearance of the forested areas, is in danger of jeopardizing the climate and drying up the wretched Sahel even more.

The Arab word 'Sahel' means 'the shore', as with the coastal zone in the Maghreb stretching from Sfax to the west of Algiers. In this case it refers to the 'shore' of the Sahara, the zone running along the southern edge of the desert. It's known that the rainfall becomes greater as you get closer to the ocean, from the Sahel of the nomads to that of the sedentary peoples, then to the Sudan zone, ending in the evergreen forest which is unfortunately in the process of vanishing for ever. It isn't just that the amount of rainfall decreases as you go further north; the rains are more variable and more irregular. And droughts have been reported there since time immemorial.

Everyone knew about them, so they were allowed for, and during good years the family granaries would be filled with pearl millet (Pennisetum) and sorghum, which grows further south and on more clayey soil. Pastoral communities would regulate the movement of livestock in areas too arid for crop growing, depending on the season and availability of water, taking care not to allow overgrazing to destroy the plant cover. Within the village communities the land chiefs were careful to ensure that the soil was protected, with long fallow periods replenishing the humus.

1 *Dakar – the town that 'does for' the peasants*

When Senegal, France's oldest colony, became independent an ironic fate saddled it with Dakar as its capital, for Dakar, single-handed, keeps Senegal dependent. This former capital of French West Africa already had a tradition of being a bureaucratic town and of sucking in tax revenue from the whole of this part of the continent. It also had ambitions to be the region's industrial centre. Léopold Senghor tried to maintain the unity of West Africa to his own advantage, but Félix Houphouët-Boigny of the Ivory Coast, who paid most of the taxes, managed to get the federation disbanded, with the help of France, who thought it better to 'divide and rule'. The micro-states set up at this time have had to shoulder an intolerable burden in the way of administrative overheads, plus the cost of government and representation abroad.

Once the federation had been broken up, Dakar still retained its luxury tastes and its leaning towards bureaucracy, even though it had lost the great majority of its revenue. How can so poor a country maintain so wasteful a town?

The nation state was set up for the benefit of its capital city, its political and economic leaders and its bureaucrats. So the only way to build up a state was to drain off resources on an even larger scale than with the *traitants*★ in the colonial era. There have always been forces that accumulated capital on the backs of the Third World's peasants, but this source wasn't now adequate on its own and it became increasingly necessary to turn to foreign aid. Dakar's scandalmongers make jokes about the aid not going into the sea, as people might think, but stopping short on the cliff road where luxury houses are springing up. While the peasants are increasingly poverty-stricken the town goes on spreading, and more and more tower blocks shoot up. There's an old French saying that when the building trade's doing well the whole country's prospering, but that certainly isn't the case here. In this schizophrenic country, growing famine, drought and malnutrition are seen by the élite as mere rumours or electoral slogans. Dakar is still a fool's paradise.

'It's the town that's done for the peasants,' one elderly peasant told us. 'Twenty years on we've come to realize what independence really meant. It was just for the towns. One of these days we'll be asking Dakar for a reckoning, you'll see. After all we're all entitled to make a living, not just the civil servants.' The peasants aren't simply sucked dry in the most shameless way, they're also penalized by a bad civil

---

★ The French word *traitant* does not have an exact equivalent. Its meaning is 'colonial-type middlemen'.

service, answerable to no one, which has piled up debts by offering poor services that don't even bring in any money. 'We're not asking for much, just a bit of help from the government. We've never been taught how to manage. If you want to be independent you've got to get hold of knowledge and skills. But they don't help us. Whenever we try to do something they just crush us.'

Here again it isn't in the interest of the urban authorities to give the peasants their freedom. After twenty years of independence the great majority of them are still illiterate and all the country's efforts go into building up an élitist education system. Any initiative liable to get out of the bureaucrats' control had better be nipped in the bud. All this is reinforced by a Jacobin concept of power in which an ultra-centralized state takes all the decisions, and does so too far away from the place where they are actually carried out, showing little consideration for the ordinary people. Civil servants are obsessed with the idea of stepping up output at all costs, so as to syphon off even more resources and channel them towards the towns and the parasitic tertiary sector of the economy.

'If we're ever going to get out of this situation, we're going to have to get rid of all the millet-eaters,'* say the peasants, who've been quick to grasp how the system works. But the tragedy is that the parasites refuse to eat the traditional millet. Dakar is the very picture of 'development', of the imported urban model incorporating the classic method of consumption. The élite have acquired these habits abroad; the middle classes follow their example and the press and broadcasting media encourage the spread of the prevailing model, whose effect is to suffocate the rural areas until they become a mere dumping ground for the towns.

2 Desertification in the Cayor de Louga in Senegal

In northern Senegal, which used to be one of the main groundnut strongholds, the road from Dakar to the former capital, Saint-Louis, goes through Louga. Whereas Saint-Louis slumbers, full of antiquated

---

* *Mange-mil* or 'millet-eater' is the French name for the quelea, a bird that feeds on millet, descending on crops like a swarm of locusts (translator's note).

charm, in its memories of Faidherbe, Mermoz and a more glorious past, in Louga time has stood still.

'In the old days there used to be forests all round here. There was plenty of work in the town, people came here to sell their groundnuts, the oil mill employed 500 people and the station was a major junction. But now it's a wilderness. You'd think you were in Mauritania and there aren't any young people left in Louga.' These disillusioned words were spoken by a man who wasn't more than forty-five. The once-prosperous town is dead; the station is crumbling and its roof tiles aren't replaced; and the oil mill's huge buildings stand empty. Faidherbe's house, where gazelles once grazed on tall grass, has become a 'man-made desert'. In an attempt to resuscitate Louga, which is now a regional capital, a new town is being built to house civil servants – the unproductive sector superseding the productive sector. In sharp contrast to the general aspect of wretchedness and desolation is the sight of a marabout's superb palace, with green domes and high walls surrounding lush grounds and a coconut grove. Economic exploitation is sometimes reinforced by appeals to religion, but in this case the marabout is investing money in Louga that was earned abroad.

The first railway line, the DSL (Dakar–Saint-Louis), was built at the end of the nineteenth century to bring down the cost of transporting the groundnut crop (though now a powerful road lobby is encouraging the government to abandon rail and ship transport in favour of lorries, which use up much more energy). The idea was also to expand the acreage under groundnuts at the expense of fallow land, and therefore of humus; and the sandy soils, known as 'Dior soils' are becoming tragically less fertile as they lose their organic content. As the population increases it has been necessary to sow more land with cereal crops, and again this means less fallow land and pasture land.

So millet, sorghum and groundnuts are increasingly eating into the fallow land. Now if the fallow land diminishes, or disappears altogether, the loss of humus deprives the soil of its binding agent. The harmattan wind blowing from the desert, especially in January, February and March, can therefore blow away all its most fragile ingredients – clay, alluvium, fine sand and the coagulated remains of the humus – leaving a skeletal soil made up of coarse sand that is shifted by the winds like a sand dune and has lost the capacity to retain water. When the first heavy rains come, pearl millet and groundnuts are sown, but if the second rains are late the sprouted seedlings wither and die and you have to start all over again, sometimes several times running, while the chance of success diminishes.

The French pedological college was set up very late in the day, starting in 1946, but Aubert and Magnien sounded the alarm, and I took up the cry in 1953.[1] But the groundnut crop swelled the colony's coffers, making a lot of money for the *traitants*, who could only import goods in proportion to the output of profitable crops – so to hell with soil protection and the country's future!

Meanwhile during the period 1932–9 the country imported rice from Indochina at rock-bottom prices, and 1 kilo of groundnuts in the shell would be traded for over a kilo of broken rice. It was therefore in the peasants' interest to grow more groundnuts and less millet or sorghum. The authorities encouraged people to consume imported cereals, changed their eating habits and thus led them into a state of dependence.

When the country became independent in 1960 plans for diversifying its agriculture were drawn up by advisers working with Father Lebret and the Minister of Planning and Development, Cheikh Amidou Kane. Attempts were made to encourage the cultivation of cereal crops, fruit and vegetables, sugar and fodder crops so as to shake off the groundnut yoke. In 1964 the Common Market announced that the price of groundnuts coming into France would no longer be 'protected' and would drop by 25 per cent.

But French interests were still keeping an eye on the situation and SATEC, a parastatal French firm offering aid and funds, promised to step up groundnut production by 25 per cent over three years, so as to make up for this loss – using a large managerial staff made up mostly of Europeans, some with a mere week of training! Grants were available only for groundnuts, and the only form of intensive research went into this one crop, since it was the only one where marketing carried no risks. The result of all this was that the average groundnut output has been falling steadily ever since – drought wasn't the only cause. The only exceptions were 1965, 1967 and 1975, when output did reach 1 million tonnes or even more. The peasants naturally changed their cropping pattern, because if they sold their groundnuts to buy rice, the rice cost them four times as much as their own millet.

Yet the government, like the colonial authorities, goes on encouraging farmers and peasants to grow cash crops, since they bring in the foreign exchange needed to pay for the imports, often of luxury goods, demanded by the privileged few in positions of power, and required if Western-style modernization is to be implemented. When the EEC was asked to provide aid it did give a subsidy, because in 1968 there were rumblings of near-revolt in the rural areas of Senegal. The price rose sharply (though inflation took care of a good deal of the rise). Yet in 1979–80 only 250,000 tonnes of groundnuts were marketed, the lowest figure since the recession of 1933 (when the population was less than half the size!). The peasants' main priority is getting enough to eat, and we don't blame them.

If we return to Louga we find that down to 1958 the output of groundnuts was higher than that of millet, except during a few short periods of drought. So the groundnut crop was developed, and the use of animal traction meant that the acreages could be expanded, which brought about the loss of yet more fallow land. When we were there in 1980 we saw a truly desolate sight. Admittedly the drought was largely responsible, but it's hard to say whether this is the result of a climatic cycle or of a full-scale change in the climate brought about by the destruction of the dense forests in the coastal regions of West Africa, as the foresters think. The French agronomist Claude Reboul refers to it as 'climatic piracy'.

Goumbo Guéoul on the Thiès–Louga road had piles of very light groundnut shells. The nuts were too small and yields were lamentably low (in some cases there was no harvest at all). Yet the chairman of Guéoul rural district had put 200,000 francs into this crop, buying three horses, fertilizers and seeds. His father cultivated two or three hectares of millet and groundnuts by hand. In a good year he could obtain yields of over $1\frac{1}{2}$ tonnes per hectare, and sometimes managed a peak yield of 2 tonnes when the rainfall was plentiful. His son, using a horse-drawn seeder and hoe, cultivated 10 hectares, but yields of even 1 tonne were becoming increasingly rare. In 1979, having spent his 200,000 francs, he harvested 228 kilograms of groundnuts on 8 hectares and 52 kilos of millet on 2 hectares. These figures spell sheer ruin. The son also used chemical fertilizers which, spread on the surface, attract the root system there: these shallow roots are more vulnerable in times of drought.

The small town of Guéoul seems to be dying where it stands. The local tailors sit behind their sewing machines waiting for a mere handful of customers, whereas in Dakar there aren't enough tailors to fulfil the huge numbers of order, particularly at holiday time. And so the towns grow richer while the rural areas grow poorer. And the people of Guéoul wear cast-off clothes, the rejects of our developed society. The textile shop will often go for days without selling anything at all. Annual sales amount to 400 metres of fabric – next to nothing. The shoemaker can't now sell his little leather slippers, made from leather he tans himself. The wealthy inhabitants are selling off their cattle, and the chairman had to spend 1,350 francs a day just on feeding his four wives and eighteen children. The poorest people appeal to *diama*, the sense of family solidarity, but if the whole family is poverty-stricken they have to borrow 100 kilos of millet at 4,000 francs, and pay back 6,500 francs six months later. The American Cathwell aid organization delivers CSM, a mixture of maize, soya bean and milk, for mothers and children. This is a useful protein supplement, but when there's a shortage of basic cereals they also need millet. We saw two hundred sacks of CSM turn up in a village that wasn't expecting it. The sacks were flung into a yard and left in the open air, and the head of the village didn't bother about getting a lean-to shed with a thatched roof built as a cheap way of keeping them dry when the rainy season came.

Inequalities are therefore growing, with rich and poor countries, and towns lording it over the villages; but a new form of inequality is emerging in the villages, with a stratum of local bigwigs losing no time in taking advantage of the situation. And against this background calamity is fast approaching. The use of draught animals means that larger acreages can be cultivated and therefore that the last traces of humus are used up.* There are increasing areas of sand dunes, stretching right to the outskirts of Dakar nowadays. For a long time there were plans to apply organic manure, but apart from a few dried-out dung heaps the agronomists have given up in sheer despair. Nothing can be done in Louga without irrigation. Not that this stops SODEVA† sending in its extension staff, though all this bureaucracy is an expensive business, and it's the peasants who pay in the end. Paying higher prices for agricultural produce would be a

---

* In the semi-arid 'virgin lands' of Soviet Kazakhstan, which Khrushchev unwisely had cultivated, the destruction of the humus has occurred even more rapidly because of the use of tractors, and yields have plummeted.
† Société de développement agricole.

better solution, but they want to make use of all those young people who refuse to do manual work. According to Pierre Biarnès[2] Senegal has 70,000 civil servants and 35,000 people employed in parastatals. This is far too heavy a burden for such a small poor country to bear.

Obviously the answer is to irrigate. But where is the water to come from, and what will it cost to get it there? The villages that lie along the route of the pipeline bringing water to Dakar from Lake Guiers are allowed to have some of it, but up to now this has been a free service, which only encourages waste. There are plans to make them pay for it, but what price will they be asked to pay? It's true that extra watering of millet and groundnuts can result in very much higher yields in return for small amounts of water. But what will the water supply system cost? Senegal can't count on the massive subsidies Israel received from the Jewish community, which helped it to develop on such an extraordinary scale. We believe that the situation is irreversible. The groundnut crop was expanded rapidly to produce profits for the profiteers during the colonial era and subsequently during the neocolonial era (you have only to look at the splendid villas along Dakar's western cliff road with their sea views, or the lavish dinner parties, and see who owns all these fine houses and private cars); and this expansion has helped to cause desertification.

This destruction caused by wind erosion, with the harmattan wind whipping away the fine particles in the soil, is characteristic of northern Senegal, but unfortunately it now has a counterpart south of the Dakar–Thiès–Dourbel road, in what is now the extensive groundnut zone in Serer territory and in Siné-Saloum. On this soil with a higher clay content and with higher rainfall, 'modernization' has resulted in land being cleared so that animal-drawn implements can be used. This takes the form of chopping down all the trees and removing the tree stumps, so that as soon as the ground slopes even very slightly, sheet erosion occurs, with the top layers of soil stripped away, and the hillsides start being criss-crossed with the rills and ravines of erosion. The authorities want to see the land reafforested, but the villagers have no tradition of looking after newly planted trees. Here too more trees are cut down than are replanted, whereas twenty times as many ought to be planted to halt soil deterioration and meet the growing demand for timber and charcoal. ENDA,* a non-

---

* ENDA, BP 3370, Dakar, Senegal.

governmental international organization under the chairmanship of Cheikh Amidou Kane, which was set up to provide backing for self-development by grassroots groups in the Third World and to train and retrain personnel in the field, is promoting the use of a small baked clay wood-burning stove which cuts the amount of wood needed for cooking by half. And methane gas, 'gas from the dung heap', will soon start being produced economically.

3 Harnessing the river Senegal from the wrong end

Although this region is suffering from desertification, the Senegal river pours huge quantities of fresh water into the sea: 24,000 million cubic metres in an average year are wasted in this way, instead of being available for crop-growing.

When the waters recede the peasants traditionally grow crops in the depressions that have been flooded. In 1950 work started on harnessing the river, beginning with the delta. But this was the worst place to start, because it is predominantly salt meadows, much of it poor land with virtually no peasant population, most of the inhabitants being shepherds. Initially the land was simply flooded, but later controlled flooding was used, with dykes and channels. But these didn't bring the waters fully under control, and the rice yields obtained were highly uneven – sometimes there was no yield at all. This naturally discouraged the colonists who had been encouraged to settle there.

The next stage was 'tertiary' development, with peripheral dykes and a full-scale and detailed irrigation and drainage system, which meant that the waters were fully controlled. Colonists were transplanted into the unlikely setting of rows of little houses with asbestos roofs; these were a success from the technical point of view, but a total failure as dwellings for human beings, and a lot of colonists refused to live in them. They either stored their crops in them and built themselves traditional houses alongside, where they felt more at home, or else abandoned these concentration-camp villages where fifteen years after they were built there was no shade and not a single tree.

Those who decided to stay in Mboundoum Est have been completely abandoned; they live in a dehumanized setting, with no clean water, no dispensary, no school, no public transport, no form of social structure whatsoever. Yet they have done their best to cultivate out of season and even have their own fodder plots, which is extremely unusual. For many years it was claimed that growing fodder crops was too expensive, but the Fulani in Louga have no pasture land and have to pay high prices for groundnut straw, groundnut meal, rice or millet bran, or even cade leaves, acacia albida. It would be more economical for them to grow fodder themselves, now that some of them are settling in Mboundoum Est.

The 'Société d'aménagement et d'exploitation du delta' or SAED (note the use of the word 'exploitation') supervises everything the peasants do. It provides them with land, mostly a hectare of irrigated land per family, which is ploughed and broken down by tractor, often in difficult conditions, since the clay is very hard in the dry season and farm implements get damaged. The peasants are given seed, broadcast it (with no bedding out), weed, at least in theory, and harvest their crop with a sickle; the paddy is threshed on the spot with sticks, or alternatively with a threshing machine, but this pushes up the cost.

So what we have here is a peasantry controlled and supervised at all times, with no opportunity to use their own initiative. The developers, whose competence and motivation are often suspect, were originally paid bonuses based on the acreage cultivated, which meant that they didn't bother about the quality of the work done and were interested only in quantity. If growing conditions are good and the tractors have been able to plough properly and on time, if the irrigation system works properly (the pumping system sometimes breaks down) and, most important of all, if the land has been levelled properly, yields of 3 to 3½ tonnes per hectare can be achieved. The settlers are charged 25,000 CFA francs per hectare for water that costs SAED 80,000 francs – a heavy subsidy, expensive for the state. Altogether, including their other expenses (soil preparation, fertilizers and seed) the peasants have to pay out 80,000 francs per hectare, the equivalent of 2 tonnes of paddy at 40 francs per kilogram. When there's a good harvest they can get by.

But good harvests are the exception rather than the rule, since the average yield is 2·8 tonnes. This means that the peasants are left with the value of 0·8 tonnes, i.e. 32,000 francs per hectare. Much of the land isn't levelled, with the result that yields may drop below a tonne per hectare. A third of the land was a sheer disaster area in 1978. So most of the time the settlers are in debt. It's true that in that case they count as 'disaster victims' and are paid 'disaster compensation', which means that they don't owe any more if the harvest is bad. But at each harvest time they must first pay off their debt; and there isn't always enough paddy left to feed their families properly; as their cash income vanishes they have to find other sources of income. This was how one disillusioned peasant summed up the situation: 'They give us water and they send administrators who put on airs and live it up at our expense. And what do we get out of it? We get more and more into debt, stuck here at the back of beyond without a hope in hell of escaping.'

A start has been made on diversifying agriculture by growing certain types of vegetable, particularly tomatoes for the concentrate factory, which keeps imports down. But in order to show a profit the factory can pay only 17 CFA francs per kilo, so the peasants prefer to sell their crop in Dakar market at 50 francs per kilo. On the other hand transport is very unreliable and it's a long way to travel with perishable goods.

So a vast development scheme has been embarked on, much too big to be well managed, and very expensive. A total of 16,500 million CFA francs had already been invested by 1978, and the eventual return on this, with 5,000 hectares of paddy fields yielding 2·8 tonnes per hectare, was 15,400 tonnes of paddy, which was worth 40 francs per kilo. There were also 800 hectares of tomatoes with a yield of 12 tonnes last year (higher yields have been known), i.e. 10,000 tonnes, for which the peasants are paid 17 francs per kilo. This means a gross income for the peasants of 600 million CFA francs from paddy and 170 million from tomatoes, i.e. a total of 770 million. The ratio of capital invested to gross income is therefore 21:1 (16,500 million: 770 million). Now this figure seems totally uneconomic. A successful business requires a capital of three to five times the value of its annual gross income.

Looked at from Dakar, the supply of water counts in theory as income, if it's properly run. But it isn't, and the only outcome for the peasants is that they're hopelessly in debt. They can perhaps be thought of as receiving welfare, but in practice they are in a subservient position and are totally dependent on the huge government machine and are allowed no responsibility. It's hard to see how this gigantic scheme could ever be profitable. Some of the peasants are starting to protest. Abdoulaye Diop has set up a youth centre in

Ronkh that has saved up enough money to pay for proper levelling of the plots cultivated by the youngsters. They do this during the slack season in the farming calendar, which in the whole of the Sahel means six months in twelve when there is virtually no production at all. It is by using the slack season, this 'hidden productive resource', for productive labour that China managed to bring about a total transformation of its agricultural landscape and enabled output to keep pace with the country's amazingly high population growth of 500 million over thirty years (the population doubled between 1950 and 1980). In Ronkh a start is being made on planting trees and organizing various devices to protect intensive crops from damage by cattle.

When the drought started, Abdoulaye Diop thought of buying up Fulani cattle very cheaply, but he later realized that it was fairer to join forces with the Fulani rather than trying to exploit them. He has set up a commission to deal with disputes between herdsmen and peasants, the idea being to settle their differences without government intervention.

The youngsters in the Ronkh centre all originally came from the village. Like Diop himself, who used to teach in Dakar, they've chosen to come back to live with the peasants, or stay there if they haven't been away, and help them to 'make ends meet'. They've introduced intensive cropping and have had to fight SAED, which thoroughly disapproved of any venture that it couldn't supervise down to the last detail. Their hard work has brought them praise from President Senghor and aid from USAID, particularly a tractor and a truck. The results of their efforts haven't been spectacular, but they've done a great deal better than the cooperative to which their parents belong. Yet the authorities always prefer to deal with the older people, who are more docile than their offspring because their only hope of survival is the land. The other villages round about comment: 'It only works in Ronkh because they go in for politics.' And in Senegal, 'If you don't go in for politics you don't get anything.'

4 *Small-scale projects pay for themselves*

Once again, we see that large-scale hydraulic schemes are too expensive. The cost is over 2 million francs per hectare developed, excluding SAED's overheads. The peasants don't feel at home because they are so closely supervised and in the end they don't work very hard. Since 1974 (though most of the work has been done since 1977) a series of small-scale projects have been set up and equipped in the middle and upper river valleys. By 1980 the 160 projects already in place covered 2,500 hectares.

Some peasant cooperatives or voluntary groups have expressed their willingness to set up a project of this kind. They are therefore encouraged to select a site, a scheme made up of a system of channels is drawn up for them and they are given a free motor-driven pump. But they have previously dug the channels themselves, set up bunds round their small plots, levelled the ground carefully and prepared the soil. The cost per hectare is then between 350,000 and 400,000 francs, five times less than with a large area. Each season the paddy yield is 4·5 to 5 tonnes, because the peasants look after it much better. Peaks of 10 tonnes are occasionally reached, and 25 per cent of the time the figure is above 6·5 tonnes. It will be possible to achieve this figure everywhere.

But the main point is that in 80 per cent of cases the fields carry two crops per year. Rainy-season rice is followed by either maize grown during the cold out-of-season period (November to March) or a kind of rice grown during the hot period (January to June). Yields are better than with rainy-season rice. So the total annual yield is between 8 and 9 tonnes, i.e. three or four times higher than with a large-scale project. The ratio of gross income to capital invested is therefore 1:1, rather than the 1:21 of SAED. So the cost-effectiveness is 21 times higher as a result of the larger amount of labour put in by the peasants.

In these small projects the peasants do all the work by hand, but their plots are too small, between 10 and 20 acres for a family of eight who need 2 tonnes of grain a year. They have to keep to their traditional crops, which can cause problems of rivalry for help with construction and irrigation. Over the last few years the river often hasn't flooded and the peasants told the minister concerned that without the irrigation projects (not that there are many of them) they would have starved to death last year. Those who didn't have any irrigated land had to leave. If they were relying solely on irrigated cultivation they would each need to farm half a hectare to ensure that they had enough food and could earn some cash income as well. But in that case to do everything by hand would involve too much back-breaking work, so the use of draught animals would have to be considered. Some people talk about small-scale mechanization, but then we would be back yet again to the problem of their becoming dependent on tractors, which is highly dangerous.

Water is pumped up with a motor pump, but if there's a shortage of foreign exchange it may not be possible to keep them supplied with petrol. So it would be better to use animal-driven pumps, with a well-sweep or Persian wheel, a bucket chain. There's no shortage of cattle, and this would increase the amount of productive labour, and lessen youth unemployment, particularly during the slack season.

Under the direction of Paul Audat, UNICEF has intervened, acting on the assumption that it is better to give assistance with production than just to hand out food. The Fund has introduced a concept of integrated development which now takes responsibility for men, women and children as well as production. Studies have therefore been made of health and education problems, reafforestation, clean water, medicinal plants, diversified crop patterns and so on.

Compared to the large-scale SAED schemes the small projects are relatively successful and the peasants are fully aware of this. As President Senghor put it: 'It's the peasants, yet again, who've proved cleverer than anyone else. When you ask them what they want they don't hesitate for a second, they ask for small-scale projects. From time immemorial they've had to battle against drought. They need help, they don't need people to think for them.'

5 *The large-scale dams*

The official goal of the Club des Amis du Sahel and the developed countries that finance it is to ensure that the Sahel will be self-sufficient in food by the end of the century. The idea is therefore to harness the two great rivers of West Africa. In the case of the river Senegal there are plans for an anti-salt dam at Diama, near the estuary. The decision to go ahead with this debatable scheme was taken before June 1981 and they can't go back on it now. Another dam was originally planned for the upper valley, at Manantali in Mali, but Jean-Pierre Cot, who came to Senegal in August 1981 (we had alerted him to the problem), wisely refused to finance the scheme, preferring to provide funds for small-scale irrigation projects. The lessons of the Aswan Dam in

Egypt must be learnt – it has made bilharziosis much more common, raised the water table in the Nile delta, and in the end has led to only a very small increase in output; yet it has made the shoreline recede and led to the disappearance of the sardine from the river's mouth.

Even if a success is made of irrigated crops, without causing too much damage and at a rate that will keep pace with population growth, when the Office du Niger irrigation network and the small dams in the Sahel have all failed, the danger is that the resulting oases of prosperity will be surrounded by virtual deserts. If wind erosion grew worse there, the dunes of moving sand would tend to shift at the mercy of the winds and be blown on to the crops and irrigation channels. In other words the basic problem is how to develop the country as a whole. Some people see the solution as taking the capitalist road with big agri-business enterprises – but they failed in Iran. Two have already been set up here. One produces sugar on one huge plantation that is linked to the factory. The other, which specialized in market-garden produce, has already gone bankrupt.

6 Sugar at Richard-Toll, and the risks of agri-business

In the mid-1950s, 5,500 hectares of paddy fields were levelled and irrigated at the town of Richard-Toll, just before the spot where the river Senegal flows into the delta. When this private initiative went bankrupt, the fields were taken over by a state-run company that was also losing a great deal of money. Yields fell and poor-quality ploughing broke up the surface. The whole operation was then transferred to the Compagnie Sucrière du Sénégal, which started growing sugar cane there instead, except in the western sector, which was too saline; the Company made up for this by extending the cane plantations further upriver.

By 1980, after desalination, a figure of over 100 tonnes of cane per hectare was reached. This is an excellent yield, but the sugar content was very low, only 8 to 9 per cent, perhaps because of overwatering (inevitable because of the presence of salt), which goes on until the crop is harvested. This overwatering is expensive.

The business is prosperous because the sugar fetches high prices, much higher than in Europe (230 CFA francs per tonne). In 1980 the cane produced only 40,000 tonnes of sugar, approximately half of the country's total consumption. The rest was imported (brown sugar for instance, from Brazil or elsewhere) and transported at vast expense from Dakar to Richard-Toll for refining – a journey of 370 kilometres by road – and then back to Dakar. No brown sugar is sold at all. But this pointless refining process (which costs four times the price prevailing elsewhere, according to the World Bank) does make price speculation and comfortable profit margins possible. Another point here is that transport costs are overestimated.

Sugar cane produces masses of dry leaves, which could provide the humus so useful for improving the difficult structure of these clayey and salt soils. And the green leaves at the top of the stalks have a fodder value equivalent to three or four tonnes of barley per hectare. Then there's the molasses, which mixed with groundnut straw and shells, straw, rice and so on could provide very valuable livestock feed. Now the Fulani are hunting high and low for cattle feed, and are in a position to pay for it, since their milk sells for 200 CFA francs a litre in Saint-Louis.

As high prices are paid for sugar, all this potential wealth goes up in smoke: the canes are burnt before being cut, which makes harvesting easier, and at the same time reduces the need for labour, although labour would be very productive, and the country suffers from high unemployment. One semi-public company manufacturing sugar near Bobo-Dioulasso in the Upper Volta doesn't burn its canes and has already noticed a distinct improvement in its soils.

Some French companies offering technical assistance have plans, once the big dams have been built, to use the Senegal's waters in two quite distinct areas. On the somewhat higher land, if small irrigation projects were organized, the peasants could grow their own food and produce a surplus to bring in a modest income. This would encourage them to stop their traditional practice of growing crops in the depressions when the waters subside. These depressions could then be allocated to the big firms, to the agri-business sector as practised at Richard-Toll. These companies could grow, say, 2,000 to 3,000 hectares of mass-produced tomatoes in the bigger depressions, and in that case would be delighted to have seasonal labour available on the small-scale irrigation projects round about at harvest time, without having to pay these workers all year round.

We should perhaps refer here to the fate suffered by the peasants practising irrigation in Khuzistan in Iran. The Shah's government expelled them from the small irrigation systems where they'd been growing crops for centuries, to make room for big companies which graciously bestowed large blocks of their shares on the Agricultural Minister or the imperial family. Only 10 per cent of those who'd been driven out of their own lands found work on the large farms that were built there, most of which incidentally were badly run. Most of the rest finished up in the poor districts in south Tehran, unemployed or virtually unemployed. As they had nothing more to lose they weren't afraid to confront the Shah's army, and thus helped to bring about his fall.

7 Aid can perpetuate beggary

In May 1981, preferably before the Agriculture Minister passed that way, the peasants living in Senegal's villages were given a 15-kilo handout of millet per person. It went to everybody, as though all the recipients were poverty-stricken, whereas some of them owned dozens of cattle. Other countries have a more sensible system whereby aid is given in return for labour, i.e. for productive human investment that can lead to an increase in output, such as building low gabion walls across the thalwegs, which means that rainwater runs off more slowly and is forced to sink into the ground. Senegal is therefore in a state of beggary, and if the population explosion continues its dependence will only grow worse.

The 'aid-givers' will only hand out gifts and loans after looking at 'development projects' drawn up in planning offices. This has resulted in a real bonanza for such offices. Electro-watt Consultant Engineers Zurich-Dakar submitted to the Senegal government a Sodagré scheme involving irrigation and mechanized rice farming for the Haute-Casamance region. The company has promised that this project will produce an annual profit of 1,829 million CFA francs between 2000 and 2030. Such an exaggerated claim assumes that the Senegalese government know nothing whatsoever about these problems. It implies a strong element of contempt for the government, some of whose advisers are sweetened by the promise of special privileges if the projects are accepted. This means that the lion's share of any aid for the Third World is creamed off at the outset by experts of all kinds and by the planning offices. On top of this they pay themselves exorbitant salaries.

8 *Dominance of top families in the groundnut cooperatives; peasants undernourished and in debt*

Paul Pélissier[3] has shown that the various peasant societies in Senegal vary widely. Yet with the exception of the Diola of Casamance, who have a democratic society, they all had a hierarchical structure, which was stronger in some cases than others, as Abdoulaye Diop shows in the case of the Tukulor.

With the arrival of Western traders and later the growth of groundnut farming, which took the place of rubber, the nineteenth century saw considerable changes. There was a large increase in the number of merchants in Saint-Louis, who also traded at the ports of call along the river, but the trading posts attached to the big colonial firms in Bordeaux and Marseilles were soon offering fierce competition. They were subsequently superseded by a generation of 'poor whites' and Lebanese. This slowed down the development of a local and independent capitalist system that might have encouraged a degree of agricultural and industrial self-development.

When Senegal became independent it tried to put a stop to exploitation of the peasants by the tax farmers. Like all the tropical African countries it aimed to achieve this by setting up cooperatives. But these too clung to the Western model, and even overlooked the indigenous forms of 'friendly societies', such as tontines, that were already well established in the country. However when independence was granted the peasants stopped handing over their groundnuts to the Lebanese and Syrian tax farmers, to whom they were heavily in debt. They never paid back any of the approximately 4,000 million francs they owed. They were able to break free from them because the cooperatives provided grants to buy food to tide them over between harvests, as the *traitants* had done before. But the cooperatives managed to cream off at least as much from the peasants, who were now led and organized. The series of state-run bodies set up to market groundnuts alone were all very badly run, with inefficiency often even more of a problem than bribery and embezzlement. They therefore relied on the cooperatives, but the cooperatives in their turn often relied on the village shopkeeper, who had premises available and knew how to keep the accounts.

As a result he would frequently become the chairman of the cooperative, and would often choose the 'weighman', whose main function was to weigh the incoming groundnuts. These would initially pay the debts of the cooperative, which had supplied the peasants with seed, fertilizers and equipment on easy terms. These debts represented a heavy burden (particularly in the case of the seed, which the peasants could produce themselves) when the harvest was poor, or even when it was average. The top families don't exploit 'their' peasants as in South America, by paying them meagre wages or charging exorbitant ground rents. They do it in a much easier, less troublesome way, by simply creaming off a considerable proportion of the peasants' surpluses at the marketing stage. The chairman doesn't always issue receipts to the peasants when they pay their entrance fee (1,000 francs). In 1980 these abuses of power necessitated the closing down of ONCAD, a state-run body that exercised control over the cooperatives. When it went bankrupt this cost the national exchequer a great deal, but made a lot of people rich. So transposing the cooperative system into a different sociological milieu enabled 'people of influence' to cream off a big share at the expense of the peasants – a bigger share indeed than that exacted by the Lebanese *traitants*. These influential people hold all the key posts in the civil service, local and national politics, the Party, and even the government.

As one minister, Djibril Sene, put it to us, 'our economic system doesn't work well, because although it claims to be socialist, credit is still handled by the banks, which means by the capitalist economy. In the case of the cooperatives, we didn't pay enough attention to the part played in them by the bigwigs who crush the peasants and grab the whole machinery of power and of the economy – shopkeepers, carriers, marabouts and political leaders.' They often lend money at 100 per cent interest for just a few months. Eighty per cent of the debts due to the cooperatives are owed by a few influential operators who don't usually intend to pay the money back.

It's true that Djibril Sene is trying to restructure the village sections of the cooperatives, where people know one another, in order to reduce the scale of the corruption. But as we have seen, the 'men of influence' are to be found at all levels in the power hierarchy. In fact as far as the peasants are concerned the cooperatives are the responsibility of the state, and they are getting more and more heavily into debt. Malnutrition is increasing in the months leading up to the harvest; the lean periods between harvests are getting longer (they now run from May to December) and are causing increasing hardship.

Provision has been made for granting loans in the form of food to tide the peasants over these lean periods, amounting to 10 per cent of the cooperatives' turnover. But this figure is nowhere near enough to meet their needs. Also, the dietary habits adopted by town dwellers (rice and wheaten bread) are spreading to the rural areas. In 1980 Kaolack had stocks of millet totalling 50,000 tonnes that no one wanted. But in a so-called normal year the country imported 240,000 tonnes of rice and 100,000 tonnes of wheat. Another 120,000 tonnes of cereals were imported in 1980, because the rains failed for the autumn 1979 harvest. If each of the country's six million inhabitants consume 130 kilos of cereals per annum, this gives a maximum figure of 900,000 tonnes. So imports account for too large a share of the country's cereal requirements, and this proportion, which is a yardstick of the country's dependence, is increasing all the time. An attempt is rightly being made to ensure a 20 per cent millet content in Pamiblé bread, but some towndwellers, whose tastes have been corrupted by the habits introduced by the colonial era, refuse to eat it, even though it is better for the health than pure wheat bread. Dakar consumes 100 kilos of rice and 29 kilos of wheat per capita per year, but only 11 kilos of millet, the only cereal crop that is produced locally in large quantities. In other words, Dakar is no longer an African city.

Meanwhile if the peasants want to produce a small surplus of pearl millet or sorghum, it is highly likely that they won't be able to sell it if they've had a good crop. The entire machinery of credit and marketing is still geared first and foremost to groundnuts, the only crop that is exported. Yet groundnuts are a poor crop; they exhaust the soil, make very little for their producer, and have been used – most ill-advisedly – as the basis of a spendthrift urban consumer society. At least Lusaka did make a living out of copper, whereas Dakar only claims to live off groundnuts – in fact, for some years now groundnuts haven't earned the city a living, and it now survives on foreign aid. The reassuring knowledge that someone will always offer a helping hand, since for some reason Senegal is viewed very favourably by the great of this world, means that the élites don't feel as if they're really up against it, as we saw in Tanzania. In Senegal the people who really are being strangled are mainly the poor peasants and the shanty town dwellers. Yet the situation is no better there than elsewhere.

Senegal is trying out a cereal policy, and during the winter of 1978–9 ONCAD bought 108,000 tonnes of millet and sorghum, which it couldn't get rid of. The towns, who are the only major customers, don't want anything but rice and wheat nowadays, especially since the arrival of massive amounts of food 'aid'. The price of imported grain would have to be raised very steeply if the country's own cereal growing is to be 'protected', as is done in the case of industry – if the real goal is self-sufficiency, that is.

9 *Heritage for sale*

President Senghor tells us that 500,000 hectares of land will be irrigated in the year 2025. God willing (*Inshallah*), and given the approval of the bodies that will finance the work, it can be done. But in what circumstances? Meanwhile, there is a shortage of funds. So, like the other countries in tropical Africa, Senegal is selling off its natural resources dirt cheap, not realizing that in so doing it is jeopardizing its own future, and that of future generations. Taïba's phosphates, like those at Lomé, in Togo, are pouring into the rich countries, when in fact the soil in both Senegal and Togo is very short of phosphate, an essential ingredient in fertile soil. In the twenty-first century only Morocco will still have large amounts of exportable phosphates, and by then it will be able to set its own prices. (It can't do so at the moment. In 1979 20 million tonnes of natural phosphates, at a price that had dropped sharply after an unsuccessful attempt to increase it by 200 per cent, only brought in enough to pay half the country's oil bill.)

The iron ore deposits beside the Falémé river on the border between Guinea and Mali have roused the interest of Europe's metallurgical industries. (Since 1977 the price of iron ore has dropped too.) There are 360 million tonnes of oxidized ore with a 62 per cent iron content, and this would work out cheaper than working Lorraine's minette. The country will need to build 720 kilometres of railway line capable of carrying large goods trucks, and an ore port on the short stretch of coast south of Dakar. This would mean that 12 million tonnes of ore a year could be exported for at least twenty years, but what would this cost? After that an even larger deposit of magnetic iron could be worked.

Senegal is bordered by coastal waters that are full of fish, and is being much more successful in developing its fisheries than its agriculture. Yet most of the catch is taken by foreign fishing fleets, particularly Soviet ones, which show little concern for planning for the future and protecting fish that are too young. And most of the catch is exported, when peasant and shanty town children are so short of proteins. One state-run fishing company has gone bankrupt, because it was badly managed and because the Soviet Union sold it faulty boats.

The United States waste ever-increasing amounts of petroleum products, but pollution is becoming almost intolerable in certain areas on its east coast. Never mind, all they need do is export their pollution. So Senegal is selling off one last resource – its atmosphere, its pure air. It has agreed to the setting up of an oil refinery, and the distillation products (5 million tonnes per annum are expected) will add to the barefaced squandering of Uncle Sam. Senegal's coastal waters have already been badly polluted by tank-cleaning by ships out at sea, and this is endangering the future potential for fish farming in coastal waters. What we say here about Senegal applies also to all the scarce and non-renewable resources on the African continent, ranging from Guinea's bauxite to uranium in Gabon and Niger and copper and cobalt in Zambia and Zaïre, not to mention oil in Libya, Nigeria and Gabon, and the immense and coveted wealth of southern Africa, which will be the deciding factor in the political future of this unhappy continent – a future already endangered in every possible way.

10 *Neocolonialist dependence: can the process be reversed?*

Some ministers who have cultivated the right contacts find it easier to get money from the banks and are piling up fortunes. If they are dismissed, as has happened in Zambia, they enter the business world. The multinationals value their contacts and some of them become company chairmen. Luxury villas are springing up along the coast. Whereas Tanzania has managed to cut its fuel consumption by 50,000 tonnes, Senegal's is 20 per cent higher, even though its population is less than a third the size of Tanzania's. And consumption is still going up there, along with the number of private cars on the roads: the figure is rising by 7 per cent per annum, at a time when the wisest policy would be to halt imports. But whenever its oil bill becomes a burden Senegal is given more overseas aid, so the privileged few are spared from giving serious thought to a policy of austerity.

As I showed in an earlier book with reference to an even poorer country, the Upper Volta,[4] this 'aid' doesn't help these countries to become independent – which requires at least a degree of self-sufficiency. By giving priority to the towns, thus encouraging people to leave the rural areas and making the privileged few even more affluent, it drives the countries into a downwards spiral of increased dependence; in other words aid eventually increases the need for foreign aid. The increasing burden of the oil bill is now added to the cost of importing cereals, another commodity whose price is liable to soar. In a normal year more than half the income derived from groundnuts in Senegal needs to be used to pay for cereal imports. In 1980 the figure for buying cereals was way above that for groundnut exports. And those who wield 'food power' will soon take control of this continent if it refuses to take the necessary steps towards ensuring a steady improvement in its self-sufficiency in food.

The total debts owed by Senegal's peasants now amount to the equivalent of two harvests of the kind that occurred in 1979. Food shortages in the periods between harvests are getting worse and worse in the rural areas, and lasting longer. They are leading people to leave the land at a faster rate than usual. By 1980 36 per cent of Senegal's population were town dwellers, and unlike Zambia there is no copper there. Yet the total number of jobs in industry, 26,000, hasn't changed since 1970. The only increase has been in the informal sector – craftsmen, tradesmen and their apprentices – but this applies only to the number of people, not to the size of the market. Nothing is being done to help this sector, yet this would be the least expensive form of job creation. Shanty towns too close to the centre of Dakar are being demolished and replaced with flats and houses for civil servants and other middle-class people who are not directly productive. The poor people who've been driven out of the centre have to spend more time and money on travelling.

While the atmosphere gets increasingly oppressive for the poor, the country as a whole is on the road to ruin – both the soil and the people. Everyone's bank account is overdrawn: private individuals, business firms, companies in both the private and semi-public sectors, and the government itself. There are no private investors and no sign whatsoever of any form of genuine development – capitalist or socialist – on the horizon. Per capita output is dropping all the time, and per capita income, according to the World Bank, fell by 40 dollars between 1977 and 1978. Yet this figure for average incomes gives no indication of the gulf caused by inequalities, which is growing wider daily. The country's oil bill swallowed up a third of its two budgets for 1980 (for basic operating costs and for capital investment), yet much of the oil is wasted. Since its foreign debt burden is going up all the time, Senegal, like most countries in tropical Africa, is threatened with bankruptcy. As with Zaïre, which has immense potential but even greater and more obvious corruption and misuse of power, it isn't in anyone's interest to declare the country bankrupt. (Incidentally, the IMF is more willing, for political reasons, to grant loans to Zaïre, which squanders any loans it receives, than to Tanzania, which would make better use of the money.) In fact the purpose of aid for Senegal is more to prevent a declaration of bankruptcy, since this would have far-reaching effects on the world economy and the whole of the capitalist system. The capitalist system shows little concern for 'developing' the country in the interests of the population as a whole.

How long can this situation last? The peasants have to shoulder the burden of an increasingly cumbersome bureaucracy that will far more often exploit than help them. They're the ones who bear the cost of the country's large-scale schemes, which seem to bring far more benefits to the privileged few. It would be interesting to know how many millions of francs were transferred to Swiss bank accounts as a result of the 1979–80 groundnut harvest, even though it was pretty mediocre. The City Bank, which is based in New York, has a branch in Dakar and has assured readers of *Le Soleil* (virtually the official gazette) that it is 'well placed for handling rapid cash transfers'. We actually saw this in a special issue celebrating twenty years of independence! It may be in the interest of the élites to keep going in the same way, refusing to admit to a state of bankruptcy that is financially advantageous to them, but the peasants are liable to tire of this situation, and to retreat into looking after themselves and their own survival rather than helping to build luxury houses in Dakar. They may even decide to stage a revolt. For the moment they're feudally exploited, but so were French peasants in the 1780s.

There's such an obsession with 'development' (developing who, and what, and how? Such questions don't seem to get asked) that the most important of the interested parties, the ordinary people, have been forgotten. And it has also been forgotten that Senegal is first and foremost an agricultural country. The élites, or at any rate the educated people, have been cut off from this prosaic reality by too sophisticated a lifestyle, too much abstract thinking and too much philosophy, all of which have been fostered by a French-style education system and Parisian tastes. The best thing would perhaps be to go back to square one, and rediscover 'the way to the villages'. At the end of a long career President Senghor himself admits: 'Our real problem lies in the rural areas.'

The country's peasants should be able to produce enough to feed themselves, plus a small surplus that would increase their purchasing power and thus create an outlet for new industries.

Supposing that the peasants can be liberated in this way, what is to be done with all those bureaucrats? Now for many years Senegal has been expanding the education system (which absorbs 30 per cent of the national budget, to produce only a 30 per cent literacy rate), but what will happen to all those managerial and executive staff in the rural areas who often have nothing much to manage, with so many overlapping institutions? The new arts faculty that's been built at vast expense on the outskirts of Saint-Louis is certainly not going to solve the problem: with five thousand students in arts subjects and 5,400 in the first year of their economics degree course, the university is merely turning out future unemployed graduates. It's all very well talking about making the peasants masters of their own destiny, but who's going to help them? It's possible that a tiny fraction of the intelligentsia is more enlightened, and does understand that the country is sinking into a state of dependence, and can't accept this decline. There may be those who are not concerned merely with foreign bank accounts, who can play a decisive part – people who can't but feel disgusted at the growing wretchedness in the rural areas and shanty towns; and who will eventually make a decision to change the prevailing atmosphere. Will the bourgeoisie allow Senegal to play the last few cards it has left? It's a matter of life or death for the poor, for the soil, for the peasants and for the climate of a country that is on the brink of being swallowed up by the desert.

In 1981 Léopold Senghor, who claims to be a socialist and relied on

the support of the socialist party sponsored by his socialist counterparts in France at the Socialist International, left his successor, Abdou
Diouf, a country suffering from desertification, a peasantry on its
knees, and a privileged class entrenched in privileges that he had never
tried to fight. Abdou Diouf, who invited us to Senegal in July and
August 1981, did dismiss three of the more corrupt ministers in
August 1981, but was reluctant to go any further. A new law was
designed to put a stop to people getting rich by illicit means, but will it
ever be properly enforced?

The report we submitted to him is called 'Peasant liberation, the
basis for a "new" rural policy in Senegal'. The campaign to revitalize
the rural areas that was conducted in the period 1960–3 was certainly
intended to liberate the peasants, but Senghor halted it and replaced it
with an innocuous 'Human improvement' campaign.

11 *Desertification and famine in the Sahel*

Apart from the coastal region, stretching from the Casamance (which
could be developed further) to Cameroun, the interior of West Africa,
and particularly its northern fringe along the Sahel, is already
endangered on a large scale. Jacques Bugnicourt[5] has stressed the
extent of the tragedy for a landscape that was once so lush and is now
being desertified, and for people who once knew how to use their land
and make provision for drought, but whose only expedient now is to
emigrate. He shows some possible ways of developing the area (which
are discussed below), but the present government is showing no sign
of carrying out the necessary adaptation. It's true that the countries
affected have set up the 'Comité inter-Etats de lutte contre la
sécheresse au Sahel' (CILSS), to coordinate the fight against desertification. A Sahel Institute has been started up at Bamako, in Mali, but an
obsession with the research workers' international status, a demand
for two hundred airconditioned offices rather than Land-Rovers to
take them into the field, and general delusions of grandeur, threaten to
take precedence over field work with the peasants, which might have
made this institute special and given it a true African quality. It has
created a 'brain drain' from the international institutes instead of
strengthening them, as it should have.

The OECD, to which the developed countries of western Europe,

North America, Japan and Australia belong, together with a number of well-known figures with respectable motivations, have set up the Club du Sahel to liaise with the CILSS. The idea is to achieve something analogous to what the Marshall Plan of 1948 aimed to do for Europe, but these rich countries have no intention of questioning either their own privileges and waste, or those of their allies, the privileged urban minorities who are in positions of power in the Sahelian states. Yet the two are closely linked. The meetings held by the Club du Sahel never tackle these problems, which should be given top priority. One privileged minority won't criticize another, and the peasants aren't invited to the meetings.

As a result of this failure to act, the Sahel is highly likely to become desertified at an increasingly fast rate. Does this mean that its half-starved peasants will have to spend the bad years waiting for food aid, a large proportion of which never leaves the towns? This aid will merely drive them into the towns. But this isn't true of the Sahel alone, for the rich coast of Africa is now being threatened in its turn.

Yet is it wise to try to keep so many people and cattle in crop growing and stock rearing in the Sahel, where attempts to introduce intensive farming will always be more expensive and chancy, and less productive? It would be easier to protect the environment if there were less overgrazing (i.e. fewer cattle), and more fallow land (fewer crops). Senegal has great unused potential in the 'Terres Neuves' of eastern Senegal and in the whole of the Casamance. Instead of people emigrating to Europe – which is anyway starting to reject them – they could be encouraged to move to another African country, providing the states who receive them treat immigrants better.

The southern parts of Mali, the Upper Volta, Niger and Chad could also be developed at less cost and more profitably than the northern regions. And then why should agriculture be thought of as the only possible activity in these semi-arid regions? Crafts and a number of small and medium-sized industries could be developed there. If ever a time comes when a West African metal-working industry is able to give added value to the region's ores instead of their being sold off cheap, the economic future of West Africa will look less terrifying, particularly in view of the fact that south of the Sahel there lies a coastal region with a much greater potential, providing care is taken not to endanger this potential. And this leads us of course to the Ivory Coast.

12 *The Ivory Coast: agriculture 'miracle' or 'mal-development'?*

The natural development along the coast, and particularly that of the evergreen rain forest, which is generally fertile, with a favourable climate, has meant that rich cash crops can be grown there. In the colonial era, coffee, cocoa, bananas and pineapples were developed in the Ivory Coast, along with forced labour for those employed by the European settlers. Félix Houphouët-Boigny's political success started with the abolition of forced labour. When the country became independent he followed the same policy of exporting cash crops, building the country's fortune on the plantations, which were rapidly developed. The Ivory Coast became the world's leading producer of cocoa (400,000 tonnes in 1980–1, though Brazil hopes to do better), superseding its rival, neighbouring Ghana, which was superseded in many other fields as well. It is the leading African coffee producer (361,000 tonnes), ranking third in the world. Other important crops are bananas (145,000 tonnes) and palm oil (118,000 tonnes), which is chiefly produced on huge nationalized plantations (based on the excellent research done by the IRHO),* even though the country claims to be economically liberal. Then there's rubber, and we mustn't forget lumber, whose consumption is nowhere near to being counterbalanced by reafforestation, which is quite inadequate.

Yet Marcel Mazoyer tells us that from the late sixties 'the development of food imports resulting from urban expansion, insufficient food crops and the shortcomings of the peasant economy curtailed profits in foreign currency. The country therefore embarked on growing food crops that were intended to replace imported food.'[6]

Soderiz, a nationalized company, wanted to see the country producing the 100,000 tonnes of rice it imported in 1971, but it envisaged intensive irrigated cultivation, which requires heavy investment (on hydraulic engineering, mechanization, fertilizers and insecticides) and the use of sophisticated technology, and therefore also a large European staff. Taken as a whole this scheme could never have cut back on imports in any substantial way, even if the planned programme had been carried out fully.

J. P. Dozon tells us that it was suggested that the Ivory Coast's peasants should have 'a method of rice development that would be laid

---

* Institut de recherche sur les huiles de palme et les oléagineux.

down in advance, in order to restructure the rural areas on a more modern and rational basis, so as to pave the way for increased agricultural output in the country'.[7]

In order to achieve this, Soderiz 'nationalized' the low-lying converted swamp land which had previously been held in common by the villages. It granted the right of use of this land to selected volunteers, and supervised their work, the idea being to create a sort of artificial peasantry. But the peasants adopted a very different policy. The local ethnic group obtained grants of land, took on paid workers or share-croppers and re-established a traditional social structure. It's true that the rice got off to a quick start, but only when the selling price shot up from 30 to 70 CFA francs per kilo, and chiefly in the form of rainy-season cultivation rather than following the technocrats' plans, which cost too much.

Having bought the rice at such high prices (from collectors who took a fat margin for themselves), Soderiz couldn't sell all of it to the wholesalers gathered in the stronghold of the chamber of commerce. The rice rotted, Soderiz closed down and ordinary business took over again at the usual exorbitant rates.

This is an example of the total failure of what Marcel Mazoyer called 'transferring advanced technologies that aren't always appropriate, affect only a tiny fraction of the Ivory Coast's peasantry, and are incapable of ensuring any far-reaching and self-sustaining development of the peasant economy'.[8] Incidentally the relative prosperity of the traditional plantations we referred to at the beginning was basically achieved at the expense of soil fertilty built up over the centuries by humus from the forest; but now the thick forest cover is fast disappearing. If it goes on being destroyed at the present rate of 450,000 hectares per year, there will be virtually nothing left by 1985. In 1956 there were 12 million hectares of forest; in 1980, only 1·4 million. A reafforestation rate of 10,000 hectares per annum was planned, but in fact only a little over 3,000 is the true figure: in other words 160 times less than is being cut down. Official development plans based on clearing forest land for cultivation are rapidly leading to the soil being abandoned and ruined after bearing food crops for only three or four years. The practice of leaving shrubland to lie fallow for long periods, which ensured that in fifteen to twenty years it was fertile once again, is tending to disappear.

This 'success' has also been achieved by exploitation of the workforce of Mossi immigrants from the Upper Volta or Mali, who are often paid half or even a third of the official wage rate, or are victimized by the share-cropping system. The poor country from which this labour force originates pays for their upbringing and looks after them when they're old, but their labour only profits the host country. The same could be said of African immigrants in France.

The relative prosperity of a few thousand planters emphasizes the relative poverty of the peasants on the savannah in the centre and north of the country, where the average family, working entirely without machinery, produces only about a tonne of cereals a year. This isn't enough to get rid of malnutrition or periods of famine before harvest time, which are still very common in the area round Korhogo, or to compete with the cereals grown on the highly mechanized farms that Léopold Senghor refers to as 'Euro-American'. Tractors are therefore being introduced, but they cost twice as much in the Ivory Coast as in France's wheat-growing Beauce region – a difference that certainly can't be justified by the extra transport costs. The difference is even greater when it comes to spare parts and after-sales service (when it's available). In its 1978 annual statement the Compagnie Ivoirienne de développement des textiles, which has been trying to develop cotton growing, admits that blocks of mechanically cleared land have an average life of seven years, after which the soil has been ruined; and that the seed-cotton yield is only 800 kilos per hectare. It goes up to one tonne per hectare with animal-drawn implements, and 1,300 kilos with purely manual labour. The area cultivated per family is higher when animal-drawn implements are used than with mechanization (2·2 hectares as compared to 2 hectares), so tractors are a failure.

The most sweeping failure of all in financial terms was that of Sodésucre, which set up huge plantations of irrigated canes equipped with ultra-modern sugar refineries. No one knows what's to be done with them, because if all the plant and equipment already set up or planned there is put into operation, there are sure to be huge losses, as the world sugar price hasn't been able to maintain its high 1974 levels. A total of 134,600 tonnes of sugar were produced in 1980–1, but the forecast of 300,000 tonnes by 1983 definitely won't be achieved. Not everyone suffers losses, however: the European firms who built the factories made huge, indeed scandalous profits, especially because a rumour was put around in 1973 that there was going to be a prolonged sugar shortage, and therefore sugar would fetch very high prices, which boosted sales of factory buildings. 'We were overcharged by 34,000 million francs for four of these agro-industrial complexes,' says Félix Houphouët-Boigny.

Most of the peasants from the savannah in the Centre-Nord district of the Ivory Coast, many of whom have been ruined, tend to emulate their fellow sufferers from poverty, the Mossi, and migrate to the plantations in the forest belt, but the need for labour is dropping fast, and so is the amount of land worth clearing. They therefore set off for the sprawling capital, Abidjan, which is yet another town with huge and growing numbers of people unemployed. A foreigner who stayed at the Hôtel Ivoire and drove past the Hollywood-style villas in the Cocody districts could easily believe – if, as is often the case, he was very ill-informed – that he was in a wealthy country. In 1968 a television announcer in the Ivory Coast tackled me with the words: 'You begrudge us our Mercedes and our villas with swimming pools, but isn't it better to arouse envy than pity?' When I reminded him of the wretched poverty of those who slept out in the streets, of the people in Treichville and Plateau, he showed no inclination to keep the discussion going.

The wealth of Abidjan's new bourgeoisie (whether employed by the state or by the free enterprise sector) is based on exploiting the planters (who themselves exploit the fertility of the forests and their immigrant labour). It's quite common for the 'Caisse de stabilisation et de soutien des produits agricoles' (Fund for Stabilizing and Funding Agricultural Produce, though it would be more logical to call it the Fund for Exploiting the Planters), which has a monopoly on exports, to pay the coffee and cocoa planters only a quarter of the sums received for sales abroad; during the coffee boom of 1975–7 the figure sometimes fell to a mere 10 per cent.

Like the 'Brazilian miracle⁹ the 'Ivory Coast miracle' is proving to be highly circumscribed. It's true that agricultural output there has expanded faster than anywhere else in tropical Africa, and a class of planters of varying degrees of prosperity has developed. But once again those who benefit from this state of affairs are the privileged urban minorities who are in positions of power, both Africans and Europeans. The national debt keeps growing, and the amount of interest payable is reaching dangerous levels; this danger is accentuated by the fact that profits earned by the French companies there, plus a large percentage of the salaries paid to the various European helpers and advisers, most of whom are French – and there are far more of them now than there were before independence – are sent out of the country. Although the Ivory Coast has been given a large amount of aid and loans – much more than the poorer countries – the net flow of capital, within this typically neocolonialist framework, may well be unfavourable. It's hard to work out the figures, but we feel pretty sure that the flow is negative for the Ivory Coast.

When I was in Lagos in 1973 I noticed that there were very few whites in the cars driving across the bridges, perhaps one in a hundred cars. But if you stand at one end of the Houphouët-Boigny bridge in Abidjan you'll see, as I did the very day after I'd been in Lagos, that one car in three has white occupants. The Ivory Coast has been, not decolonized, but overcolonized. Félix Houphouët-Boigny, the chief architect of a form of prosperity that is fast breaking down, still hasn't assured his succession. But the curtain has come down and belief in the miracle is fading. A reversal of the former trend is beginning to emerge, with the country's increasing debt burden, rapid destruction of the natural environment, and increasingly marked inequalities.

13 Guinea-Bissau: Amilcar Cabral and attempted recolonization by stealth

'If you fed all the [economic] data available for our country into a computer, it would come up with the answer that we don't exist.' The speaker was Luis Cabral, then the president of the very small country which was formerly called Portuguese Guinea. It played a well-known part in the progressive movements during the fight for liberation that was led by the agronomist Amilcar Cabral until his assassination in January 1973. People still remember the schools beneath the trees – illiteracy reached record levels here – and the 'people's stores' working on the barter principle in the liberated areas. The Friendship Institute in Conakry used to train those who would have managerial jobs in the future state. Cabral had spent a lot of time visiting the villages, analysing his country's social structure, which is feudal in the Fulani and Mandingo areas and democratic in the villages where Balante rice-growers live. Yet, true to his Marxist principles, even the agronomist Cabral thought that 'the peasantry doesn't represent the main revolutionary force', even if 'we have based the whole of our armed struggle on them. . . . Unlike the Chinese communists, we've had to win their support by working very hard at it.'[10]

He claimed that the African petty bourgeoisie 'take power – I don't know on whose behalf, but the fact is that they take it. . . . [They have to choose] between joining forces with imperialism to defend their existence as a petty bourgeoisie, or joining forces with the workers and the peasants, who are obliged to take and control power with an eye to the coming Revolution. In short, what is being asked of the petty bourgeoisie? That they should commit suicide – the Revolution excludes them from power.'

When we were in Bissau in autumn 1979 we found that the 'petty bourgeoisie' was alive and well. It held the administrative posts and in the last analysis most of the power in the country, since it is the only social class capable of operating the machinery of government in yet another would-be 'modern' state. It has inherited from the Portuguese what has been referred to as a 'non-colony', with no industries other than twenty-three distilleries run on a semi-industrial basis and producing a nation of alcoholics, and a modern brewery built mainly to serve the army, but finished just in time for independence. (It has also inherited, however, the unwieldy and inefficient bureaucracy of the Portuguese, and hasn't yet been able to replace it, though the civil servants claim to have been 'converted to the spirit of the struggle'.)

But Guinea-Bissau, with fewer than a million people living on 36,000 square kilometres, is surrounded on all sides by countries that are heirs to the former French empire: Senegal, which is very much a neo-colony, and Guinea, where France is rebuilding its links. The country is being showered from all sides with the most modern plant and equipment, i.e. the most ill-suited to its true situation, which involves a shortage of capital and technicians and a surfeit of unskilled labour.

The seven industrial schemes that were decided in 1976–7 provided for 12 million dollars' worth of investments, but were expected to create only 373 jobs. This meant that each new job would cost 32,000 dollars, in a country where the population was increasing by at least 15,000 per annum, and where government revenue was only 600 million pesos. A scheme that was going to create a mere handful of jobs was intended to absorb an investment of about 10 per cent of GNP. But since then even more colossal errors have been committed, reaching such a pitch that we believe that they are likely to jeopardize the whole economic future of this small country, and therefore its policy of independence.

Guinea-Bissau has virtually no roads, and although the waterways are more economical, they inevitably serve only very restricted areas. Yet a 'developed' company has somehow managed, by using methods that are somewhat suspect, to sell them an absolutely crazy scheme. A huge factory is planned at Cumere, very close to Bissau, the capital, to husk most of the country's paddy – to produce rice. The paddy is to be concentrated in this one spot, at vast expense, which means that the husk encircling the grain, which ought to stay in the villages, will have to be transported as well. If small-scale workshops were set up in the areas where the rice is grown, the added value involved in the processing stage would stay there and could be invested in the villages.

The urge to build everything on a giant scale adds to the costs at every stage, and has already led to many bankruptcies. The Belgian agronomist H. Dupriez cites the Ivory Coast as an example. The large nationalized factories there notched up a cost price of 70 francs per kilo for husked rice, compared with 42 francs when Diola craftsmen used small diesel-driven husking machines housed in straw huts. On top of this, the nationalized factories made an average loss of 20 francs per kilo, and two days' pay for the experts 'advising' these factories was equal to the average annual income of an African farm labourer.

The Cumere scheme envisages most of the country's groundnut output being processed there to make refined oil (which has less food value than crude oil), cattle cake for the export market, soap and so on. Here too the idea of concentrating the whole output in one place would mean heavy transport costs for the groundnut shells and would add to the cost price. The whole Cumere scheme is going to be disastrous for the country's agriculture and for the economy as a whole.

A scheme for a vast sugar refinery at Gambiel that was supposed to produce 60,000 tonnes of sugar a year has been abandoned (thank goodness it has – it was heading straight for bankruptcy). The scheme that is now being implemented, which provides for 10,000 tonnes, still seems too grandiose to us, because in 1979 it was costed at 35 million dollars (the price has gone up since then), which means 3,500 dollars per tonne of sugar! The irrigation dam alone was expected to cost 5 million dollars. We were told that the 27 hectares of canes planted in 1979 were already causing management problems, so what is going to happen with the 1,500 hectares envisaged in the scheme? Is the soil really suitable for irrigation? Part of the existing distilleries could have been used to produce unrefined sugar at very little cost. The cost of the additional plant needed (for evaporating the cane juice) would have represented some hundreds of dollars a time for a few dozen tonnes of crude sugar, i.e. 10 to 20 dollars per tonne of sugar.

We ended by criticizing the pumping system for the dry-farming method of rice-growing in Contubuel, feeling that the soil was on the whole too sandy to be suitable for rice growing. In every case you could sense the looming presence of the plant and equipment salesmen, who are often of questionable honesty, and tend to exploit the inexperience of the country's leaders by dangling shiny new 'modern' projects before them. They couldn't care less about a really healthy economic development for Guinea-Bissau – i.e. one that benefits the whole of the population, and therefore the peasants.

And yet here too the peasants are in danger of being drawn towards a capital that may still be modest now, but is once again already growing too fast, and is the only town to benefit from considerable amenities. Bissau already consumes six times as much electricity as the whole of the rest of the country, and the schemes that are being carried out will make this gap even wider.

Yet the peasant communities in Guinea-Bissau are first-rate, the most remarkable being no doubt the Balante, who grow rice in the coastal regions. When we came to a Balante village we saw a whole lot of people busy building a hut. The women were pugging clay to make adobe bricks. Other people were bringing wooden poles to make the basic structure and the framework for the walls. We asked them how much they were being paid for doing this work, but our innocent question was met by indignant stares – they were building a house for an old man in the village: and of course they weren't being paid for it. This reveals a very different morality from our own, which is not a good model.

By their hard work, the Balante are gradually turning the coastal mangrove swamp into high-yield rice fields, once the rains, which are very heavy in the south of the country, have desalinated them. One elderly peasant asked us for 'honey and cloth' so that the rice output could be pushed up faster. (Here too rice is in short supply.) The honey is used to make hydromel, which is an added incentive to crop-growers. And if they make some money from their rice, they'd like to be able to buy their womenfolk some cloth.

In 1981 food shortages in Guinea-Bissau were getting worse and creating a dangerous situation.

In a note on the industrial development strategy being followed in Guinea-Bissau, the Brazilian economist Ladislaw Dowbor offers a timely reminder that industry is an expensive process that requires a very high turnover, and that it is more likely to throw an economy off balance than to make it dynamic. Guinea-Bissau has had the good fortune not to inherit an industrial sector geared to exports or to satisfying the luxury tastes of the privileged few. If the country sets up large and expensive units such as those we've referred to, with large factories supplied with immediate possession, using the fallacious argument of economies of scale, it would be building its economy upside-down, and forcing its agriculture to adapt accordingly – a method that has led to failure everywhere else. You can't supply a sophisticated factory with agricultural produce that's been cultivated with hoes and wooden swing ploughs and emerge unscathed. On top of this, this type of factory needs an entire economic, financial and technical infrastructure, roads, ports with boats that call there regularly, and a whole trading network. Dakar has got all this, but Bissau hasn't.

Dowbor sensibly advises Guinea-Bissau to set up a whole series of small units throughout the country, since this would raise the overall level of technology and create a more dynamic process of industrialization. We outlined a similar proposal in our 1979 report. The villages would be equipped with small machines for husking rice and groundnuts, grain mills, and small pumps worked by hand or driven by motors or animals. Farm implements would be made on the spot, to be worked by hand or drawn by animals. The next stage would be to set up a textile industry to use the cotton output and provide clothing for the home market. Fishing, which has great potential, and lumbering, which must have value added locally, would produce the first supplies of foreign exchange, to tide the country over until agriculture, helped by locally made means of production, started producing surpluses, though the country's food needs must first be taken care of, and even improved. When he sent us this note Ladislaw

213

pointed out: 'It's very down-to-earth, but unfortunately that's where out problems are.'

14 Cape Verde: 'an implacable war on desertification'

The Cape Verde archipelago lies off Dakar, halfway between Portugal and Brazil, and is generally referred to as part of Africa, though it isn't at all like the mainland. The people look different, and so does the landscape, which, though desolate, is one of the most astonishing anywhere in the world. It seems like a lunar landscape, with arid soil and broken stones, then suddenly you round a jagged mountain and come across a fertile valley, an oasis covered with canes growing in the shade of coconut palms, lush vegetation. Yet in spite of these contrasts the overall picture is arid, and nature seems barren here. It rarely rains, or if it does the rain is no use: some of the mountain tops get almost as much rain in a couple of nights as falls on Paris in a whole year; this torrential rain washes away the soil, scours the valleys and then hurtles into the sea. And meanwhile the country suffers from a water shortage! The goats eat paper and the coffee shrubs soak up the moisture brought by the fogs through their leaves.

The Portuguese reached these islands in about 1460. They were uninhabited, and the Portuguese thought of them originally as a stopping-off place from which to settle Africa's coastal fringe, then subsequently as a base for the voyage to South America. Having started as a mere port of call the islands later became the first centre for the slave trade (before Gorée). The Portuguese continued to control them right down to 1975, when they achieved independence as a result of the guerrilla warfare waged, with their help, in Guinea-Bissau. Amilcar Cabral, who was born in Batafa in Guinea, but whose parents came from Cape Verde, was keen to maintain links between the countries. A single party has survived, and the president of Cape Verde, Aristide Pereira, is its general secretary. Since the fall of Luis Cabral in Bissau the links between the countries have weakened.

Merchant adventurers and explorers from Portugal and Flanders brought slaves there and went in for intensive cross-breeding right from the start. By the eighteenth century the islands had become too small for their growing population and a series of droughts led to appalling famines, forcing large numbers of people to emigrate.

This strong tradition of emigrating has disturbed the islands' cultural patterns, what with the constant toing and froing, the emigrants coming back from the United States or Europe, and money being sent home from abroad. The villages seem more like those in the Algarve or the Alentejo in southern Portugal than in Senegal or Guinea-Bissau, except that the colour of people's skins is darker than in Portugal, especially in Santiago, which was colonized earlier. In Santiago there were latifundia farmed by share-croppers, who were so ruthlessly exploited that they staged several revolts. They had to hand over half their annual harvest in rent, and the landowner would take all the fruit grown there (mangoes, coconuts and so on), plus even the castor oil beans that grow wild there. The northern islands were colonized later, in the eighteenth and nineteenth centuries, and a system of peasant farming developed there, with very small holdings worked by the owners. Cane is still grown at Santo Antão on hillside terraces, and is used to distill the famous rum that is one of the island's major activities and a goldmine for bars all over the archipelago. But over the years these small farms have been broken up and they are no longer capable of providing enough work or income. The government pays modest wages for road building and work to prevent erosion, so as to avoid having a population living off begging or welfare payments. In fact the country has decided that in order to overcome its unpromising natural conditions it must switch from fighting the Portuguese to fighting erosion and desertification. When we were in Fogo, a volcano masquerading as an island, the local people were busy all over the place building dry stone walls crisscrossing the hillsides. The women were carrying the stones on their heads on trays. Other people were using mallets to bed small, irregular paving stones to make steep roads, getting them absolutely straight by using lengths of string – a real engineering feat!

Every Sunday the peasants emerge from their hamlets, and come flocking down the hillsides to the churches in the bigger villages, the women wearing their smartest clothes. The Party flag is carried at the head of the procession, but is left outside the church. On Good Friday there was a procession to Mindelo followed by a crowd of worshippers, and on Easter Sunday a grander one wended its way down the hillside from the old town to Ribeira Grande. Half the local population crowded into the church, but strong competition came from the music and dancing across the road, with Cape Verdean music playing

– another facet of daily life on these islands. They clearly aren't really part of Africa, though they rightly want to set up close contacts with the newly emerged nations on the mainland. Yet from the point of view of climate the country is more like an extension of the Sahel in the Atlantic.

Imagine that there was a world government, with the task of deciding where agriculture is to be developed. If it looked into the natural conditions prevailing in Cape Verde (the fickle climate, scarce water supplies, steeply mountainous landscape, the great difficulties with communications, etc.), it might well decide to leave the archipelago out of its investment projects, since it could find more profitable territory virtually anywhere else. Yet this new nation has already embarked on the very difficult process of agricultural development, seeing it as a logical follow-up to its struggle for independence, since it is an essential basis for economic independence. Apart from the stone walls to combat erosion, they've built countersloped earth banks along the contour lines, to break the force of the torrential rains and make them soak into the soil. When these are ready, they plant mesquite or parkinsonia at 1·5-metre intervals to provide wood and, more important, fodder for the goats, to protect the soil, and to act as a windbreak for the upland crops they cultivate – maize mixed with beans, *niébés* (the cow-pea: *Vigna unguiculata* or *V. caljang*) or pigeon-peas (*Cajanus cajan*). It is extraordinarily hardy, and will protect hillsides on its own, as well as giving both seeds, fodder (its leaves) and wood (its stalks), though only in very small quantities. Maize is tending to grow higher up, because the rainfall increases with the altitude, especially on the side where the wind blows; but on steeper hillsides it aggravates erosion. It would be a good idea to plant trees instead of annuals, because with their deep roots they make better use of the irregular rainfall, particularly where the soil covering is thick. With tenant farming – the share-cropping system was abolished in 1976, though rents are still high – the custom of keeping all the fruit for the landowner doesn't encourage the tenant to look after these trees.

The landowners seem even more like parasites where the land is irrigated. This is the only land that produces large and, most important, regular yields, and rents are exorbitant. We came across a rent of 1,100 francs per hectare near the capital, Praia. The recent string of years with little rainfall has reduced the water flow, and as a result yields are dropping on land that isn't well watered. One tenant farmer was forced into selling off some of his cattle to pay his rent. The Portuguese courts of arbitration used to be presided over by magistrates who inevitably acted as upholders of property, so when the country became independent it set up people's courts that were more favourable to tenants. But they were closed down as a result of repeated protests and shrieks of complaint from the landowners (there were a lot of them now and the authorities, whose first concern was to create a united nation, didn't want to alienate them).

We believe that this was a retrograde move, particularly regrettable in that the ground rent doesn't apply to the soil but to the crucial prerequisite for any form of agriculture, water for irrigation, which has in theory been nationalized. At least half the traditional rent could therefore be allocated for water supplies, and transferred, not to the state (the *Communist Manifesto* of 1848 insisted that ground rent should be confiscated for the benefit of the state), but to the local authorities, to pay for public works.

A little over half of the total area that is being irrigated at present, nearly 1,000 hectares out of 1,850, is used for growing sugar cane, which initially produced crude sugar that was at first exported to Brazil. The cane is still crushed with a *trapiche*, which consists of three steel cylinders turned by a pair of oxen, but the juice is left to ferment – nowadays in metal drums, instead of the old wooden casks. After ten days the resulting cane 'wine' is distilled to produce the rum which, with its roughly 21° alcohol content, is very popular with the local people – virtually all of the two million or more litres produced in this way per annum are consumed by the home market of slightly over 300,000 inhabitants living on 4,000 square kilometres. A distillate of fermented sugar and water is also made, plus various other even more noxious substances that work out cheaper.

As well as anti-erosion measures, great effort is being expended on reclaiming surface water by filtering it or storing it behind dams, then building wells and galleries at vast expense to draw up the subterranean water. It is hoped that as a result the country will have 130 million cubic metres of water per annum available for irrigation by 2005, i.e. enough to irrigate 8,600 hectares. But this will involve very heavy expenditure, and at least twenty-five years' work.

This can never be achieved without international aid, large quantities of which are being paid to Cape Verde at the moment. Without it, thousands of the inhabitants would have died of starvation, because there has been scarcely any respite from droughts since 1969. The official records refer to fifty-eight famines and 250,000 deaths from starvation in the period 1747 to 1900. In our glorious twentieth century this figure has gone up by 135,000, which explains why 700,000 Cape Verdeans are living abroad. Their families left the country to avoid starvation, going initially to the United States, where they were welcome new recruits to the whaling industry, and nowadays to various European countries – Portugal, Holland, Italy and France.

The country therefore couldn't have managed without aid, and has made good use of it on the whole, better than in Guinea-Bissau. Whereas the Portuguese confined themselves to roads, major expenditure now goes on anti-erosion measures, reafforestation and water collection. Yet there are only enough jobs for one member of the family to be in work. If, as so often happens, a woman has been abandoned and is bringing up her children alone, she can't manage on wages of 6 francs a day, in return for very hard work. There are still apparently 30 per cent unemployed, and in the rural areas virtually everyone is under-employed. We saw children waiting outside restaurants to beg for even a tiny piece of bread, clearly as hungry as those we saw in Andalusia in 1951. Malnutrition is still a serious problem in the rural areas and on the outskirts of towns.

We repeat that the country couldn't have managed without the aid, but it does have its negative side. The donors provide their own equipment and technology, which isn't necessarily the most appropriate for the country concerned. Lorries and small vans driving along paved roads and tracks pass by women and little girls walking in single file carrying water containers on their heads, a few donkeys weighed down with more of the precious liquid, but not a single cart. The nationalized farms are getting a few tractors (which aren't easy to use in the narrow valleys), but animal-drawn ploughs are quite unknown. Nowhere near enough is being done to develop wind power and solar energy, and virtually the only source of energy used is oil, while the country can afford it, that is. (Seeing Guinea-Bissau piling up debt upon debt the World Bank said politely: 'We'll come back and see you in a couple of years, when you need our help.') Exports only pay for 5 per cent of imports, a record low, but for the time being the country is getting all the foreign exchange it needs in the form of aid and money sent home by emigrants (though this is spent on eating better, buying land and building attractive houses, rather than on productive investment – it's high time this was realized). As a result it is squandered: for instance tonnes of building cement are used, when the traditional stone houses, which are very attractive, would result in more jobs and wouldn't require anything in the way of foreign exchange, since pozzolana mixed with lime can be used as mortar. But the technical colleges teach their students all about cement and nothing about ashlar. Aid is unlikely to maintain its present level, and the acquired habit of squandering funds will constitute an extra handicap.

Greater economic stringency is therefore needed. On the island of Fogo a sea-level spring has been tapped in order to pump the water to an altitude of 400 metres and irrigate a small plateau covering 15 hectares. This involves investment expenditure of at least 80,000 francs per hectare, plus the electricity system. The water comes to 2·2 francs per cubic metre, which is too expensive for crop growing, and this figure will rise with the price of oil. (The desalination plant at Mindelo produces water at 11 francs per cubic metre. Thirty years ago we were promised that by 1980 desalinated water would be available cheaply.) As the water in this case was an underground stream that ran down the sides of the volcano it would have been better to tap it high enough for gravity to do the carrying. Also, the geothermal activity of the volcano ought to be made into a source of energy.

Priority ought to be given to saving water. At the moment large amounts are being wasted both in the towns, chiefly because of the use of Western-style lavatories, and in the fields, with clay water channels, crops too sparsely sown, low-yield varieties of cane, with low sugar content, and zones that are flooded. Using watering cans would represent a saving, but it wouldn't be 'modern'. The only way to force people to economize is to stop subsidizing water and sell it at cost price. Wood is in short supply too, yet it's being wasted all over the country. Stills could be as airtight as baker's ovens. And the potters bake their clay pots in the open air, whereas if they used a kiln they wouldn't waste so much fuel, straw and dung, which are so badly needed for other uses.

The byproducts of the various crops, such as banana tree leaves and stems, could be used much more widely for cattle. Cassava leaves, which are so popular in Africa, aren't eaten here at all, and nor are vegetable leaves. Yet the forage trees that I've been recommending in vain for so many years are miraculously beginning to turn the arid hillsides green. They form the basic ingredient of a form of development covering agriculture, forestry and stock rearing that can eliminate reliance on irrigation. By the beginning of the twenty-first century it is hoped that on top of the 8,000 hectares that will have been irrigated by then, there will be another 100,000 hectares that have been reafforested (i.e. over 100 million trees). They are taking root now, and the island's goats are kept firmly tethered, whereas in Mali, near the border with Mauritania, a Canadian reafforestation scheme was abandoned because the Canadians refused to call in the army to restrain the goats – or their owners. It's true that agriculture is the starting point for the country's development and should still be given priority, at least during the eighties. But in view of its many limitations the accent will subsequently have to be put on other activities. The first thought that springs to mind is fishing, including deep-sea fishing, since the coastal waters are nowhere near as full of fish as those of the continental shelf round Africa. Experiments in fish farming would be well worth the effort, and the same applies to algae. But the essential ingredient in the country's future development will be industry and the service sector (providing a stopping-off point for ships and planes), and this means that thought will have to be given to the training of young people. Most of those who will be at work at the end of the century are already alive. The country's population is very young, and this tendency has been accentuated by the number of adult males who emigrate. But the schools still disregard manual work entirely.

There is one positive aspect amidst all these problems though, and in an area where we have directed much of our criticism of Africa. Cape Verde has suffered hardly at all from the teething troubles associated with independence that have afflicted other countries ranging from Senegal to Zambia. It has considerable political determination, and the prime minister, Pedro Pires, whose personal aspirations are as modest as his aspirations for his country, told us that he wanted it 'to go forward slowly but surely'. The Cape Verdeans may talk firmly of putting an end to 'man's exploitation of man', but no one refers to building socialism by forced marches. Private enterprise still plays a part in the economy, and no one contemplates nationalizing a small business that is playing its part – in that it is distributing income – and creating a lot of jobs.

The Party here isn't monopolized by a small vanguard and a tiny political committee of the sort that only too often claims to be in possession of the Truth with a capital T. Instead it tries to educate its members, to instil a sense of responsibility and to organize participation by the people. It knows that dialogue is more difficult than issuing diktats, but tries to get a dialogue going all the same. People who've come back from Angola or Mozambique, where they had executive jobs and were used to giving orders, aren't always 'politically sound', but they're all welcomed. The constant coming and going of those who've emigrated abroad is a dangerous factor because it tends to Westernize the country and to lead to cultural dominance from abroad, but it's important to take into account all the objective conditions.

This flexible but firm political will, plus the aid the country receives (but the Cape Verdeans know how to use it productively), means that whereas on the African continent people talk about erosion and desertification a great deal, here in Cape Verde, which suffers from much worse conditions than the great majority of the Sahelian states, and even more than the rest of the continent, an efficient step-by-step struggle is being waged against them. *A lutta continua*, as they say in Mozambique.

7 Conclusions

Must Africa Starve? by René Dumont

Two development decades, twenty years of failure

The idea was that the two development decades trumpeted in the United Nations and publicized all over the affluent world by the mass media were supposed to free the Third World – providing they listened to the proper authorities, the rich and powerful – 'from poverty, disease and ignorance', and first and foremost to protect them from the most appalling sword of Damocles, the scourge of famine. In order to achieve this, tens of thousands of experts were mobilized. They came in every shape and size and at every level of competence and commitment, which cost very dear at first. Working with local people with Western education, they drew up hundreds and thousands of plans and development schemes for specific sectors or whole countries and for one- or five-year spans. They took as their starting-point – and still do, only too often – the philosophy developed by a 'leading' economist, W. W. Rostow, which claims that the poor nations have only to follow the Western 'model' to arrive surely (if slowly) at a position where all their people will enjoy great wealth, the wealth of the 'Mass consumer society'.

Some people still believe this, refusing to question the famous Western model and putting the blame solely on the inadequacy of the people who put it into effect. Yet repeated failures have occurred in every possible field, and ought to disqualify the model. Malnutrition is increasing, though it's still difficult to give exact figures. It is the major cause of infant mortality, which is still high, and is a fair gauge of the problem. The fact that in many villages half the children die before the age of five emphasizes the failure of the health services, which have put an end to traditional medicine, yet have been unable to provide an effective substitute, except for those town dwellers who can afford it. This failure is as obvious in West Africa as it is in Tanzania and Zambia.

According to the International Labour Office's figures for 1973, more than two thirds of the people of Africa were still living in conditions of extreme poverty. And the absolute number of very poor people is rising all the time. This is tied up with the problem posed by the continent's ten million unemployed and fifty-three million markedly underemployed, most of them in the villages. These ILO figures, which exclude South Africa, seem to us extremely optimistic. And since 1973 they have been increasing at an even faster rate. Remember that the World Bank has already said that it is absolutely incapable, under any circumstances, of stamping out this poverty before the end of the century.

The most serious problem is posed by the failure of agriculture, which is the main cause of malnutrition, unemployment and the growing number of imports. A great deal of hard work has gone into developing rice growing in West Africa, and output almost doubled between 1962 and 1977. But as consumption grew much faster than output, imports had to be stepped up at the same time – they have increased by over 300 per cent and now amount to well over 1 million tonnes. Food aid has helped to increase the consumption of bread, and therefore wheat imports. Imports of foodstuffs rose by 35 per cent between 1962 and 1972, whereas per capita output went down by at least 4 per cent. Since 1972, with widespread droughts – though they are not the only reason – declining output and increasing imports have been an ever more serious problem.

Apart from Egypt, the Sudan and Tunisia – and to a certain extent the Ivory Coast and Tanzania – no other African country has really given priority in its investment programme to agricultural development. Very small amounts of government expenditure were earmarked for agriculture, since the lion's share went on administrative buildings and other equipment, the urban areas and industry. Food crops have received – and still are receiving – the least attention of all, since the only substantial effort has been made in the direction of cash crops for export.

Despite the priority it has been given, industrial development still has not been adequate. Its share of Africa's GNP rose only 2½ per cent between 1960 and 1970 (from 9 to 11·5 per cent). Africa accounts for only 8 per cent of industrial activity in the Third World, and here too it ranks bottom in the world, as it does for the overall growth of its GNP. It is still handicapped by a deterioration in the terms of trade, which have been worsening steadily for twenty years – a process accelerated in the last few years largely because of the rise in the price of petroleum products. Let's think about these figures for a moment: Tanzania, with a population of 18 million, can't manage to pay for the 750,000 tonnes of oil it consumes each year. The foreign exchange it has left is barely enough to pay for building one bridge a year, when several hundred are urgently needed.

France, with a population three times greater, consumes 100 million tonnes of oil, i.e. 33 times as much, or 40 times as much per head of the population. In order to pay for this oil, France sells 2,200 million dollars' worth of arms per annum, 2,000 million worth to the Third World, which buys three times as much in the way of arms as it receives in aid. There were hopes of developing inter-African trade, but its share of the overall trade figure dropped from 5·4 per cent in 1970 to 4 per cent in 1974. There were failures all along the line. But the worst failure of all is that the African environment is being destroyed so fast – by deforestation, erosion and desertification. This is the most appalling crime against future generations, and unfortunately it isn't unique to Africa. Let us repeat the figures yet again: every minute of every day 20 hectares of tropical rain forest disappear.[1]

The last but by no means the least failure is education. During the 1960 Unesco conference held in Addis Ababa, the African countries set the target of universal primary education by 1980. Admittedly Tanzania, Zambia and some of the coastal states in West Africa are close to achieving this goal, but from the Sahelian states to Ethiopia, and in central Africa, school enrolment figures are way below 100 per cent. In the Upper Volta 11 per cent of children of school age attend primary school, but in the capital the figure is 75 per cent, whereas in the rural areas it is only 3 per cent. In Egypt, the Sudan and many other countries there are far fewer girls attending school than boys (the ratio is often 1:5). And in 1975 the overall figure for illiteracy in Africa was still 74 per cent.[2]

Worse still, the élitist Western model of education, in which primary schools hardly do anything except prepare their pupils for secondary education, continued to predominate. As we have seen, virtually all those who 'fail' secondary school, and are given the elegant label of 'educational drop-outs', refuse to do manual work and to tackle the hard work needed in the fields; and no attempt has been made to make this work less strenuous by looking for the most appropriate technologies. As long ago as 1962, when I wrote *False Start in Africa*, I spoke of the problem of schools versus agriculture, and since then this virtually mortal illness has only got worse. The few graduates who are found work generally go into the public or parastatal sector, which isn't directly productive. And this leads to a worsening of the nation's overheads, which are in the last analysis shouldered by Africa's peasants – the stranglehold on them is tighter than on any other peasant class, and they are suffering from absolute impoverishment, in a sector that Marx may not have foreseen (but would it be fair to blame him for this?). When these bureaucrats were students they were always ready to attack the ruling classes and accuse them of exploiting the peasants. But as soon as they're settled into a job it never enters their heads to go out and live 'in the backwoods' to help the selfsame peasants.

Young unemployed people from the villages congregate hopelessly in the shanty towns, which are the focus for epidemics, extreme poverty, and insanitary 'dwellings' (though that's scarcely the right word), with no clean water on tap, no sewerage and no areas for the children to play. Yet it is there, in these 'peri-urban' and 'infra-urban' districts, that the most genuine community spirit can be created, and that what is known as the 'informal' labour sector can best develop.

2 *If this pseudo-development continues it will destroy the whole of Africa*

'Towards a projection for the future of the environment and development in Africa' is the title of a study carried out by ENDA* for a meeting in Addis Ababa in February 1979 attended by representatives of African governments and organized by the United Nations Environment Programme and the United Nations Economic Commission for Africa on the theme of Africa's future. This study clearly shows that if what it rightly refers to as 'growing independence' continues, the first outcome will be even more rapid environmental damage:

This would mean that most of the African governments were

---

* Environnement et Développement en Afrique.

letting themselves be guided by the world economy and by the interests of the social groups that benefit most from the present situation. . . . The sale of raw materials abroad would remain the most important source of income . . . the outlook for iron ore, bauxite, copper and oil is promising. . . . Import substitution industries are geared to customers in a high-income bracket. . . . Technological dependence is going to increase . . . the urban centres (paying low wages) will be an even greater pole of attraction.

However, according to Wassily Leontief, it is highly unlikely that the price of iron ore and bauxite will rise much between now and the end of the century, though the prospects are brighter for copper and excellent for oil.

According to this scenario, Africa's natural environment would be pillaged, as indeed we have already pointed out with reference to places ranging from the Sahelian states to the Ivory Coast. Timber is still the main source of energy in the rural areas, and its consumption in the Sahelian states is likely to have increased by 100 per cent between 1975 and 2000. So if the tree cover is to be maintained and the demand for timber satisfied, 4·5 million hectares in the Sahel alone would have to be reafforested before the end of the century. If present trends continue, the already deforested areas around the towns will spread and merge. Present levels of reafforestation represent only 2 per cent of the necessary minimum.

Half of Africa is in danger of desertification, some areas more than others. In North Africa the desert is gaining ground at the rate of 100,000 hectares every year, and the green belt of forest land that has been planted in Algeria, on the north face of the Saharan Atlas, has done nothing to halt its advance. During the UN Conference on Desertification in Nairobi in 1977 Kurt Waldheim said that if present trends continued, three or four African states were liable to disappear altogether before the end of the century. In refusing to make any substantial contribution to the battle to head off this appalling threat, the rich countries have failed to understand that a catastrophe of this kind would affect them too.

The many different types of erosion, by both wind and water, have been accentuated by deforestation, overgrazing and the loss of fallow land, and are resulting in a dangerous lowering of tropical Africa's output potential. Wind erosion is blowing away all the finer particles in the soil of the Sahel, and there is a real danger that unless production methods are changed the harmattan winds that blow from the desert from January to March will carry a growing freight of sand, the first step towards the spread of desert. From the southern edge of the desert, where the rainfall is slight but can be very heavy on occasions, to the edge of a dense forest that is gradually disappearing, water erosion will go on getting worse. Even the areas infested with the tsetse fly may spread, as has happened in recent years in East Africa.

The great majority of the continent's fishing resources, ranging from Agadir in Morocco to Windhoek in Namibia, are being grabbed by foreign fishing fleets, which now take 85 per cent of the total catch. Almost half of it goes to the Soviet Union, which has treated its peasants so badly that it has made a total mess of its stock breeding, and now finds it simpler to sail the high seas in search of proteins; the Soviet boats use the most sophisticated equipment, which threatens long-term fishing prospects because it nets all available fish, whatever their size. If present trends continue, the overfishing that is now taking place is liable to get worse, at the expense of future generations of Africans.

If we accept this scenario, it is highly likely that poverty and inequalities will get worse, and the basic needs of those who are worst off, in the way of food, clothing and housing, education and health care, will be taken care of less and less well. In the period 1934–8 Africa was a cereal exporter; in 1950 the continent was self-sufficient; in the 1980s it is becoming increasingly short of cereals, having to import 10 million tonnes in 1976 and 12 million in 1978. If present policies aren't changed, the shortfall will have become unendurable by 1990, with a deficit of 5·6 million tonnes for Egypt, about the same for the Sahel and the Maghreb, double that figure for East Africa and three times that figure for Nigeria, making a total of 45 million tonnes. It is expected that the shortfall in southern Asia will be much higher still, so there's no way the rich countries' surpluses will be able to fill the gap. Even if the surpluses were available, most of the African countries are already virtually bankrupt and would be unable to afford to buy them. They would have to appeal to charity, which is incompatible with true independence, and with the love of dignity that is one of the Africans' basic values.

The continent therefore relies on industry. But if the rich countries go on looting the best ores, a crucial basis for autonomous industrialization will vanish. If it continues in the same way as now, industry will add to the disparities that have already been caused by differing availability of essential non-renewable resources, both oil and ores. Too many people will go on flocking from the villages to the capital cities and major ports to seek work, and these same capitals and ports will go on having cheap food available as a result of the very low wages paid to people from the rural areas who've come to live in the shanty towns – a wound that will go on deepening and festering.

Urban growth and housing policy will always benefit the mansions of the rich, and therefore property speculators and building firms that are too closely modelled on the West. The chances of achieving a genuinely popular form of housing, based on self-help and local materials (such as the attractive Adaoua complex in Rosso in Mauritania, though it is too expensive for the poorest families in the shanty towns), will be lessened or even nullified. The majority of the funds available will go on cars and other forms of transport, for which urban roads and a number of motorways will be developed even further. The imbalance between urban and rural areas will then become worse.

All this would damage any likelihood of achieving genuine agricultural development. Some see such a development in terms of 'agri-business', as at Richard-Toll and the former BUD, which turns the peasants into a rural proletariat. Or else they foresee ranches with rich pasture land for the cattle, which would deprive local herdsmen and arable farmers of their best land in order to supply the towns with the meat that they prefer, but which is a wasteful food. Another thing that could happen is that small peri-urban plantations could develop, owned by civil servants or shopkeepers who have managed to get their hands on the best low-lying land and make it private property, where formerly it was common land administered by the villages. The few dynamic peasants who have already embarked on using animal-drawn implements or tractors will forge ahead, leaving the mass of poor peasants way behind and thus creating new forms of inequality, as Claude Reboul has already shown. The children of the poor peasants will refuse to slave away over their hoes once they've received a bad education and seen at first hand the privileges enjoyed by the towns, and the wastage that goes on there. The continent will therefore rely on food aid, which will suck in even more people to the towns, since it is there that most of it is distributed. Now this aid will depend on how much the United States and Canada have available for export, and stocks are likely to diminish because both countries are squandering more and more in the form of meat.[3] This aid develops an assistance mentality, plunges the country further into dependence and stands in the way of any form of independent cereals policy.

So ENDA wonders whether Africa's future will bring:

> even faster destruction of the natural environment in the various regions of Africa . . . virtually total destruction of the dense forest cover . . . tree planting in the Sahel and the Sudan completely halted. . . . A continuation of the precarious situation in the shanty towns . . . not enough food for the underprivileged in urban and rural areas, and an unacceptable level of public health.

But another scenario can and must be envisaged, even though it may be hedged with difficulties, and likely to come up against various obstacles, both natural and official. We must adopt it, if we do not want to see Africa strangled.

3 *The death of ideologies*

For many years the 'revolutionaries' in Africa thought that revolution was going to solve all their problems. They shouted as much to me in December 1962, when the original French edition of *False Start in Africa* was published. I replied that the best way of helping them would be for me to study the countries that had actually staged a revolution, and see what 'problems' they still faced. I found that in countries as diverse as the Soviet Union and China, Cuba and Hungary, and many others too, a large number of difficulties had persisted and others had arisen in the post-revolutionary period. Anyway, revolution often means no more than the arrival of a new group of leaders. Jean-Claude Pomonti quotes Okot p'Bitek as saying that African socialism can be defined as popular government for and by the educated classes.[4]

The new group of leaders, like their predecessors, have to rely on the administrative machine, on a bureaucracy that has its own ideas about what's good for the peasants (and the country), and sees no need to consult them. The trouble is that the colonial era fostered the idea that education was a matter of prestige, and thus that workers, the 'masses', were to be despised. There is a wide gulf between the educated minority, who like to think of themselves as an 'élite', and the vast majority of the population, most of whom are virtually illiterate. (When we were in Dakar people used to ask us: 'What can we, the "élite", do *for* the masses?' What they should have been asking surely was: 'What can we do *with* the masses' or '*to serve* the masses?')

As a general rule socialist 'élites' haven't turned out, in practice, to be any better than the rest. In fact they have been more likely to use authoritarian methods to impose their version of the 'truth', which is so often inappropriate. Although there have unquestionably been some achievements – an end to some types of foreign domination and exploitation, frequent support for national languages, wider availability of some public services and so on – revolutionary slogans are only too often a façade for a form of dictatorship that is incapable of organizing development from the grassroots upwards. Attempts are made to put the land under collective production, but although the peasants will make a success of this when they want to, in order to achieve objectives that they have set themselves, they hate having the system forced on them. Premature schemes are devised for totally changing the pattern of crop growing and stock breeding as practised by family groups, since no one realizes that they provide an unbreakable link between the economy and social relationships. Sometimes villages will be reorganized without their inhabitants being properly consulted. Supply channels have often been pointlessly rearranged. And in every case so-called 'modern' methods and techniques are introduced, sometimes with a great deal of coercion, without the planner bothering about what the peasants think of it all. On top of all this there is unwarrantable interference in the daily lives of groups, families or individuals – it's frequently far from clear that this serves the common good.

If the new leaders like the Soviet model they'll give priority to industry, rejecting intermediate technologies as old-fashioned. The real problem isn't how to set up a socialist economy or socialist structures, but how to emerge from the dependence and under-development that involves slotting into a world economic system only too adept at exploiting people. The only way to escape this is to call into question the whole Western model of development, the consumer society, and the supremacy of urban areas and of industry (as has been tried in China). This complete rethink must go much further than anything Africa's socialists have managed so far. And it would be wrong to refer to it as socialism if socialism is still defined as meaning the 'nationalization of the major means of production and exchange'. Anyway, these 'major means' are virtually nonexistent in many African states. Africa must break free from a Eurocentrist form of socialism that is totally unsuited to the needs of the Third World.[5]

I had an opportunity to explain to the students at Dar es Salaam University what could be achieved by a form of development based on the peasants. These opponents used a half-baked version of Marxism to ascribe all Africa's failures to imperialism, central capitalism and outside factors, yet they enjoyed living in an environment that is very much pleasanter than that of many students in the richer countries, in the socialist camp for instance. They even refused to acknowledge the sufferings endured by the peasant women whose hard work earns them their privileges. Though they wouldn't say this, they were getting ready to join the privileged few themselves.

Their fellow-students in Lusaka reminded us that Engels had said such-and-such about the peasant question and Lenin had said such-and-such. We merely reminded them that neither Marx nor Lenin had ever been to Zambia, or even to tropical Africa, and therefore hadn't been able to share in the struggles and thinking of the workers and those who lived in the shanty towns in the various countries.

To treat the problems facing Africa's peasants on the basis of economic, social and political analyses conducted in Europe in the early days of industrialization goes right against the grain of the fruitful approach and method put forward by Marxism. We have seen how attempts to apply socialist principles in Africa failed in Guinea, Mali and Ghana, when their leaders tried to take them a stage further. Anyway, this so-called socialism is essentially *étatisme* or state socialism.

The students at the United Nations Institute of Economic Development and Planning in Dakar took us to task for not having made a thorough enough analysis of the mechanisms of power and of the state. After spending nine months at the Institute doing theoretical work they will go back to their very easy administrative work, without having even tried either to see with their own eyes – and with their hands – what life is like in the working-class districts and Serer or

Wolof villages in Senegal; or to give concrete evidence of their solidarity with the most underprivileged people; or to discuss *with them* their problems and how to tackle them with the means at their disposal. The room for manoeuvre is small, but it's a mistake not to make the fullest possible use of it.

We have already underlined the overall failure of the parastatals in Zambia and the difficulties they are having to face in Tanzania. Although in theory these companies were set up so that the state could 'control the commanding heights of the economy', in practice they enable the group of people who run them – and who've been appointed by those in power, as with benefices under the *ancien régime* in France – to claim exorbitant privileges for themselves by flouting the rules laid down for those in public office, which are a legacy of our own rules, and working as often as not without any proper supervision. The parastatals often set up links with the multinationals, who like having them as customers. The sophisticated equipment they buy means that their country's technological dependence will last even longer. An attempt by Mozambique to set up nationalized farms all over the country was a failure and the minister in charge was dismissed: he was helping to starve the country to death, when it had already suffered quite enough from the Rhodesian raids. Robert Mugabe in Zimbabwe is trying, on the advice of Samora Machel, to persuade the white settlers to stay, because of their technical efficiency. In Angola, on the other hand, criticisms published by Samora Machel concerning the errors committed there in the immediate post-independence period (most of which have since been put right) were banned from distribution. Angola now finds itself in a highly critical situation, with a handful of political commissars completely cut off from the peasant masses, who refuse in their turn to work hard when their efforts would mainly benefit the towns. We mustn't forget the damage caused by the South African raids, whose perpetrators were closely associated with the Unità guerrillas. In both Mozambique and Angola output will take a long time to recover from the large-scale departures of the Portuguese. Their governments are trying to persuade some of them to come back.

This in no way diminishes the guilt of imperialism, whose ideology of pillage and exploitation is obviously indefensible. The imperialists have never been squeamish about getting rid of African leaders who show signs of not being sufficiently amenable and obedient, and this is still true today. We need only think of the assassination of my friend Mehdi Ben Barka of Morocco, aided and abetted by the French police; or that of some of the leaders of the Union of the Peoples of the Cameroons by the French secret service; or of Amilcar Cabral and Eduardo Mondlane at the instigation of the Portuguese, not to mention all those people who have been and still are being executed, tortured or killed in unequal combat in South Africa and Namibia, and who suffered the same fate in Rhodesia. Another example is Patrice Lumumba, who could have made something better of the newly independent Belgian Congo than Mobutu (for no one could do worse). And I should also mention the massacres perpetrated by Macias Nguema in Equatorial Guinea, Idi Amin in Uganda, the 'Emperor' Bokassa in the Central African Republic; it's true that all these crimes can be attributed to Africans, but the nations still exercising influence could perfectly easily have prevented them, as the French army proved in 1979 in Bangui – but it intervenes only when French interests are at stake.

4 *Third World hunger demands new schemes*

Africa isn't the only continent that's being strangled. Southern Asia, which is much more densely populated, is facing an even more difficult situation, particularly on the Indian subcontinent, but also in places ranging from Indonesia (especially Java) to the Philippines. The shortage of land there is more acute, and the villages are far too often ruled by petty potentates who exploit the poor peasants to the hilt, chiefly by means of low wages, exorbitant interest rates and ground rents. The peons on the latifundia in Latin America are just as badly exploited:[6] the estate owners underpay them and strip them of the land they need for growing food crops, while at the same time under-using the vast tracts of ranch land that they hold by brute force.

The Food and Agriculture Organization of the United Nations is in charge of this problem, and has been since it was set up in 1944 in Quebec. As early as 1947, in Copenhagen, it had to bow to the pressures exercised by the multinational firms trading in large-scale agricultural produce and give up the idea of organizing distribution on any base other than profit plain and simple. When the United States joined in the war against the Nazis – because they'd been attacked by the Japanese – they announced that they were fighting to achieve 'freedom from want' for mankind. The FAO holds annual meetings in Rome attended by representatives from all member nations; it recruits thousands of experts, who spend more of their time in their offices than in the fields or villages. It organizes major international conferences, such as the one in 1974 on food and the one in 1979 on agrarian reform and rural development. They are attended by delegates from the various governments and from the 'agri-business' sector, and a few large-scale farmers, but not a single peasant. A counter-conference had to be organized in Rome in 1979 to give them a chance to air their views. Like the other specialized agencies within the United Nations (with the possible exception of UNICEF), the FAO spends hundreds of millions of dollars and pays its so-called experts high salaries. Yet in spite of this vast organization and all this money, world hunger has got steadily worse over this period. A 1974 forecast spoke of a cereal shortfall in the Third World of 85 million tonnes by 1985, but a figure of 88 million had already been reached by 1980. The total cost of cereal imports is 20,000 million dollars. According to the FAO committee which met between 27 March and 3 April 1980 to discuss the worrying world food situation, expenditure on cereal imports is rising by over 20 per cent per annum, and the shortfall in 1985 will be much higher than forecast.

In 1966 I was writing *Nous allons à la famine* with Bernard Rosier, which was published in English as *The Hungry Future*.[7] But at that time we didn't appreciate the full extent of the problem as it already existed. We must now speak of the 'hungry *present*', for famine is with us each and every day, and not only in a highly dramatic and spectacular form, as in India and Bangladesh (1966 and 1974), the Sahel and Ethiopia (1972 and 1973), Uganda (1980) and Ethiopia once again since 1977–8, as soon as the peasants lost the power that the revolutionary authorities granted them in the early days. Every single day thousands of children die of malnutrition, in the Nordeste in Brazil, on the Sierras in the Andes, in Colombia and Bolivia; in central eastern Java, on most of the Indian subcontinent, in parts of the Philippines and so on.

In 1979 the FAO published another document, this time on how agriculture would look towards the end of the century.[8] This certainly deplores the existence of world hunger, but announces the FAO's attachment to the new international economic order. It underlines the fact that if present trends continue the shortfall of cereals in the so-called developing countries is liable to be twice as big as the supplies now available in North America, which wields the world's biggest food weapon.

So what does the FAO suggest as a way to counter the danger? That we carry on pretty much as before, even though it has just emphasized the shortcomings of present policies! It speaks of plans to quintuple supplies of chemical fertilizers by the end of the century; the number of tractors is expected to increase by 7·5 per cent per annum, but the number of draught animals 'only slowly', while the use of hand and animal-drawn implements is expected to grow by 0·6 per cent per annum. You'd think they had never heard of the oil crisis, the need for humus, erosion, desertification and all the problems that are closely bound up with such trends. Figures for poultry and pigs (food for the rich) are expected to rise, but no mention is made of whether there'll be enough grain to feed the poor. Everything is calculated in dollars and in cash investments, which are expected to be in excess of 100,000 million dollars by the end of the century. There is no mention of what could be achieved by mobilizing the peasants, i.e. by the human investment on which China's progress has been based since 1950.

It is already clear that the agricultural programme drawn up by the 1974 conference for 1985 will be a complete failure. Instead of the so-called developing countries (what a euphemism!) moving towards self-sufficiency in food, as forecast, this goal is receding with every year that passes. So there's nothing particularly clever about our saying that the schemes of the Club du Sahel and the FAO for achieving self-sufficiency by the end of the century are bound to fail. This failure will be inevitable unless and until they recognize that their development 'model', which has never really worked, must be completely rethought; and unless and until power is no longer in the hands of those who go on exploiting their peasants, both abroad and at home, instead of helping them.

5 *An outline for village development centred on local needs*

In discussing Zambia we put forward a solution appropriate to the prevailing political wind, which consisted of setting up village units.

There is no such unit there at the moment, but they did exist, in another form, in the precolonial era, as Mungo Park clearly shows in describing his expedition along the river Niger.[9] The land chief used to ensure that the fertility of the land was respected, since it belonged not merely to the community now alive but to their ancestors and descendants as well, and it was a moral obligation to hand it on in good condition. This obligation has been unknown in our society since the entitlement under Roman law to 'use and abuse' your own property.

The rural communities set up by the authorities in Senegal go far beyond the village framework. Yet the peasants of Africa could achieve their full potential within that framework provided, first, that they were given the necessary basic powers, and the possibility of developing it as it suited them; second, that excessive checks and supervision were removed; third, that no attempts were made to integrate them too fast and too fully into the cash economy; and fourth, that they were allowed to use the surpluses obtained by their own work to improve and develop their village, thereby creating productive work.

The ENDA report we referred to earlier argues the possibility of 'environmental development' carried out with the peasants, the idea being to sit down with them to discuss their problems and their future. No one should be entitled to call himself an 'expert' if he hasn't gone to live in the village with the peasants and help them understand the situation they're in, discussing workable solutions day in and day out. If he does that the villagers will refer to him as their 'brother'. Incidentally an interdisciplinary group of researchers on the Sahel met for the first time in January 1980 in Niamey and in the rural districts around Ayorou, in Niger. The purpose of the meeting was to try to draw up a definition of the ideal researcher working for the peasants and herdsmen, and working *with* them, on topics put forward by them.

The excessive deforestation of the Senegal valley makes it advisable to plant trees in and round the village, and to recreate the tree cover in the fields. A variety of cactus without spines could be used to provide forage supplies directly usable by browsing livestock, with none of the hard work involved in collecting hay and silage forage reserves of the European type. A backwater creek and the surrounding flood area could be converted, with embankments made from compacted earth, to form a pond at Tilapia. Donkeys (which are put to work for only a few weeks in the year, to transport the harvest) or oxen could be used to draw enough water from the wells to meet domestic requirements and for irrigating dry-season gardens and orchards, on which any improvements to nutrition will be based. If the well is too far away from the village, donkeys and oxen could again be used to transport the water on their backs (I've seen oxen being used as a means of transport in Chad). Later on, carts could be used; they'd be made by cartwrights – one of the trades that would be included under the new education system, which would offer classes in working with iron and wood, joinery and furniture making. Gardening and keeping goats for milk would be encouraged, among other things.

Well-meaning souls in the rich countries protest about child labour. Admittedly children were taken advantage of in Europe in the nineteenth century, and in the Nordeste in Brazil some people do expect them to do work that is too hard for them at that age. But if the effort involved is kept within reason, child labour, which is both very common in Africa and very necessary, seems to us to perform a very useful function, in that it not only helps production, but also furthers the children's education, giving them a chance to take responsibility at an early age. The best way would be for them to organize themselves into working groups (from one school, or age group and so on) and to benefit in some way from the money they earn, or at any rate decide how it should be used.

The next stage would involve trying to find a local energy source, such as water in highland areas with adequate rainfall and plenty of streams; or animals – say a pair of oxen driving a treadmill or other implement; or wind (perhaps even solar?) energy elsewhere. This new source of energy would be used initially to work a pump or a bucket chain to provide water for the animals and, after filtering, for the villagers. It could also be used to work a maize or millet crusher, thus avoiding the expense of motor-driven implements, and completely transforming the life of the women. This would mean that more of the girls could go to school. The new energy source could subsequently be used to provide the electricity needed to light the school, the youth centre and then the whole village; in due course it could give a boost to education by supplying radio and television. But the peasants would have to be in charge of programme planning; the current saturation diet of lunatic Western pap turns the programmes into a tool that alienates viewers from traditional culture, de-Africanizes them (this applies to Zambia Television among others) and encourages frenzied urbanization.

This outline scheme will have to be adapted to suit each specific situation. Most important of all, it must be worked out with the peasants concerned, by which I mean the elderly farmers and land chiefs as well as young people who've been to school and have enough courage to stay in the villages. Will we ever come to realize that the initiative shown by the chaps who do the work is the prime resource available to development? It can fit into a collective framework – for instance when part of Niamey's 'Fulani village' burnt down all the inhabitants got together to rebuild it. This type of scheme can be compared to a certain extent with the one that the Ruvuma Development Association had started to implement before the Arusha Declaration and which the Party suddenly broke up because it didn't want the surplus produced by the peasants to be of direct benefit of them.

So the surplus was channelled instead towards the privileged few who have a firm grip on all forms of power, via cash crops for export, which are still encouraged, or even imposed on farmers. Will these minority groups ever understand that they are ruining their countries? And will we, the privileged inhabitants of the rich world? When they do eventually come to their senses, once the peasants have worked out their schemes, they will have to make the authorities respect them enough to allow them to go ahead. The chairman of a farm union in Bouaké in the Ivory Coast didn't mince his words in pointing out the extent to which they feel they are despised, yet know that they're necessary: 'The peasant is the arse-hole of the world. But when the arse-hole gets bunged up, the world can't keep going.'

6 *What can be done in the shanty towns?*

The first thing to do is to slow down the fatal spread of the shanty towns, by making village life more attractive and more interesting, and restoring the real powers of decision which the bureaucrats have frequently stolen from the peasants. Obviously absolute priority will have to be given to the villages, but the movement away from the rural areas is becoming so widespread that it will take some time even to slow it down. In the case of the young people it's less a matter of stopping them leaving than of encouraging them to come back of their own accord, in favourable circumstances. Community groups could organize the equipment of their districts with essential services (water and drainage, roads, schools and dispensaries). After that it would be possible to improve the productive activities already being carried out there, such as craft work involving the use of all the refuse produced by modern urban living (wood, metal, etc.) to make highly functional objects which would be produced and sold very cheaply. This applies to towns ranging from Nairobi to Abidjan.

There are many obstacles in the path of a programme of this kind, but they could be removed. The only reason for demolishing the shanty towns and moving the poor away from the town centres is so that the privileged few will no longer be offended by the sight of them, so that foreign visitors arriving from the airport won't see them, and so that they will no longer represent a latent social threat in the heart of such fine towns. But if they have no security of tenure the inhabitants of the shanty towns will have no incentive to improve their environment. They must be helped to use the most suitable technology and given technical advice and grants and loans for the necessary amenities (up to now both advice and loans have only too often been restricted to the friends of those in power). The first step will be to allocate local authority expenditure on a fairer basis. They must be helped to improve output and to market their produce; for instance they must be allowed to supply government markets, without too much red tape. They should be given instruction in reading and writing, which must have a practical basis and could be linked to technical training, again run on practical lines and suited to their specific situation, so that they can put it to use immediately.

Allotments could be laid out round the outside of these peri–urban districts. If each family had 5 ares of irrigated land this would provide productive labour and would help to combat malnutrition in women and children. These gardens would be more productive if technical advice, seed, fertilizer and small tools were available, and the same applies to orchards.

7 *Power to the peasants and the villages – our own responsibilities*

When President Nyerere gave the opening speech at the international conference on agrarian reform and rural development (in which, incidentally, the secretary-general, Herman Santa Cruz, wouldn't let me take part), he stressed that even the best-intentioned governments, including his own, tended to talk about rural development as if the ordinary people had no ideas of their own. He claimed that political power automatically goes to the 'haves', whereas both political and economic power ought to be in the hands of the people at village, regional and national level, and that it was essential to ensure that the surpluses produced by those in the rural areas remained there, so that the rural economy could be diversified by means of alternative sources of production and labour. Nyerere is undoubtedly a man of good will, but as we've seen, his own bureaucracy still forces his own peasants in his own country to grow a high proportion of export crops, even in places where they're by no means sure to do well.

In his book *Les Leçons d'une crise*, Claude Raynaut, who has spent a long time working in the area round Maradi in Niger, reminds us very appositely that the crisis in the Sahel isn't tied up solely or chiefly with the unreliable climate, the population explosion and the degradation of the natural environment, but with:

> the disorganization of the old methods of distribution and circulation of staple foodstuffs (warehousing, redistribution within closely knit communities). . . . The gradual dominance of an economic system based on credit . . . local agricultural produce traded for cash, then the cash sucked back again via taxes and the sale of imported produce . . . at the time of Independence led to the emergence – at the expense of the peasant masses – of a national, administrative and commercial bourgeoisie.[10]

He therefore recommends that 'the agricultural economy should be enabled to fuel its own development by building up surpluses within its own system . . . leading to a form of collective saving at village level', and speaks of agrarian societies regaining control over the system of agricultural production, and of 'the need for rural communities to become less and less dependent on their monetary transactions with the outside world' (which, incidentally, would necessitate an expansion of the craft sector, particularly in the textile field). This brings us to a crucial point. It would be helpful for the countries of Africa to cut back on their trade with the capitalist countries, so as to give them fewer opportunities for exploitation. They should also make changes to the framework within which such trade is conducted. And we believe that this also applies to the villages, since they are exploited twice over – by the outside world and by their country's rulers. More power must therefore be given both to the peasants and to the villages.

Yet you can't give real economic and political power to the peasants if they're not ready to take it; in other words if they haven't organized themselves into groups to be reckoned with. Resistance movements opposed to the authorities are being reported in various places, and in 1968 the peasants of Senegal started what was cautiously referred to as 'peasant unrest', which resulted in their obtaining better conditions for themselves merely by reducing their acreage of groundnuts. After the very bad harvest in 1979 there was again talk, in 1981, of putting up the price of groundnuts. Debts have been cancelled, which is scarcely an incentive to those who pay promptly, since only the bad payers benefit.

The peasants' first priority is to have enough to eat. They must therefore concentrate mainly on food crops, since the climate is so unreliable. And as in the good old days before the colonial era they must start building up reserves for their families, or even communal granaries. Rather than cooperatives imposed and supervised by the authorities, and benefiting their rulers before anyone else, they must once again set up economic, social and political groups run by themselves, supervised by the masses and capable of providing effective and non-violent* opposition to the authorities who are exploiting them.

After all, the authorities aren't going to give up their prerogatives and privileges without a fight, especially when they know that they can expect support from the dominant developed powers. This underlines the fact that the decisive responsibility lies with us, with our privileges and our squandering of resources, which are destroying

---

* It isn't for foreigners to start extolling the virtues of violent revolutions, when they won't be taking part in them. But we mustn't forget that when the French aristocrats gave up their privileges during the night of 4 August 1789, they were clearly influenced by the handful of châteaux that had been burnt down by the peasants. The rich and powerful were so afraid of losing everything that they decided to make some sacrifices.

our small planet while we look on unconcerned. Europe can't manage without Africa and the Third World, since they supply it with cheap energy – oil is still much too cheap, considering that we're still wasting it in such an extravagant fashion – plus cheap metals, timber and exotic produce. It is therefore in Europe's long-term interest to make sure that Africa survives, rather than backing those who allow it to be pillaged and destroyed.

In the long term it would run completely counter to our interests to have Africa strangled and the Third World destroyed, since this would result in the break-up of the Western economic system. Nor will the socialists in the West be in a position to step in effectively until they've started showing genuine concern for the Third World. They will then try to set up an international economic system whose first move will be to lessen inequalities, rather than talking all the time about increasing our standard of living. Priority must also be given to cutting back the squandering of the world's scarce resources. This means a series of austerity measures, initially for the rich, but also for the great majority of people in North America and Europe, Australia and Japan, and even later on for the socialist bloc. Such a policy could well accord with a life that is more interesting and more convivial, because it is less selfish. Writing in *Le Monde* on 6 May 1980, Jacques Madaule put it this way:

> The American people must in the long run realize that the standard of living they enjoy – and which is shared by a few other nations, including our own – is based on massive iniquities that brute force won't always be strong enough to maintain. If we don't want to experience catastrophes all over the world we must accept some sacrifices. The terms of trade between the North and the South must be made fairer. We must not convince ourselves that we have deserved the prosperity we now enjoy, when what we have mainly done is to take advantage of a few lucky breaks that others haven't had.

The Party's Over, by Marie-France Mottin

In 1944 the Belgian writer Jean-Paul Harroy referred to Africa as 'a dying land.'[1] The continent seems fated to be pillaged, to be a magnet for our greed and for our dreams of expansion, which we find very hard to give up as we stew in our cosy mediocrity. It acts as a prop for our ideological abstractions and, increasingly nowadays, as a graveyard for our disappointed hopes.

Africa has been thrown off course by developments imported from elsewhere or merely contemplated; soils have been destroyed and desertified, whole landscapes torn away; societies broken up or disrupted, with nothing to replace them. Peasants are exploited and despised; privileged minorities still swan around in capitals that only really govern themselves and their lush residential districts; self-important and allegedly omniscient experts go on talking in millions and gushing hot air. All this adds up to a thoroughly damning balance sheet, a funereal dirge. Socialist systems devised in the eastern bloc and capitalist systems introduced from the West have proved equally incapable of rescuing Africa from the wreckage of underdevelopment. And it wasn't long before the so-called 'miracles' achieved in Kenya and the Ivory Coast revealed their true colours. Rather than 'developing', Africa is heading for bankruptcy, with famine either just round the corner or already present. Our plans have failed.

When a catastrophe occurs a scapegoat must be found, so everyone is busy shifting the blame. Some people brand the West as the criminal (though it is guilty of hypocrisy and greed rather than of true crime). Others condemn corrupt and profiteering élites. But the man in the street in the West and the man on the savannah in Africa feel equally uninvolved. Why not admit that everyone shares some blame for the failure and start up a genuine dialogue, using language untainted by self-interest, ideology and grudges?

What is the point of the cynical epitaphs, and didactic pontificating

243

of the intellectuals, or the good intentions of activists who are powerless to do anything? Cynically optimistic reports, and even some that sound a warning – many of them written in technocratic jargon, yet naive and devoid of real content – will go on piling up on the shelves of international organizations, local authorities and ministerial waiting rooms.

But what do all those millions of Africans care about our cynicism, our pity, our objectivity or our despair, when their main concern is survival? They couldn't care less about our assessments and our books (including this one).

'We aren't guinea pigs, we're people,' was how Amin Jamal, Tanzania's Finance Minister, put it to the delegates at the joint ACP and EEC meeting held in Arusha in March 1980. We've been so busy with our analyses, our abstract concepts, our schemas, that we've forgotten that Africa is first and foremost men and women, and that they can't agree to be sacrificed while we look on unconcerned. When Africans wondering what the future held, and genuinely trying to find solutions to their problems, asked us how Europe was reacting to Africa's disastrous situation, what else could we do but repeat their own words: 'They don't give a damn . . .'?

In our discretion we didn't tell them that the average Frenchman or woman, caught in the trap of development, is primarily concerned with his or her motor car and the petrol to run it, with saving up for the next holiday (preferably on an underdeveloped beach somewhere), and with getting more free time. Nor did we confess that we get ill from over-eating (in 1979 the West Germans spent 5,000 million marks on preventing and curing obesity). Meanwhile in Africa the sick die because there's no transport to get them to hospital or medicines aren't obtainable, and what ordinary people worry about is not being able to get hold of soap, salt, maize, rice, and particularly millet.

Every society has its own problems and its own preoccupations. The odd thing is that two such different worlds can exist side by side in a world that claims to be civilized. Fidel Castro, the chairman of the non-aligned nations, emphasized this when he asked the thirty-fourth session of the United Nations Assembly in New York on 12 October 1979:

Why must some people go barefoot so that others can drive in limousines? Why must some people live thirty-five years so that others can live seventy? Why must some be wretchedly poor so that others can be extravagantly rich? Some countries have outlets to the sea, and others don't; some have energy resources, and others don't; some have plenty of land for growing food, and others don't; some are so crammed with machines and factories that you can't even breathe the air of their poisoned atmosphere, others have nothing but their own bare hands to earn their bread. In other words, some countries have abundant resources while others have none. What is the fate of these last? To die of hunger? To remain forever poor? What use is civilization then? What use is the conscience of mankind? What use are the United Nations? What use is the world?

One of the worst forms of stranglehold on Africa, the one that hits the continent hardest, is our indifference. It all seems such a long way away. Yet is it really? In the old days distances seemed long and any journey was certainly an adventure, yet although it gave you the sense of a complete change of scene, you didn't feel that you were entering a completely different way of life, as you do now. Air travel has shortened physical distances – in a few hours you can be in Bamako or Dar es Salaam. But the true distance has become much greater. Some experts will refer to a ratio of 1 : 120, others to 1 : 40, but what does this mean to the man in the street? You'd have to work out a detailed and matter-of-fact comparison between a day in the life of a wealthy Texan (or quite simply a comfortably off middle-class citizen in Western Europe) and that of a peasant woman in one of the Sahelian states. With all our technology and so-called intelligence we haven't been able to shorten the distance between those two lives. The only difference is that once we weren't aware of this, whereas now we are. What of it? The Third World is a mere sideshow as far as we're concerned. We snuggle comfortably into our armchairs, our feet shod in cosy slippers, to watch images of famine parade across our television screens, scenes from the carnival of wretchedness and poverty. We're so used to such sights that we can't tell fact from fiction any more. The appalling statistics and horrifying photos are meaningless: we've reached saturation point. The mass media, far from creating public awareness, have merely sent people to sleep. We're so well informed nowadays that we know how people die in India, Africa or Latin America. But that's as far as it goes. When the situation gets too dramatic, when the skeletal figures of the children of Cambodia huddle together to die before our bleary eyes and well-filled bellies, we do feel a twinge of emotion for just a second as the image flashes by, because our lives have become so drab that we need the sufferings of others to give us a lift. It's a question of contrast. But no one bothers about the ordinary malnutrition that's devastating Africa and the Third World, except when it reaches sensational proportions in the Sahel, in which case we may sit up and take notice, but only for a short while. It's all such a long way away, we can't really believe it's true. Or rather we don't want to.

We make a great song and dance about insisting on human rights, but what are we doing about the hundreds of millions of people living below the 'absolute poverty line' – as if there were such a thing! – or about the fifteen million children who die of malnutrition every year? Their freedom doesn't interest us, because as far as we're concerned these ordinary people don't really exist, and it seems perfectly natural that the only human right they enjoy is the right to die. That is their freedom. And even those intellectuals who get so worked up about the restrictions placed on the freedom of their counterparts in Eastern Europe or elsewhere, as if they deserved priority treatment, forget that in the last analysis our freedom carries an aftertaste of exploitation and our privileges carry the taint of pillage. How can they refer to the tens of thousands of people who die of malnutrition every day without questioning the very society that grants them special status? Our intelligentsia wouldn't be what it is without slavery, colonization and continuing pillage. As Fidel Castro told the UN assembly: 'People talk a lot about human rights, but they should also talk about the rights of mankind.' In the same way, the French working classes won't normally admit that the true twentieth-century proletariat is made up of the peasants on the savannah, and especially the peasant women.

Our ardent feminists find it hard to imagine what the life of an African peasant woman can be like. At the end of the eighteenth century Mungo Park could already write of the black female slaves of the Moors that their condition was utterly lamentable. He described how from dawn to dusk they had to carry water in heavy goatskins, pound and prepare the maize, sweep out the tents and do all the other heavy work, in the full heat of the sun, and yet they were poorly fed and often cruelly punished. Two hundred years later this is still true only too often, though nowadays the women are no longer slaves – in the literal sense of the term – and are not so harshly punished. (The world does still have some slaves, mainly in Mauritania, which also cuts off the hands of thieves!) We can add to the list of female duties the drudgery of fetching and carrying firewood, work in the fields and transporting the crops at harvest time, as we saw in Tanzania. But we no longer see things through the ingenuous eyes of Mungo Park, so it all seems quite natural. And lo and behold, the generous West, with its feeling for the dramatic and for strong emotions that are only skin-deep, has embarked on a crusade, not against the terrible poverty endured by these women, which it takes for granted, but against ritual sexual mutilations (infibulation, for example). Of course these are horrible, and we condemn them, but they are essentially an African problem. Even the lesbians in the United States are getting involved. In claiming to be helping 'our African sisters' we merely make another indecent assault on the modesty of women who have suffered such a traumatic experience. But of course it creates more of a stir than campaigning against the fact that they are exploited every day of their lives, as the whole of their society is exploited – to our advantage once again.

We've so completely lost a sense of proportion and reality, things are in so confused a state, that it's pointless referring to the need for a dialogue.

After so many formulations and abstractions, perhaps the time has come for simplicity, though not for simplification. It is time to go back to the villages, on what may well be the path of common sense. Once we've got back to our starting point we can ask the basic question of what development really is. By which I mean our own development as a first step, before we move on to talking about theirs. After all, now that we have come round to warning the Africans against the model we're so proud of (after all those years of telling them the opposite), how do we know that it's such a good model for us? The phenomena we're now observing in all these poorly structured countries are after all the same as those occurring in our own countries, but on a more spectacular scale – the destruction of rural society, the exodus from villages to towns, growing unemployment and frustration. Our schools too are turning out a generation of unemployed people, who would once have been given higher aspirations. Illnesses of 'affluence' are increasing in towns that will soon have one doctor per 250 inhabitants (in rural districts in Africa the figure is one for 10,000 to 70,000 people). Paris has even got one magnificent hospital that will never open because it would cost too much to run. Africa's failure is perhaps our failure too. Britain, which once ruled the waves, and was the birthplace of the Industrial Revolution, is now showing signs of 'underdevelopment'. And just look at the presidential candidates recently put forward by the United States, in spite of all her power and brains (many of them 'drained' from less developed countries).

Yet even supposing no major crisis has occurred, by the beginning of the twenty-first century there will be 10 per cent of us with well-filled bellies compared to 90 per cent living in extreme poverty and trapped in one vast ghetto of hunger and poverty. It may be that those arms we persist in manufacturing will come in useful after all, to protect us in our own luxury ghettoes. Can we expect apartheid on a world scale? To quote Fidel Castro again:

> If we don't find a wise and peaceful solution to present injustices and inequalities, the future will be apocalyptic. The clash of arms, threatening talk and arrogance in the international arena must stop. Enough of this belief that problems can be settled by nuclear weapons. Bombs can kill the hungry, the sick and the ignorant, but they can't kill hunger and sickness and ignorance. Nor can they kill the just rebellion of the people, and the cataclysm would also remove the rich, who are the ones who have most to lose in this world.

Can the affluent (if frustrated) West go on flaunting its abundance – which is anyway heavily dependent on oil and other forms of imperialism – when there are millions of starving, forgotten, despised people lying at its feet? What sort of world do we want to live in? The time has perhaps come for us to work out new relationships, and to look at the situation with new eyes. After all that is more or less the only choice open to us. We must adopt a new attitude before it's too late.

But who's going to set the tone, unless they're forced into it? The looters in the West aren't going to give up without a fight – too many interests are at stake, and the economic machinery has been running smoothly for too long. They scarcely give a thought to the long term and to the future of our planet. At most they may feel concerned about their own children's future, but they have the nerve to hope that they'll be able to take over in their turn. Meanwhile the élites who are in power in Africa, who work and think solely in the short term, with the frenzy bred of insecurity, have no more reason to move into reverse. Let the future take care of itself! We're too inclined to forget that Africa's history isn't made up merely of black culture and values and Ujamaa, and there's a long tradition of Africans exploiting other Africans. The slave trade started before the Europeans came to Africa's coasts. Joseph Ndiaye, the curator of the Slave House on Gorée Island, used to say: 'It's easy enough to see what the white slave-traders looked like, but it's hard to envisage the black traders.' And he added: 'If no one had been selling, there wouldn't have been any buyers.' The West has always found local allies willing to sell off their brothers and their country cheap. The people who complain about pillaging, and often benefit from it themselves, don't always realize that they're being manipulated by large-scale interests and that no one really takes them seriously. The sight of them knocking back the champagne and caviar in the name of the underprivileged during Third World meetings (generously organized by the international organizations) must raise some chuckles in New York and Geneva. What influence can they bring to bear now? Not all the heads of state are corrupt, as we saw in Tanzania and the Sahel among other places, but the eagle eyes of the multinationals and other profiteers will soon spot someone close to them – a top civil servant or the head of a parastatal – who is. If all the people in leading positions really did represent the interests of their country as a whole, the peasants and the workers, there's no doubt that the dialogue would be conducted in a different tone. Anyway, is it really in their interest to lock themselves away in their luxury villas, their grounds and their swimming pools, when unemployment, hunger and frustration are escalating all around them? At best their new slaves may refuse to go on producing. And since they've been brought up on textbooks of European history, it might be a good thing if they turned to the chapter on France and looked up what happened on the night of 4 August 1789.

This change of attitude shouldn't be restricted to those in positions of power and authority. If it is to have any real effect it must come about at all levels of society, for what is really needed is a complete rethink of development. And this should even go as far as questioning aid giving (though we mustn't sink to the niggardly attitude of those who say that we should give to our own countries before handing out foreign aid). But what's the point of going on tossing the crumbs left over when our cattle have finished feasting to the millions who are starving? (Each of the monstrous creatures in the feedlots in the United States – which are stuffed with a diet worked out by computer, while sweet canned music plays – consumes the same amount of cereals as seventeen Indians.) It would be much better to help them produce more, taking into account the needs and aspirations of the ordinary men and women who make up the vast majority of the population. We must accept once and for all that they are people, not guinea pigs. We must find another solution – rethinking our research programmes, since they've been a failure (they were too simplistic for such very complicated situations), and our technical assistance and cooperation policies in terms of the true needs of the countries concerned and in the interests of those who are worst off. We've been trying to farm without the peasants and to develop without the people. And there's a heavy price to pay.

But we need to change our attitude too. This applies both to those of us who watch what is going on – even those who are clear sympathizers – and to the man in the street who feels that it hasn't got anything to do with him. We must admit that the so-called 'Third' World is merely the other side of the coin of our world, and that over and above any form of racism, paternalism and do-gooding, we're all in the same boat. This problem of survival may well apply to us as well. Europe can't survive if it's cut off from the Third World, or even from Africa.

We'll be accused of being prophets of doom, of being Cassandras or of being wet blankets and killjoys. But the party really is over, and it's too late for crystal-gazing because the catastrophe has already occurred. How can we avoid an emotional response, after all we've seen, when on our return we found ourselves confronting the indifference of the developed world? If attitudes don't change everywhere what's the point of almsgiving and palliatives and makeshift solutions that won't solve a thing?

Throughout all those months of travelling thousands of kilometres in the back of beyond, as we happened upon villages, small towns and shanty towns, we'd come across the faces of African men, women and children. The guinea pigs are just like us – peasants immersed in the daily round and practising genuine solidarity; upright ministers (there are some) who speak lucidly of their presentiments about the future even while coping with endless difficulties; young people trying to find a reason to hope, and dreaming of a country that can give them hope.

'They're going to strangle us,' said Edward Sokoine. Are we – and by this I mean everyone who's busy strangling them, both black and white – going to haul on the rope? Or are we going to get together and try to untie it?

Notes and references

CHAPTER I

1 *Evolution des campagnes malgaches* (Madagascar 1958); *Reconversion de l'économie agricole, Guinée, Côte-d'Ivoire, Mali (Cahiers du Tiers-Monde)* (Paris: PUF–IDES 1961).
2 *Afrika inakwenda Kombo* (East African Literature Bureau, Nairobi, 1974).
3 Jean-Jacques Servan-Schreiber, *Le Défi américain* (Paris: Denoël 1967); English translation, *The American Challenge*, tr. Ronald Steel (London: Hamish Hamilton 1968; Harmondsworth: Penguin 1969).
4 René Dumont, *Paysans écrasés, terres massacrées* (Paris: Laffont 1978).
5 See Bernard Granotier, *La Planète des bidonvilles* (Paris: Le Seuil 1980).
6 Cf. *New African*, December 1979.

CHAPTER 2

1 David Livingstone to Robert Livingstone, 31 May 1859, quoted in George Seaver, *David Livingstone: His Life and Letters* (1957), p. 345; it is also quoted in Andrew Roberts, *A History of Zambia* (London: Heinemann 1976), which was very helpful to me when I wrote this paragraph.
2 John Gunther with Sam and Beryl Epstein, *Meet Southern Africa* (London: Hamish Hamilton 1959), pp. 175–6.
3 Frantz Fanon, *Peaux noires et Masques blancs* (Paris: Maspero 1961).
4 Kenneth Kaunda, *Humanism in Zambia*, vol. I (Zambia Information Services 1967).
5 J.-P. Harroy, *L'Afrique terre qui meurt* (Brussels 1944).
6 A. Marter and D. Honeybone, *The Economic Resources of Rural Households and the Distribution of Agricultural Development* (Lusaka: UNZA, Rural Development Studies Bureau 1977).
7 Ben Turok (ed.), *Development in Zambia: A Reader* (London: Zed Press 1979).
8 Ben Turok, 'The Penalties of Zambia's Mixed Economy', loc. cit., p. 72.

CHAPTER 3

1   H. J. Simons, 'Zambia's Urban Situation', in *Development in Zambia*, ed. Turok, p. 19.
2   Frankenburg and Leeson, in an article on health in Zambia.

CHAPTER 4

1   Mwalimu Julius K. Nyerere, *Tanzania Ten Years after Independence, Report by the President of Tanu*, submitted to TANU National Conference, Dar es Salaam, September 1971 (Dar es Salaam: Ministry of Information and Broadcasting, n.d.), pp. 4–5.
2   *The Arusha Declaration and Tanu's Policy on Socialism and Self-Reliance* (Dar es Salaam: Publicity Section, TANU 1967), pp. 5–18, passim.
3   Ibid., p. 19.
4   Julius K. Nyerere, *Socialism and Rural Development* (Dar es Salaam 1967), pp. 8–31, passim.
5   Ibid., p. 30.
6   Note submitted to the economic research unit at Dar es Salaam University on 16 October 1979.
7   J. Boesen, B. S. Madsen and T. Moody, *Ujamaa, Socialism from Above* (Uppsala: Scandinavian Institute of African Studies).
8   *Socialism and Rural Development*, p. 21.
9   Sylvain Urfer, *Une Afrique socialiste, la Tanzanie* (Paris: Editions Sociales 1976).
10   Bernard Joinet, in *Revue des études coopératives*, no. 192 (Paris 1978).
11   P. Kammerer and B. Vaissière, *Un Village tanzanien*, roneoed note submitted by two young French agronomists (students at the Institut National Agronomique in Paris), based on a study carried out in summer 1979.
12   *Socialism and Rural Development*, p. 16.
13   Joinet, op. cit.
14   *Socialism and Rural Development*, p. 3.
15   *Arusha Declaration*, p. 15.
16   Julius K. Nyerere, *Education for Self-Reliance*, pamphlet published by the Information Services Division, Ministry of Information and Tourism, Dar es Salaam (1967), p. 1.
17   Ibid., p. 3.
18   Ibid., p. 6.
19   Ibid., pp. 8–9.

CHAPTER 5

1   Cf. my earlier book, *Paysans écrasés*.
2   Fosbrooke, paper read to the United Nations Conference on Desertification, held in August 1977 in Nairobi.
3   Article in *Le Monde dimanche*, 10 February 1980.

4   René Dumont, *Paysanneries aux abois: Ceylan, Tunisie, Sénégal* (Paris: Le Seuil 1972).
5   See René Dumont, *Is Cuba Socialist?* (London: André Deutsch 1972) and Marie-France Mottin, *Cuba quand même, vies quotidiennes dans la révolution* (Paris: Le Seuil 1980).
6   See Dumont, *Utopia or Else* . . . (London: André Deutsch 1974).

CHAPTER 6
1   René Dumont, *Economie agricole dans le monde* (Paris: Dalloz 1953).
2   Article in *Le Monde*, 16 April 1980.
3   *Les Paysans du Sénégal* (Saint-Yriex 1966).
4   Dumont, *Paysans écrasés*.
5   Jacques Bugnicourt, 'Paysages déchirés, environnements menacés dans le delta et la vallée du Sénégal', *Environnement africain* (ENDA), August 1976.
6   Marcel Mazoyer in conversation with the author.
7   *Cahiers Orstom*, Sciences Humaines, 1–2 (1979).
8   Mazoyer, in conversation with author.
9   Cf. our book *Le mal-développement en Amérique latine* (Paris: Le Seuil 1981), which we wrote for our friends in Africa as well; the Ivory Coast is already on the way to 'mal-development'.
10 Amilcar Cabral, *L'Arme de la théorie* (Paris: Maspero 1975).

CHAPTER 7
1   Cf. Erik P. Eckholm, *Losing Ground: environmental stress and world food prospects* (New York: Norton 1976; Oxford: Pergamon 1978).
2   Figures given in M. Doo Kingue's report prepared for the OAU summit in Monrovia in February 1979, *Quelle sorte d'Afrique en l'an 2000?*
3   In her book *How the Other Half Dies* (Harmondsworth: Penguin 1979), which is otherwise extremely interesting and courageous, Susan George refuses to condemn this.
4   In *L'Afrique trahie* (Paris: Hachette 1979).
5   See the work done by ENDA, including the journal *L'Environnement africain*, and its many other publications.
6   See Robert Linhart, *Le Sucre et la faim* (Paris: Minuit 1980) and our own book *Mal-développement*.
7   René Dumont and Bernard Rosier, *The Hungry Future*, foreword by Lord Balogh (London: André Deutsch 1969).
8   *Agriculture in the year 2000* (FAO: 1979).
9   Mungo Park, *Travels in the Interior Districts of Africa* (1799).
10 Claude Raynaut, *Les Leçons d'une crise.* (Paris: Centre National de la Recherche Scientifique 1980).
11 J.-P. Harroy, *Afrique, terre qui meurt* (Brussels: 1944).

Select Bibliography

Samir Amin, *Neo-Colonialism in West Africa* (Harmondsworth: Penguin 1973).

Paul Bairoch, *Le Tiers-Monde dans l'impasse* (Paris: NRF 1971).

G. Ballandier, *L'Afrique ambiguë* (Paris: Plon 1969).

Josué de Castro, *The Geopolitics of Hunger* (New York & London: Monthly Review Press 1979).

Erik P. Eckholm, *Losing Ground: environmental stress and world food prospects* (New York: Norton 1976; Oxford: Pergamon 1978).

Susan George, *How the Other Half Dies: the real reasons for world hunger* (Harmondsworth: Penguin 1979).

Pierre Jalée, *The Pillage of the Third World* (New York: Monthly Review Press 1968; London: Monthly Review Press 1970).

Frances Moore Lappé and Joseph Collins, *World Hunger: ten myths*, 4th edn (San Francisco: Institute for Food and Development Policy; Birmingham: Third World Publications 1979).

Michael Lipton, *Why Poor People Stay Poor, A study of urban bias in world development* (London: Maurice Temple Smith 1977).

Andrew Roberts, *A History of Zambia* (London: Heinemann 1976).

Albert Tévoédjvè, *Poverty, Wealth of Mankind* (Oxford: Pergamon 1979).

Ben Turok (ed.), *Development in Zambia* (London: Zed Press 1979).

Sylvain Urfer, *Ujamaa, espoir du socialisme africain en Tanzanie* (Paris: Aubier 1971).

Sylvain Urfer, *Une Afrique socialiste, la Tanzanie* (Paris: Editions ouvrières 1976).

Ki Zerbo, *Histoire de l'Afrique noire* (Paris: Hatier 1972).